7 The
HA
of Highly Effective
TEENAGERS

'Excellent! This book is possibly the best book I have ever read and makes complete sense to me and my teenage brain . . . It's not a book that you read once and stuff it in a box under your bed, it's a book that you can read over and over again and each time you can pick up something that you might have missed last time around. It helps you to communicate better with other people and view their mistakes and your mistakes in a different light'

—A reader from Hereford, aged 14

'The best! I am a teenager, and having recently read this book, it has now become a second bible. I have only had the book a few months, and it is already falling to bits I have read it so many times, and used it in so many real-life situations. This book is very easy to read, and you can pick it up many times. PLEASE give it a go . . . You will love it. NB, this is not just for teens, my mum has read it as well!'

—A reader from London

'This is one amazing book. It manages to put all the points across wonderfully well whilst still being worth reading for the humour alone. In fact this book is so good I came to this page to order one for a friend's birthday! Every teenager should read this book'

—A reader from Basingstoke, aged 17

'I bought this book for my daughter – now it's one of the most read books in her room and she's started lending it to her friends!'

—A reader from Warwickshire

'I was amazed at what I was reading, it seemed like the book was breaking through any doors I had previously thought to be closed to me . . . This book is great'

—A reader from Leeds, aged 15

'Outstanding! As a teacher I thought this was great. It manages to be both realistic and humorous without preaching. Buy it for a teenager or for a teacher. I have used it in the classroom very successfully'

—A reader from Essex

More Praise for *The 7 Habits of Highly Effective Teenagers*

'Sean Covey's *The 7 Habits of Highly Effective Teenagers* is a true gift for the "teenage soul". No matter what issues you may be struggling with in life, this book offers hope, vision and the strength to overcome your challenges'

—JACK CANFIELD and KIMBERLY KIRBERGER,
co-authors of *Chicken Soup for the Teenage Soul*

'What? Sean Covey wrote a book? You've got to be kidding!'

—SEAN'S English teacher

'Unlike my book on the 7 Habits, this book by my son Sean speaks directly to teenagers in an entertaining and visual style (and Sean, I never thought you listened to a word I said). As prejudiced as this may sound, this is a remarkable book, a must-read!'

—STEPHEN R. COVEY, author of *The 7 Habits of Highly Effective People*

'The best way to "make it happen" in your life is to make the right choices as a teenager. *The 7 Habits of Highly Effective Teenagers* lets teens see themselves as the principal force in their lives, regardless of their background or current walk of life'

—STEDMAN GRAHAM, author of *You Can Make It Happen* and founder of Athletes Against Drugs

'Whether to sink in self-pity or swim in the ocean of knowledge is a choice we are called upon to make in life. Here is an excellent guide for youth, by a youth, to make life meaningful'

—ARUN GHANDI, grandson of Mahatma Ghandi and founder of the Ghandi Institute

'Our youth today are facing ills their parents and grandparents never imagined. They are searching for answers, and *The 7 Habits of Highly Effective Teenagers* provides the tools to enable them to find those answers within themselves. With the help of loving parents, teachers and friends, may our teens be blessed to grow to be happy, healthy, contributing adults'

—DR ROBERT SCHULLER, author of *If You Can Dream It, You Can Do It*

'This book has many positive, inspirational and motivational strategies to help teenagers live up to their potential'

—LAURA C. SCHLESSINGER, Ph.D., author of *Ten Stupid Things Women Do to Mess Up Their Lives*

SEAN COVEY was born in Belfast and raised in Utah; he has lived in South Africa, Boston and Dallas. He is currently Vice President of Product Innovation at FranklinCovey, one of the world's leading time and life leadership authorities. He graduated with honours from Brigham Young University with a Bachelor's degree in English and later earned his MBA from Harvard Business School. As the starting quarterback for BYU, he led his team to two bowl games and was twice selected the ESPN Most Valuable Player. Before joining FranklinCovey, he worked at Deloitte & Touche Management Consulting, Trammell Crow Ventures, and Walt Disney. He is a popular speaker to youth and adult groups and is the author of *Fourth Down and Life to Go*.

Sean's favourite activities include going to movies, working out, riding his dirt bike, hanging out with his family, eating (anything in large quantities) and writing poor poetry. Sean and his wife, Rebecca, are the parents of six children and live in the Rocky Mountains of Utah.

Other books from FranklinCovey Co.

The 7 Habits of Highly Effective People
Daily Reflections for Highly Effective People
Living the 7 Habits
The Power Principle
Principle-Centred Leadership
First Things First
What Matters Most
The 7 Habits of Highly Effective Families
Business Think

The
7 HABITS
of Highly Effective
TEENAGERS

The Ultimate Teenage Success Guide

Sean Covey

SIMON &
SCHUSTER

London · New York · Sydney · Toronto · Dublin

A CBS COMPANY

First published in Great Britain by Simon & Schuster UK Ltd, 1999
This edition published by Simon & Schuster UK Ltd, 2004
A CBS Company

9 10 8

Simon & Schuster UK Ltd
1st Floor,
222 Gray's Inn Road,
London WC1X 8HB

www.simonandschuster.co.uk

Simon & Schuster Australia
Sydney

A CIP catalogue record for this book is available from the British Library

ISBN 13: 978-0-7434-8426-8

Printed and bound by
CPI Group (UK) Ltd, Croydon, CR0 4YY

TO MUM
FOR ALL THE LULLABIES
AND LATE-NIGHT TALKS

What's Inside

What's Inside

Who am I?

I am your constant companion. I am
your greatest helper or heaviest burden.
I will push you onward or drag you down
to failure. I am completely at your command.
Half the things you do you might just as
well turn over to me and I will be able to do
them quickly and correctly.

I am easily managed – you must merely
be firm with me. Show me exactly how you
want something done and after a few
lessons I will do it automatically. I am the
servant of all great individuals and, alas, of
all failures, as well. Those who are great, I
have made great. Those who are failures,
I have made failures.

I am not a machine, though I work
with all the precision of a machine plus
the intelligence of a human. You may run
me for a profit or run me for ruin – it
makes no difference to me.

Take me, train me, be firm with me,
and I will place the world at your feet. Be
easy with me and I will destroy you.

Who am I?

I am
Habit.

PART I

The Set-up

Get in the Habit
They Make You or Break You

Paradigms and Principles
What You See Is What You Get

Get in the Habit

THEY MAKE YOU OR BREAK YOU

Welcome! My name is Sean and I wrote this book. I don't know how you got it. Maybe your mum gave it to you to shape you up. Or maybe you bought it with your own money because the title caught your eye. Regardless of how it landed in your hands, I'm really glad it did. Now you just need to read it.

A lot of teenagers read books, but I wasn't one of them. (I did read several Cliffs Notes book summaries, however.) So if you're like me, you may be ready to shelve this book. But before you do that, hear me out. If you promise to read this book, I'll promise to make it an adventure. In fact, to keep it fun, I've stuffed it full of cartoons, clever ideas, great quotes and incredible stories about real teenagers from all over the world . . . along with a few other surprises. So will you give it a try?

Okay? Okay!

Now, back to the book. This book is based on another book that my dad, Stephen R. Covey, wrote several years ago entitled *The 7 Habits of Highly Effective People*. Surprisingly, that book has become one of the best-selling books of all time. He owes a lot of the credit for its success to me and my brothers and sisters,

> We first make our habits, then our habits make us.
>
> ENGLISH POET

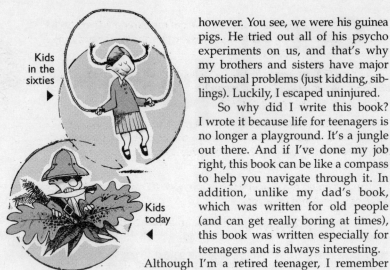

Kids in the sixties ▶

Kids today ◀

however. You see, we were his guinea pigs. He tried out all of his psycho experiments on us, and that's why my brothers and sisters have major emotional problems (just kidding, siblings). Luckily, I escaped uninjured.

So why did I write this book? I wrote it because life for teenagers is no longer a playground. It's a jungle out there. And if I've done my job right, this book can be like a compass to help you navigate through it. In addition, unlike my dad's book, which was written for old people (and can get really boring at times), this book was written especially for teenagers and is always interesting.

Although I'm a retired teenager, I remember what it was like to be one. I could have sworn I was riding an emotional roller coaster most of the time. Looking back, I'm actually amazed that I survived. Barely. I'll never forget the time I turned thirteen when I first fell in love with a girl named Nicole. I told my friend Ben to tell her that I liked her (I was too scared to speak directly to girls so I used interpreters). Ben completed his mission and returned and reported.

'Hey, Sean, I told Nicole that you liked her.'

'What'd she say!?' I giggled.

'She said, "Ooohhh, Sean. He's fat!"'

Ben laughed. I was devastated. I felt like crawling into a hole and never coming out again. I vowed to hate girls for life. Luckily my hormones prevailed and I began liking girls again.

I suspect that some of the struggles that teenagers have shared with me are also familiar to you:

'There's too much to do and not enough time. I've got school, homework, job, friends, parties and family on top of everything else. I'm totally stressed out. Help!'

'How can I feel good about myself when I don't match up? Everywhere I look I am reminded that someone else is smarter, or prettier, or more popular. I can't help but think, "If I only had her hair, her clothes, her personality, her boyfriend, then I'd be happy."'

'I feel as if my life is out of control.'

'My family is a disaster. If I could only get my parents off my back I might be able to live my life. It seems they're constantly nagging, and I can't ever seem to satisfy them.'

'I know I'm not living the way I should. I'm into everything – drugs, drinking, sex, you name it. But when I'm with my friends, I give in and just do what everyone else is doing.'

'I've started another diet. I think it's my fifth one this year. I really do want to change, but I just don't have the discipline to stick with it. Each time I start a new diet I have hope. But it's usually only a short time before I blow it. And then I feel awful.'

'I'm not doing too well in school right now. If I don't get my grades up I'll never get into university.'

'I'm moody and get depressed often and I don't know what to do about it.'

These problems are real, and you can't turn off real life. So I won't try. Instead, I'll give you a set of tools to help you deal with real life. What are they? The 7 Habits of Highly Effective Teenagers or, said another way, the seven characteristics that happy and successful teenagers the world over have in common.

By now, you're probably wondering what these habits are so I might as well end the suspense. Here they are, followed by a brief explanation:

Habit 1:   **Be Proactive**
            Take responsibility for your life.

Habit 2:   **Begin with the End in Mind**
            Define your mission and goals in life.

Habit 3:   **Put First Things First**
            Prioritize, and do the most important things first.

Habit 4:   **Think Win-Win**
            Have an everyone-can-win attitude.

Habit 5:   **Seek First to Understand, Then to Be Understood**
            Listen to people sincerely.

Habit 6:   **Synergize**
            Work together to achieve more.

Habit 7:   **Sharpen the Saw**
            Renew yourself regularly.

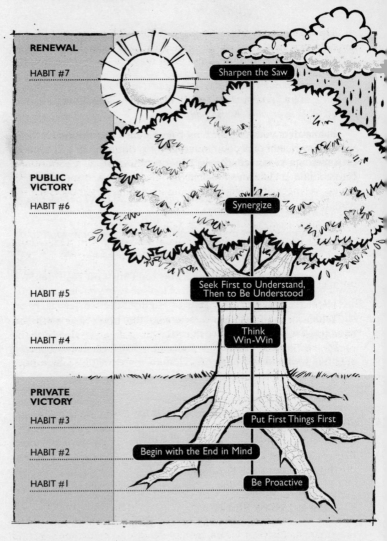

RENEWAL

HABIT #7 — Sharpen the Saw

PUBLIC VICTORY

HABIT #6 — Synergize

HABIT #5 — Seek First to Understand, Then to Be Understood

HABIT #4 — Think Win-Win

PRIVATE VICTORY

HABIT #3 — Put First Things First

HABIT #2 — Begin with the End in Mind

HABIT #1 — Be Proactive

As the above diagram shows, the habits build upon each other. Habits 1, 2 and 3 deal with self-mastery. We call it the 'private victory'. Habits 4, 5 and 6 deal with relationships and teamwork. We call it the 'public victory'. You've got to get your personal act together before you can be a good team player. That's why the private victory comes before the public victory. The last habit, Habit 7, is the habit of renewal. It feeds all of the other six habits.

The habits seem rather simple, don't they? But just wait till you see how powerful they can be! One great way to understand what the 7 Habits are is to understand what they are not. So here are the opposites, or:

The 7 Habits of Highly Defective Teenagers

Habit 1: _React_

Blame all of your problems on your parents, your stupid teachers, your lousy neighbourhood, your boy- or girlfriend, the government or something or somebody else. Be a victim. Take no responsibility for your life. Act like an animal. If you're hungry, eat. If someone yells at you, yell back. If you feel like doing something you know is wrong, just do it.

Habit 2: _Begin with No End in Mind_

Don't have a plan. Avoid goals at all costs. And never think about tomorrow. Why worry about the consequences of your actions? Live for the moment. Sleep around, get wasted and party on, for tomorrow we die.

Habit 3: _Put First Things Last_

Whatever is most important in your life, don't do it until you have spent sufficient time watching repeats, talking endlessly on the phone, surfing the internet and lounging around. Always put off your homework until tomorrow. Make sure that things that don't matter always come before things that do.

Habit 4: _Think Win-Lose_

See life as a vicious competition. Your classmate is out to get you, so you'd better get him or her first. Don't let anyone else succeed at anything because, remember, if they win, you lose. If it looks like you're going to lose, however, make sure you drag that sucker down with you.

Habit 5: _Seek First to Talk, Then Pretend to Listen_

You were born with a mouth, so use it. Make sure you talk a lot. Always express your side of the story first. Once you're sure everyone understands your views, then pretend to listen by nodding and saying 'uh-huh'. Or, if you really want their opinion, give it to them.

Habit 6: _Don't Cooperate_

Let's face it, other people are weird because they're different from you. So why try to get along with them? Teamwork is for the dogs. Since you always have the best ideas, you are better off doing everything by yourself. Be your own island.

I'M GONNA **ACE** THIS TEST. I STUDIED ALL NIGHT!

Habit 7: *Wear Yourself Out*

Be so busy with life that you never take time to renew or improve yourself. Never study. Don't learn anything new. Avoid exercise like the plague. And, for heaven's sake, stay away from good books, nature or anything else that may inspire you.

As you can see, the habits listed above are recipes for disaster. Yet many of us indulge in them . . . regularly (me included). And, given this, it's no wonder that life can really stink at times.

WHAT EXACTLY ARE HABITS?

Habits are things we do repeatedly. But most of the time we are hardly aware that we have them. They're on autopilot.

Some habits are good, such as:
- Exercising regularly
- Planning ahead
- Showing respect for others

Some are bad, like:
- Thinking negatively
- Feeling inferior
- Blaming others

And some don't really matter, including:
- Taking showers at night
- Eating yogurt with a fork
- Reading magazines from back to front

Depending on what they are, our habits will either make us or break us. We become what we repeatedly do. As writer Samuel Smiles put it:

> Sow a thought, and you reap an act;
> Sow an act, and you reap a habit;
> Sow a habit, and you reap a character;
> Sow a character, and you reap a destiny.

Luckily, you are stronger than your habits. Therefore, you can change them. For example, try folding your arms. Now try folding them in the opposite way. How does this feel? Pretty strange, doesn't it? But if you folded them in the opposite way for thirty days in a row, it wouldn't feel so strange. You wouldn't even have to think about it. You'd get in the habit.

At any time you can look yourself in the mirror and say, 'Hey, I don't like that about myself', and you can exchange a bad habit for a better one. It's not always easy, but it's always possible.

Not every idea in this book will work for you. But you don't have to be perfect to see results, either. Just living some of the habits some of the time can help you experience changes in your life you never thought possible.

The 7 Habits can help you:

- Get control of your life
- Improve your relationships with your friends
- Make smarter decisions
- Get along with your parents
- Overcome addiction
- Define your values and what matters most to you
- Get more done in less time
- Increase your self-confidence
- Be happy
- Find balance between school, work, friends and everything else

One final point. It's your book, so use it. Get out a pencil, pen or highlighter and mark it up. Don't be afraid to underline, highlight or circle your favourite ideas. Take notes in the margins. Scribble. Reread the stories that inspire you. Memorize the quotes that give you hope. Try doing the 'baby steps' at the end of each chapter, which were designed to help you start living the habits immediately. You'll get a lot more out of the book if you do.

You may also want to call or visit some of the hotlines and websites I have listed at the back of the book for additional help or information.

If you're the kind of reader who likes to skip around looking for cartoons and other interesting tidbits, that's just fine. But at some point you ought to read the book from start to finish, because the 7 Habits are sequential. They all build on each other. Habit 1 comes before Habit 2 (and so on) for a reason.

So what do you say? Make my day and read this book!

COMING ATTRACTIONS

Up next, we'll take a look at ten of the dumbest statements ever made. You don't want to miss them. So read on!

Paradigms and Principles

The following is a list of statements made many years ago by experts in their fields. At the time they were said they sounded intelligent. With the passing of time, they sound idiotic.

Top 10 All-Time Stupid Quotes:

10 'There is no reason for any individual to have a computer in their home.'

KENNETH OLSEN, PRESIDENT AND FOUNDER OF DIGITAL
EQUIPMENT CORPORATION, IN 1977

9 'Airplanes are interesting toys but of no military value.'

MARSHAL FERDINAND FOCH, FRENCH MILITARY STRATEGIST
AND FUTURE WORLD WAR I COMMANDER, IN 1911

8 '[Man will never reach the moon] regardless of all future scientific advances.'

DR LEE DE FOREST, INVENTOR OF THE AUDION TUBE AND FATHER
OF RADIO, ON 25 FEBRUARY 1967

7 '[Television] won't be able to hold on to any market it captures after the first six months. People will soon get tired of staring at a plywood box every night.'

DARRYL F. ZANUCK, HEAD
OF 20TH CENTURY–FOX,
IN 1946

> Better keep yourself clean and bright; you are the window through which you see the whole world.
>
> GEORGE BERNARD SHAW
> PLAYWRIGHT

6 'We don't like their sound. Groups of guitars are on the way out.'
DECCA RECORDS REJECTING THE BEATLES, IN 1962

5 'For the majority of people, the use of tobacco has a beneficial effect.'
DR IAN G. MACDONALD, LOS ANGELES SURGEON, AS QUOTED IN *NEWSWEEK*, 18 NOVEMBER 1969

4 'This "telephone" has too many shortcomings to be seriously considered as a means of communication. The device is inherently of no value to us.'
WESTERN UNION INTERNAL MEMO, IN 1876

3 'The earth is the centre of the universe.'
PTOLEMY, THE GREAT EGYPTIAN ASTRONOMER, IN THE SECOND CENTURY

2 'Nothing of importance happened today.'
WRITTEN BY KING GEORGE III ON 4 JULY 1776 (AMERICAN INDEPENDENCE DAY)

1 'Everything that can be invented has been invented.'
CHARLES H. DUELL, US COMMISSIONER OF PATENTS, IN 1899

Having read these, let me share with you another list of statements made by real teenagers just like you. You've heard them before, and they are just as ridiculous as the list above.

'No one in my family has ever gone to university. I'd be crazy to think I could make it.'

'It's no use. My stepdad and I will never get along. We're just too different.'

'Being smart is a "white" thing.'

'My teacher is out to get me.'

'She's so pretty – I'll bet she's stuck up.'

'You can't get ahead in life unless you know the right people.'

'Me? Thin? Are you kidding? My whole family is full of fat people.'

'It's impossible to get a good job around here 'cause nobody wants to hire a teenager.'

So What's a Paradigm? What do these two lists of statements have in common? First, they are all *perceptions* about the way things are. Second, they are all inaccurate or incomplete, even though the people who said them are convinced they're true.

Another word for perceptions is *paradigms* [pair-a-dimes]. A paradigm is the way you see something, your point of view, frame of reference or belief. As you may have noticed, our paradigms are often way off the mark, and, as a result, they create limitations. For instance, you may be convinced that you don't have what it takes to get into university. But, remember, Ptolemy was just as convinced that the earth was the centre of the universe.

And think about the teenager who believes she can't get along with her stepdad. If that is her paradigm, is she likely to ever get along? Probably not, because that belief will hold her back.

Paradigms are like glasses. When you have incomplete paradigms about yourself or life in general, it's like wearing glasses with the wrong prescription. That lens affects how you see everything else. As a result, what you see is what you get. If you believe you're stupid, that very belief will make you stupid. If you believe your sister is stupid, you'll look for evidence to support your belief, find it and she'll remain stupid in your eyes. On the other hand, if you believe you're smart, that belief will cast a rosy hue on everything you do.

A teenager named Kirsty once shared with me how much she loved the beauty of the mountains. One day she went to visit her eye doctor and, to her surprise, discovered that her sight was much worse than she had thought. After putting in her new contacts, she was astonished at how well she could see. As she put it, 'I realized that the mountains and trees and even the signs on the side of the road have more detail than I had ever imagined. It was the strangest thing. I didn't know how bad my eyes were until I experienced how good they could be.' That's often the way it is. We don't know how much we're missing because we have messed-up paradigms.

We have paradigms about ourselves, about other people and about life in general. Let's take a look at each.

PARADIGMS OF SELF

Stop right now and consider this question: Are your paradigms of yourself helping or hindering you?

When my wife, Rebecca, was in Sixth Form, a sign-up sheet for a talent contest was passed around in class. Rebecca, along with many other girls, signed up. Linda, who sat next to Rebecca, passed without signing.

'Sign up, Linda,' insisted Rebecca.

'Oh, no. I couldn't do that.'

'Come on. It will be fun.'

'No, really. I'm not the type.'

'Sure you are. I think you'd be great!' chimed Rebecca.

Rebecca and others continued to encourage Linda until she finally signed.

Rebecca didn't think anything of the situation at the time. However, seven years later, she received a letter from Linda describing the inner struggle she had gone through that day and thanking Rebecca for being the spark that helped her change her life. Linda related how she suffered from a poor self-image in school and was shocked that Rebecca would consider her a candidate for a talent contest. She had finally agreed to sign up just to get Rebecca and the others off her back.

Linda said she was so uncomfortable about being in the contest that she contacted the organizer the following day and demanded her name be removed from the list. But, like Rebecca, she insisted that Linda participate.

Reluctantly, Linda agreed.

But that was all it took. By daring to participate in an event that demanded the best in her, Linda began to see herself in a new light. In her letter, Linda thanked Rebecca from deep within for, in essence, taking off her warped glasses, shattering them against the floor and insisting she try on a new pair.

Linda noted that although she hadn't won a single title or award, she had overcome an even bigger obstacle: her low perception of herself. Because of her example, her two younger sisters participated in the contest in later years. It became a big thing in her family.

The following year Linda became a prefect, and, as Rebecca relates, developed a vivacious and outgoing personality.

Linda experienced what is called a 'paradigm shift'. It means that you suddenly see things in a new way, as if you just tried on a new pair of glasses.

Just as negative self-paradigms can put limitations on us, positive self-paradigms can bring

out the best in us, as the following story about the son of King
Louis XVI of France illustrates:

*King Louis had been taken from his throne and imprisoned. His
young son, the prince, was taken by those who dethroned the king.
They thought that inasmuch as the king's son was heir to the throne,
if they could destroy him morally, he would never realize the great
and grand destiny that life had bestowed upon him.*

*They took him to a community far
away, and there they exposed the lad to
every filthy and vile thing that life could
offer. They exposed him to foods the
richness of which would quickly make
him a slave to appetite. They used vile
language around him constantly. They
exposed him to lewd and lusting
women. They exposed him to dishonour
and distrust. He was surrounded
twenty-four hours a day by everything that could drag the soul of a
man as low as one could slip. For over
six months he had this treatment – but*
*not once did the young lad buckle under pressure.
Finally, after intensive temptation, they questioned him. Why had he
not submitted himself to these things – why had he not partaken?
These things would provide pleasure, satisfy his lusts, and were
desirable; they were all his. The boy said, 'I cannot do what you ask
for I was born to be a king.'*

Prince Louis held that paradigm of himself so tightly that nothing could shake him. In like manner, if you walk through life
wearing glasses that say 'I can do it' or 'I matter', that belief will put
a positive spin on everything else.

At this point you may be wondering, 'If my paradigm of myself
is all contorted, what can I do to fix it?' One way is to spend time
with someone who believes in you and builds you up. My mother
was such a person to me. When I was growing up, my mum always
believed in me, especially when I doubted myself. She was always
saying stuff like 'Sean, of course you should run for head boy,' and
'Ask her out. I'm sure she would love to go out with you.'
Whenever I needed to be affirmed I'd talk to my mum and she'd
clean my glasses.

Ask any successful person and most will tell you that they had a person who believed in them . . . a teacher, a friend, a parent, a guardian, a sister, a grandmother. It only takes one person, and it doesn't really matter who it is. Don't be afraid to lean on this person and to get nourished by them. Go to them for advice. Try to see yourself the way they see you. Oh, what a difference a new pair of glasses can make! As someone once said, 'If you could envision the type of person God intended you to be, you would rise up and never be the same again.'

At times, you may not have anyone to lean on and may need to go solo. If this is the case with you, pay special attention to the next chapter, which will give you some handy tools to help build your self-image.

● PARADIGMS OF OTHERS

We have paradigms not only about ourselves, but also about other people. And they can be way off track too. Seeing things from a different point of view can help us understand why other people act the way they do.

Becky told me about her paradigm shift:

In the lower Sixth at school, I had a friend named Kim. She was essentially a nice person, but as the year progressed, it became more and more difficult to get along with her. She was easily offended and often felt left out. She was moody and difficult to be around. It got to the point where my friends and I started calling her less and less. Eventually we stopped inviting her to things.

I was gone for a good part of the summer after that year, and when I returned I was talking to a good friend of mine, catching up on all the news. She was telling me about all the gossip, the different romances, who was dating who, and so on, when suddenly she said, 'Oh! Did I tell you about Kim? She's been having a hard time lately because her parents are going through a really messy divorce. She's taking it really hard.'

When I heard this, my whole perspective changed. Rather than being annoyed by Kim's behaviour, I felt terrible about my own. I felt I had deserted her in her time of need. Just by knowing that one little bit of information, my whole attitude toward her changed. It was really an eye-opening experience.

And to think that all it took to change Becky's paradigm was a smidgen of new information. We too often judge people without having all the facts.

Monica had a similar experience:

I had a lot of good friends at my old school. I didn't care about anybody new because I already had my friends and I thought that new people should deal with it in their own way. Then, when I moved, I was the new kid and wished that someone would care about me and make me part of their group of friends. I see things in a very different way now. I know what it feels like to not have any friends.

From now on, Monica will treat new kids very differently, don't you think? Seeing things from another point of view can make such a difference in our attitude toward others.

FRANK & ERNEST ® by Bob Thaves

The following anecdote from *Reader's Digest* (contributed by Dan P. Greyling) is a classic example of a paradigm shift:

A friend of mine, returning to South Africa from a long stay in Europe, found herself with some time to spare at Heathrow Airport. Buying a cup of coffee and a small packet of biscuits, she staggered, laden with luggage, to an unoccupied table. She was reading the morning paper when she became aware of someone rustling at her table. From behind her paper, she was flabbergasted to see a neatly dressed young man helping himself to her biscuits. She did not want to make a scene, so she leaned across and took a biscuit herself. A minute or so passed. More rustling. He was helping himself to another one.

By the time they were down to the last biscuit in the packet, she was very angry but still could not bring herself to say anything. Then the young man broke the biscuit in two, pushed half across to her, ate the other half and left.

Some time later, when the tannoy called for her to present her ticket, she was still fuming. Imagine her embarrassment when she opened her handbag and was confronted by her packet of biscuits. She had been eating his.

Consider this lady's feelings toward the neatly dressed young man before the turn of events: 'What a rude, presumptive young man.'

Imagine her feelings after: 'How embarrassing!? How kind of him to share his last biscuit with me!'

So what's the point? It's simply this. Our paradigms are often incomplete, inaccurate or completely messed up. Therefore, we shouldn't be so quick to judge, label or form rigid opinions of others, or ourselves, for that matter. From our limited points of view, we seldom see the whole picture, or have all the facts.

In addition, we should open our minds and hearts to new information, ideas and points of view, and be willing to change our paradigms when it becomes clear that they're wrong.

Most important, it is obvious that if we want to make big changes in our lives, the key is to change our paradigms, or the glasses through which we see the world. Change the lens and everything else follows.

If you'll look closely, you'll find that most of your problems (with relationships, self-image, attitude) are the result of a messed-up paradigm or two. For instance, if you have a poor relationship with your dad, it's likely that both of you have a warped paradigm of each other. You may see him as being totally out of touch with the modern world, and he may see you as a spoiled, ungrateful brat. In reality, both of your paradigms are probably incomplete and are holding you back from real communication.

As you'll see, this book will challenge many of your paradigms and, hopefully, will help you create more accurate and complete ones. So get ready.

● **PARADIGMS OF LIFE**

Besides having paradigms about ourselves and others, we also have paradigms about the world in general. You can usually tell what your paradigm is by asking yourself, 'What is the driving force of my life?' 'What do I spend my time thinking about?' 'Who or what is my obsession?' Whatever is most important to you will become your paradigm, your glasses, or, as I like to call it, your life-centre. Some of the more popular life-centres for teenagers include Friends, Stuff, Boyfriend/Girlfriend, School, Parents, Sports/Hobbies, Heroes, Enemies, Self and Work. They each have their good points, but they are all incomplete in one way or another, and, as I'm about to show you, they'll mess you up if you centre your life on them. Luckily, there is one centre that you can always count on. We'll save it for last.

Friend-Centred

There's nothing better than belonging to a great group of friends and nothing worse than feeling like an outcast. Friends are important but should never become your centre. Why? Well, occasionally they're fickle. Now and then they're fake. Sometimes they talk behind your back or develop new friendships and forget yours. They have mood swings. They move.

In addition, if you base your identity on having friends, being accepted and being popular, you may find yourself compromising your standards or changing them every weekend to accommodate your friends.

Believe it or not, the day will come when friends will not be the biggest thing in your life. During school I had a fabulous group of friends. We did everything together – gorged at all-you-can-eat buffets, went skinny-dipping in the dark, dated each other's girlfriends . . . you name it. I loved these guys. I felt that we'd be friends forever.

After leaving school and moving away, however, I've been amazed at how seldom we see each other. We live far apart, and new relationships, jobs and family take up our time. As a teenager, I never could have fathomed this.

Make as many friends as you can, but don't build your life on them. It's an unstable foundation.

SORRY, GUYS, WE CAN'T DO **EVERYTHING** TOGETHER!

Stuff-Centred

Sometimes we see the world through the lens of possessions or 'stuff'. We live in a material world that teaches us that 'He who dies with the most toys wins'. We have to have the fastest car, the nicest clothes, the latest stereo, the best hairstyle and the many other *things* that are supposed to bring us happiness. Possessions also come in the form of titles and accomplishments, such as head boy or girl, lead in the play, prefect, top of the class or team captain.

There is nothing wrong with accomplishing and enjoying our stuff, but we should never centre our lives on *things*, which in the end have no lasting value. Our confidence needs to come from within, not from without, from the *quality of our hearts*, not the *quantity of things* we own. After all, he who dies with the most toys . . . still dies.

I once knew a girl who had the most beautiful and expensive wardrobe I'd ever seen. She seldom wore the same outfit twice. After getting to know her better, I began to notice that she got much of her self-confidence from her clothes and had a bad case of 'elevator eyes'. It seemed that whenever she talked with another girl, she'd eye her from head to foot to see if her outfit was as nice as her own, which usually gave her a superiority complex. She was stuff-centred, which was a real turnoff to me.

I read a saying once that says it better than I can: 'If who I am is what I have and what I have is lost, then who am I?'

Boyfriend/Girlfriend-Centred

This may be the easiest trap of all to fall into. I mean, who hasn't been centred on a boyfriend or girlfriend at one point?

Let's pretend James centres his life on his girlfriend, Natasha. Now, watch the instability it creates in James.

NATASHA'S ACTIONS	JAMES'S REACTIONS
Makes a rude comment:	'My day is ruined.'
Flirts with James's best friend:	'I've been betrayed. I hate my friend.'
'I think we should date other people':	'My life is over. You don't love me anymore.'

The ironic thing is that the more you centre your life on someone, the more unattractive you become to that person. How's that? Well, first of all, if you're centred on someone, you're no longer hard to get. Second, it's irritating when someone builds their entire emotional life around you. Since their security comes from you and not from within themselves, they always need to have those sickening 'where do we stand' talks.

When I began dating my wife, one of the things that attracted me most was that she didn't centre her life on me. I'll never forget the time she turned me down (with a smile and no apology) for a very important date. I loved it! She was her own person and had her own inner strength. Her moods were independent of mine.

If who I am is what I have and what I have is lost, then who am I?

ANONYMOUS

You can usually tell when a couple becomes centred on each other because they are forever breaking up and getting back together. Although their relationship has deteriorated, their emotional lives and identities are so intertwined that they can never fully let go of each other.

Believe me, you'll be a better boyfriend or girlfriend if you're not centred on your partner. Independence is more attractive than dependence. Besides, centring your life on another doesn't show that you love them, only that you're dependent on them.

Have as many girlfriends or boyfriends as you'd like, just don't get obsessed with or centred on them, because, although there are exceptions, these relationships are usually about as stable as a yo-yo.

School-Centred

Among teenagers, centring one's life on school is more common than you might think. Lisa regrets being school-centred for so long:

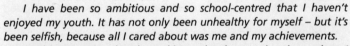

I have been so ambitious and so school-centred that I haven't enjoyed my youth. It has not only been unhealthy for myself – but it's been selfish, because all I cared about was me and my achievements.

At thirteen I was already working as hard as a university student. I wanted to be a brain surgeon, just because it was the hardest thing I could think of. I would get up at six every morning all through school and not go to bed before two A.M. in order to achieve.

I felt teachers and peers expected it of me. They would always be surprised if I didn't get perfect marks. My parents tried to loosen me up, but my own expectations were as great as that of teachers and peers.

I realize now that I could have accomplished what I wanted without trying so hard, and I could have had a good time doing it.

Our education is vital to our future and should be a top priority. But we must be careful not to let it take over our lives. School-centred teenagers often become so obsessed with getting good marks that they forget that the real purpose of school is to learn. As thousands of teenagers have proved, you can do extremely well in school and still maintain a healthy balance in life.

Thank goodness our worth isn't measured by our exam results.

Parent-Centred

Your parents can be your greatest source of love and guidance and you should respect and honour them, but centring your life on your parents and living to please them above everything else can become a real nightmare. (Don't tell your parents I said that or they might take away your book . . . just kidding.) Read what happened to this young girl:

I worked so hard all term. I just knew that my parents would be pleased – six A's and one B+. But all I could see in their eyes was disappointment. All they wanted to know was why the B+ wasn't an A. It was all I could do not to cry. What did they want from me?

And I spent the next two years trying to make my parents proud of me. I played netball and I hoped that they would be proud – they never came to see me play. I was top of the class – but after a while straight A's were just expected. I was going to go to college to be a teacher, but there was no money in that, and my parents felt that I would be better off studying something else – so I did.

UMMM...
I NEED TO
GO TO WORK
NOW, HONEY.

Every decision I made was prefaced with the questions – What would Mum and Dad want me to do? Would they be proud? Would they love me? But no matter what I did, it was never good enough. I had based my whole life on the goals and aspirations my parents thought were good, and it didn't make me happy. I had lived to please my parents for so long that I felt out of control. I felt worthless, useless, and unimportant.

Eventually I realized that my parents' approval wasn't coming, and if I didn't get my act together, I would destroy myself. I needed to find a centre that was timeless, unchanging and real – a centre that couldn't shout, disapprove, or criticize. So I started to live my own life, by the principles that I thought would bring me happiness – like honesty (with myself and my parents), faith in a happier life, hope for the future and belief in my own goodness. In the beginning I sort of had to pretend that I was strong, but, over a period of time, I became strong.

Finally I struck out on my own and had a falling out with my parents, but it made them see me for who I was, and they loved me. They apologized for all the pressure they put on me and expressed their love. I was eighteen years old before I ever remember my dad saying 'I love you', but they were the sweetest words I have ever heard, and well worth the wait. I still care about what my parents think, and I am still influenced by their opinions, but, ultimately, I have become responsible for my life and my actions, and I try to please myself before anybody else.

Other Possible Centres

The list of possible centres could go on and on. *Sports/hobbies-centred* is a big one. How many times have we seen someone build his identity around being a great athlete only to suffer a career-ending injury? It happens all the time. And the poor guy is left to rebuild his life from scratch. The same goes for hobbies and interests, such as dance, drama, music or clubs.

And what about being *hero-centred?* If you build your life around a movie or rock star, famous athlete or powerful politician, what happens if they die, do something really stupid or end up in jail? Where are you then?

Sometimes we can even become *enemy-centred,* and build our lives around hating a group, a person or an idea, like Captain Hook whose entire existence revolved around hating Peter Pan. This is often the case with gangs and with bitter divorces. What a warped centre this one is!

Becoming *work-centred* is a sickness that usually afflicts older people but can also reach teenagers. Workaholism is usually driven by a compulsive need to have more stuff, like money, cars, status or recognition, which feeds us for a season but doesn't ever fully satisfy.

Another common centre is being *self-centred,* or thinking the world revolves around you and your problems. This often results in being so worried about your own condition that you're oblivious to the walking wounded all around you.

As you can see, all these and many more life-centres do not provide the stability that you and I need in life. I'm not saying we shouldn't strive to become excellent in something like dance or debate or strive to develop outstanding relationships with our friends and parents. We should. But there's a fine line between having a passion for something and basing your entire existence on it. And that's the line we shouldn't cross.

Principle-Centred – *The Real Thing*

In case you were starting to wonder, there is a centre that actually works. What is it? (Drumroll, please.) It's being *principle-centred*. We are all familiar with the effects of gravity. Throw a ball up and it comes down. It's a natural law or principle. Just as there are principles that rule the physical world, there are principles that rule the human world. Principles aren't religious. They aren't American or Chinese. They aren't mine or yours. They aren't up for discussion. They apply equally to everyone, rich or poor, king or peasant, male or female. They can't be bought or sold. If you live by them, you will excel. If you break them, you will fail (hey, that sort of rhymes). It's that simple.

Here are a few examples: Honesty is a principle. Service is a principle. Love is a principle. Hard work is a principle. Respect, gratitude, moderation, fairness, integrity, loyalty and responsibility are principles. There are dozens and dozens more. They are not hard to identify. Just as a compass always points to true north, your heart will recognize true principles.

For example, think about the principle of hard work. If you haven't paid the price, you may be able to get by for a while, but eventually it'll catch up to you.

I remember one time being invited to play in a golf tournament with my football coach. He was a great golfer. Everyone, including my coach, expected that I'd be a fine golfer as well. After all, I was an athlete and all great athletes should be great golfers. Right? Wrong. You see, I stank at golf. I'd only played a few times in my life and I didn't even know how to hold a club properly.

I was nervous about everyone finding out how bad I was at golf. Especially my coach. So I was hoping that I could fool him and everyone else into thinking I was good. On the very first hole there was a small crowd gathered around. I was first up to tee off. Why me? As I stepped up to hit the ball, I prayed for a miracle.

Swooooossssssshhhhh. It worked! A miracle! I couldn't believe it! I had hit a long shot, straight down the middle of the fairway.

I turned around and smiled to the crowd and acted as if I always hit like that. 'Thank you. Thank you very much.'

I had them all fooled. But I was only fooling myself because there were 17½ more holes to go. In fact, it took only about five more shots for everyone around me, including my coach, to realize that I was awful. It wasn't long until the coach was trying to show me how to swing the club. I'd been exposed. Ouch!

You can't fake playing golf, tuning a guitar or speaking Arabic if you haven't paid the price to get good. There's no shortcut. Hard work is a principle. As the American basketball great Larry Bird put it, 'If you don't do your homework, you won't make your free throws.'

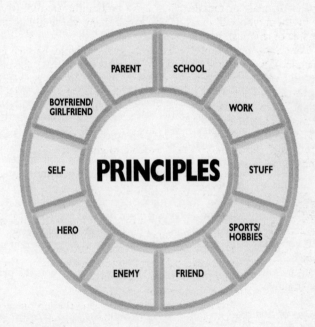

Principles Never Fail

It takes faith to live by principles, especially when you see people close to you get ahead in life by lying, cheating, indulging, manipulating and serving only themselves. What you don't see, however, is that breaking principles *always* catches up to them in the end.

Take the principle of honesty. If you're a big liar, you may be able to get by for a while, even for a few years. But you'd be hard-pressed to find a liar who achieved success over the *long haul*. As Cecil B. DeMille observed about his classic movie *The Ten*

Commandments, 'It is impossible for us to break the law. We can only break ourselves against the law.'

Unlike all the other centres we've looked at, principles will never fail you. They will never talk behind your back. They don't get up and move. They don't suffer career-ending injuries. They don't play favourites based on skin colour, gender, wealth or body features. A principle-centred life is simply the most stable, immovable, unshakable foundation you can build upon, and we all need one of those.

To grasp why principles always work, just imagine living a life based on their opposites – a life of dishonesty, loafing, indulgence, ingratitude, selfishness and hate. I can't imagine any good thing coming out of that. Can you?

It is impossible for us to break the law. We can only break ourselves against the law.

CECIL B. DEMILLE
MOVIE DIRECTOR

Ironically, putting principles first is the key to doing better in all the other centres. If you live the principles of service, respect and love, for instance, you're likely to pick up more friends and be a more stable boyfriend or girlfriend. Putting principles first is also the key to becoming a person of character.

Decide today to make principles your life-centre, or paradigm. In whatever situation you find yourself, ask, 'What is the principle in play here?' For every problem, search for the principle that will solve it.

If you're feeling worn out and beaten up by life, perhaps you should try the principle of *balance.*

If you find no one trusts you, the principle of *honesty* might just be the cure you need.

In the following story by Walter MacPeek, *loyalty* was the principle in play:

One of two brothers fighting in the same company in France fell by a German bullet. The one who escaped asked permission of his officer to go and bring his brother in.

'He is probably dead,' said the officer, 'and there is no use in your risking your life to bring in his body.'

But after further pleading the officer consented. Just as the soldier reached the lines with his brother on his shoulders, the wounded man died.

'There, you see,' said the officer, 'you risked your life for nothing.'

'No,' replied Tom. 'I did what he expected of me, and I have my reward. When I crept up to him and took him in my arms, he said, "Tom, I knew you would come – I just felt you would come."'

In the upcoming chapters, you'll discover that each of the 7 Habits is based upon a basic principle or two. And that's where they get their power from.

The long and short of it is *principles rule*.

★★★

COMING ATTRACTIONS

Up next, we'll talk about how to get rich, in a way you probably never thought of. So carry on!

A Word About Baby Steps   One of my family's favourite movies is *What About Bob?* starring Bill Murray and Richard Dreyfuss. It is the story of a dysfunctional, phobia-laden, immature, pea-brained leech named Bob who never, ever goes away. He attaches himself to Dr Marvin, a renowned psychiatrist, who wants nothing more than to get rid of Bob and finally gives him a book he wrote called *Baby Steps*. He tells Bob that the best way to solve his problems is not to bite off too much at once but to just take 'baby steps' to reach his goals. Bob is delighted! He no longer has to worry about how to get all the way home from Dr Marvin's office, a big task for Bob. Instead, Bob only has to baby step his way out of the office, and then baby step his way onto the elevator, and so on.

So I'll give you some baby steps at the end of each chapter, starting with this one – small, easy steps that you can do immediately to help you apply what you just read. Though small, these steps can become powerful tools in helping you achieve your larger goals. So, come along with Bob (he really becomes very likeable after you accept the fact that you can't shake him) and take some baby steps.

BABY STEPS

1. The next time you look in the mirror say something positive about yourself.

2. Show appreciation for someone's point of view today. Say something like 'Hey, that is a cool idea'.

3. Think of a limiting paradigm you might have of yourself, such as 'I'm not outgoing'. Now, do something today that totally contradicts that paradigm.

4. Think of a loved one or close friend who has been acting out of character lately. Consider what might be causing them to act that way.

5. When you have nothing to do, what is it that occupies your thoughts? Remember, whatever is most important to you will become your paradigm or life-centre.

   What occupies my time and energy? _____

   _____

6. 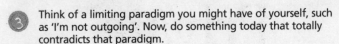 The Golden Rule rules! Begin today to treat others as you would want them to treat you. Don't be impatient, complain about leftovers or bad-mouth someone, unless you want the same treatment.

7. Sometime soon, find a quiet place where you can be alone. Think about what matters most to you.

8. Listen carefully to the lyrics of the music you listen to most frequently. Evaluate if they are in harmony with the principles you believe in.

9. When you do your chores at home or work tonight, try out the principle of hard work. Go the extra mile and do more than is expected.

10. The next time you're in a tough situation and don't know what to do, ask yourself, 'What principle should I apply (i.e., honesty, love, loyalty, hard work, patience)?' Now, follow the principle and don't look back.

PART II

The Private Victory

The Personal Bank Account
Starting with the Man in the Mirror

Habit 1 – Be Proactive
I Am the Force

Habit 2 – Begin with the End in Mind
Control Your Own Destiny or Someone Else Will

Habit 3 – Put First Things First
Will and Won't Power

The
Personal
Bank Account

Before you'll ever win in the public arenas of life, you must first win private battles within yourself. All change begins with you. I'll never forget how I learned this lesson.

'What's wrong with you? You're disappointing me. Where's the Sean I once knew?' the coach glared at me. 'Do you even want to be out there?'

I was shocked. 'Yes, of course.'

'Oh, give me a break. You're just going through the motions and your heart's not in it. You better get your act together or the younger players will pass you up and you'll never play here.'

It was my second year at Brigham Young University (BYU) during preseason football camp. Coming out of high school, I was recruited by several colleges but chose BYU because they had a tradition of producing great quarterbacks like Jim McMahon and Steve Young, both of whom went on to the pros and led their teams to Super Bowl victories. Although I was the third-string quarterback at the time, I wanted to be the next great player!

> I'm starting with the man in the mirror
> I'm asking him to change his ways
> And no message could have been any clearer
> If you wanna make the world a better place
> Take a look at yourself, and then make a change.
>
> 'MAN IN THE MIRROR'
> BY SIEDAH GARRETT
> AND GLEN BALLARD

When the coach told me that I was 'stinkin' up the field', it came as a cold, hard slap in the face. The thing that really bugged me was that he was right. Even though I was spending long hours practising, I wasn't truly committed. I was holding back and I knew it.

I had a hard decision to make – I had to either quit football or triple my commitment. Over the next several weeks, I waged a war inside my head and came face-to-face with many fears and self-doubts. Did I have what it took to be the starting quarterback? Could I handle the pressure? Was I big enough? It soon became clear to me that I was scared, scared of competing, scared of being in the limelight, scared of trying and perhaps failing. And all these fears were holding me back from giving it my all.

I read a great quote by Arnold Bennett that describes what I finally decided to do about my dilemma. He wrote, 'The real tragedy is the tragedy of the man who never in his life braces himself for his one supreme effort – he never stretches to his full capacity, never stands up to his full stature.'

Having never enjoyed tragedy, I decided to brace myself for one supreme effort. So I committed to give it my all. I decided to stop holding back and to lay it all on the line. I didn't know if I would ever get a chance to be first string, but if I didn't, at least I was going to try my best.

No one heard me say, 'I commit'. There was no applause. It was simply a private battle I fought and won inside my own mind over a period of several weeks.

> The real tragedy is the tragedy of the man who never in his life braces himself for his one supreme effort—he never stretches to his full capacity, never stands up to his full stature.
>
> ARNOLD BENNETT

Once I committed myself, everything changed. I began taking chances and making big improvements on the field. My heart was in it. And the coach took notice.

As the season began and the games rolled by one by one, I sat on the bench. Although frustrated, I kept working hard and kept improving.

Midseason featured the big game of the year. We were to play nationally ranked Air Force on ESPN, in front of 65,000 fans. A week before the game, the coach called me into his office and told me that I would be the starting quarterback. Gulp! Needless to say, that was the longest week of my life.

Game day finally arrived. At kickoff my mouth was so dry I could barely talk. But after a few minutes I settled down and led our team to victory. I was even named the ESPN Player of the Game.

Afterward, lots of people congratulated me on the victory and my performance. That was nice. But they didn't really understand.

They didn't know the real story. They thought that victory had taken place on the field that day in the public eye. I knew it happened months before in the privacy of my own head, when I decided to face my fears, to stop holding back, and to brace myself for one supreme effort. Beating Air Force was a much easier challenge than overcoming myself. Private victories always come before public victories. As the saying goes, 'We have met the enemy and he is us.'

AHH, FORGET ADDITION TABLES, LET'S DO SOME ALGEBRA!

• INSIDE OUT

We crawl before we walk. We learn arithmetic before algebra. We must fix ourselves before we can fix others. If you want to make a change in your life, the place to begin is with yourself, not with your parents, or your boyfriend, or your teacher. All change begins with you. It's inside out. Not outside in.

I am reminded of the writings of an Anglican bishop:

> *When I was young and free and my imagination had no limits, I dreamed of changing the world;*
>
> *As I grew older and wiser I realized the world would not change.*
>
> *And I decided to shorten my sights somewhat and change only my country. But it too seemed immovable.*
>
> *As I entered my twilight years, in one last desperate attempt, I sought to change only my family, those closest to me, but alas they would have none of it.*
>
> *And now here I lie on my death bed and realize (perhaps for the first time) that if only I'd changed myself first, then by example I may have influenced my family and with their encouragement and support I may have bettered my country, and who knows I may have changed the world.*

This is what this book is all about. Changing from the inside out, starting with the man or woman in the mirror. This chapter ('The Personal Bank Account') and the ones that follow on Habits 1, 2 and 3 deal with *you* and your character, or the private victory. The next four chapters, 'The Relationship Bank Account', and Habits 4, 5 and 6 deal with *relationships*, or the public victory.

Before diving into Habit 1, let's take a look at how you can immediately begin to build your self-confidence and achieve a private victory.

The Personal Bank Account

How you feel about yourself is like a bank account. Let's call it your *personal bank account* (PBA). Just like a current or savings account at a bank, you can make deposits into and take withdrawals from your PBA by the things you think, say and do. For example, when I stick to a commitment I've made to myself, I feel in control. It's a deposit. *Cha-ching.* On the other hand, when I break a promise to myself, I feel disappointed and make a withdrawal.

So let me ask you. How is your PBA? How much trust and confidence do you have in yourself? Are you loaded or bankrupt? The symptoms listed below might help you evaluate where you stand.

Possible Symptoms of a Poor PBA

- You cave in to peer pressure easily.
- You wrestle with feelings of depression and inferiority.
- You're overly concerned about what others think of you.
- You act arrogant to help hide your insecurities.
- You self-destruct by getting heavily into drugs, pornography, vandalism or gangs.
- You get jealous easily, especially when someone close to you succeeds.

Possible Symptoms of a Healthy PBA

- You stand up for yourself and resist peer pressure.
- You're not overly concerned about being popular.
- You see life as a generally positive experience.
- You trust yourself.
- You are goal driven.
- You are happy for the successes of others.

If your personal bank account is low, don't get discouraged about it. Just start today by making £1, £5, £10, or £25 deposits. Eventually you'll get your confidence back. Small deposits over a long period of time is the way to a healthy and rich PBA.

With the help of various teen groups, I've compiled a list of six key deposits that can help you build your PBA. Of course, with every deposit, there is an equal and opposite withdrawal.

PBA DEPOSITS	PBA WITHDRAWALS
Keep promises to yourself	Break personal promises
Do small acts of kindness	Keep to yourself
Be gentle with yourself	Beat yourself up
Be honest	Be dishonest
Renew yourself	Wear yourself out
Tap into your talents	Neglect your talents

KEEP PROMISES TO YOURSELF

Have you ever had friends who seldom come through? They say they'll call you and they don't. They promise to pick you up for the match and they forget. After a while, you don't trust them. Their commitments mean nothing. The same thing occurs when you continually make and break self-promises, such as 'I'm going to get up at six tomorrow morning' or 'I'm going to get my homework done right when I get home'. After a while, you don't trust yourself.

We should treat the commitments we make to ourselves as seriously as those we make to the most important people in our lives. If you're feeling out of control in life, focus on the single thing you can control – yourself. Make a promise to yourself and keep it. Start with real small £10 commitments that you know you can complete, like committing to eat healthier today. After you've built up some self-trust, you can then go for the more difficult £100 deposits, such as deciding to break up with an abusive boyfriend or not going after your sister for wearing your new clothes.

DO SMALL ACTS OF KINDNESS

I remember reading a statement by a psychiatrist who said that if you ever feel depressed, the best thing to do is to do something for someone else. Why? Because it gets you focussed outward, not inward. It's hard to be depressed while serving someone else. Ironically, a by-product of helping others is feeling wonderful yourself.

I remember sitting in an airport one day, waiting for my flight. I was excited because I had been upgraded to a first-class ticket. And in first class, the seats are bigger, the food is edible and the flight attendants are actually nice. In fact, I had the best seat on the entire plane. Seat 1A. Before boarding, I noticed a young lady who had several carry-on bags and was holding a crying baby. Having just finished reading a book on doing random acts of kindness, I heard my conscience speak to me, 'You scumbag. Let her have your ticket'. I fought these promptings for a while but eventually caved in:

'Excuse me, but you look like you could use this first-class ticket more than me. I know how hard it can be flying with kids. Why don't you let me trade you tickets.'

'Are you sure?'

'Oh yeah. I really don't mind. I'm just going to be working the whole time, anyway.'

'Well, thank you. That's very kind of you,' she said, as we swapped tickets.

As we boarded the plane, I was surprised at how good it made me feel to watch her sit down in seat 1A. In fact, under the circumstances, seat 24B or wherever the heck I was sitting didn't seem that bad at all. At one point during the flight I was so curious to see how she was doing that I could hardly stand it. So I got up out of my seat, walked to the first-class section, and peeked in through the curtain that separates first class from economy. There she was with her baby, both asleep in big and comfortable seat 1A. And I felt like a million pounds. Cha-ching. I've got to keep doing this kind of thing.

This sweet story shared by a teenager named Jenny is another example of the joy of service:

There is a girl in our neighbourhood who lives in a flat with her parents, and they don't have a lot of money. For the past three years, when I grew out of my clothes, me and my mum took them over to her. I'd say something like 'I thought you might like these', or 'I'd like to see you wearing this'.

When she wore something I gave her, I'd think it was really cool. She would say, 'Thank you so much for the new shirt'. I'd reply, 'That colour looks really good on you!' I tried to be sensitive so that I didn't *make her feel bad, or give her the impression that I thought she was poor. It makes me feel good, knowing that I'm helping her have a better life.*

Go out of your way to say hello to the most lonely person you know. Write a thank-you note to someone who has made a difference in your life, like a friend, teacher, or coach. The next time you're at a toll booth, pay for the car behind you. Giving gives life not only to others but also to yourself. I love these lines from *The Man Nobody Knows* by Bruce Barton, which illustrate this point so well:

There are two seas in Palestine. One is fresh, and fish are in it. Splashes of green adorn its banks. Trees spread their branches over it and stretch out their thirsty roots to sip of its healing waters.

. . . The River Jordan makes this sea with sparkling water from the hills. So it laughs in the sunshine. And men build their houses near to it, and birds their nests; and every kind of life is happier because it is there.

The River Jordan flows on south into another sea.

Here is no splash of fish, no fluttering leaf, no song of birds, no children's laughter. Travellers choose another route, unless on urgent business. The air hangs heavy above its water, and neither man nor beast nor fowl will drink.

What makes this mighty difference in these neighbour seas? Not the River Jordan. It empties the same good water into both. Not the soil in which they lie; not in the country round about.

This is the difference. The Sea of Galilee receives but does not keep the Jordan. For every drop that flows into it another drop flows out. The giving and receiving go on in equal measure.

The other sea is shrewder, hoarding its income jealously. It will not be tempted into any generous impulse. Every drop it gets, it keeps.

The Sea of Galilee gives and lives. This other sea gives nothing. It is named the Dead.

There are two kinds of people in this world. There are two seas in Palestine.

BE GENTLE WITH YOURSELF

Being gentle means many things. It means not expecting yourself to be perfect by tomorrow morning. If you're a late bloomer, and many of us are, be patient and give yourself time to grow.

It means learning to laugh at the stupid things you do. I have a friend, Charles, who is extraordinary when it comes to laughing at himself and never taking life too seriously. I've always been amazed at how this hopeful attitude of his attracts friends by the score.

Being gentle also means forgiving yourself when you mess up. And who hasn't done that? We should learn from our mistakes, but we shouldn't beat ourselves up over them. The past is just that, past. Learn what went wrong and why. Make amends if you need to. Then drop it and move on. Throw that voodoo doll out with the rubbish.

'One of the keys to happiness,' says Rita Mae Brown, 'is a bad memory.'

A ship at sea for many years picks up thousands of barnacles that attach themselves to the bottom of the ship and eventually weigh it down, becoming a threat to its safety. Such a ship ultimately needs its barnacles removed and the least expensive and easiest way is for the ship to harbour in a freshwater port, free of salt water. Soon the barnacles become loose on their own and fall off. The ship is then able to return to sea, relieved of its burden.

Are you carrying around barnacles in the form of mistakes, regrets and pain from the past? Perhaps you need to allow yourself to soak in fresh water for a while. Letting go of a burden and giving yourself a second chance may just be the deposit you need right now.

> Always be a first-rate version of yourself, instead of a second-rate version of somebody else.
>
> JUDY GARLAND
> SINGER-ACTRESS

Truly 'learning to love yourself,' as Whitney Houston sings, 'is the greatest love of all.'

BE HONEST

I looked up synonyms for the word *honest* the other day and these are a few I found: upstanding, incorruptible, moral, principled, truth-loving, steadfast, true, real, right, good, straight-shooting, genuine. Not a bad set of words to be associated with, don't you think?

Honesty comes in many forms. First there's self-honesty. Is what people see the genuine article or do you appear through smoke and mirrors? I find that if I'm ever fake and try to be something I'm not, I feel unsure of myself and make a PBA withdrawal. I love how singer Judy Garland put it, 'Always be a first-rate version of yourself, instead of a second-rate version of somebody else'.

Then there's honesty in our actions. Are you honest at school, with your parents and with your boss? If you've been dishonest in the past, and I think we all have, try being honest, and notice how whole it makes you feel. Remember, you can't do wrong and feel right. This story by Jeff is a good example of that:

In my second year at university, there were three kids in my class who didn't do well in maths. I was really good at it. I would charge them £5 for each test that I helped them pass. The tests were multiple choice, so I'd write on a little tiny piece of paper all the right answers, and hand them off.

At first I felt like I was making money, kind of a nice job. I wasn't thinking about how it could hurt all of us. After a while I realized I shouldn't do that anymore, because I wasn't really helping them. They weren't learning anything, and it would only get harder down the road. Cheating certainly wasn't helping me.

It takes courage to be honest when people all around you are getting away with cheating on tests, lying to their parents and stealing at work. But, remember, every act of honesty is a deposit into your PBA and will build strength. As the saying goes, 'My strength is as the strength of ten because my heart is pure'. Honesty is always the best policy, even when it's not the trend.

● RENEW YOURSELF

You've gotta take time for yourself, to renew and to relax. If you don't, you'll lose your zest for life.

You might be familiar with the book *The Secret Garden* by Frances Hodgson Burnett. It's a story about a young girl named Mary who goes to live with her wealthy uncle after her parents are killed in an accident. Her uncle has become cold and withdrawn since the death of his wife several years earlier. In an effort to escape his past, he now spends most of his time travelling abroad. He has a son who is miserable, sickly and confined to a wheelchair. The boy lives in a dark room in the vast mansion.

After living in these depressing conditions for some time, Mary discovers a beautiful, overgrown garden nearby the mansion that has been locked up for years. Upon finding a secret entrance, she begins to visit the garden daily to escape her surroundings. It becomes her place of refuge, her secret garden.

It's not long before she begins to bring her crippled cousin to the garden. The beauty of the garden seems to cast a spell on him, for he learns to walk again and regains his happiness. One day, Mary's withdrawn uncle, upon returning from a trip, overhears someone playing in the forbidden garden and angrily rushes to see who it could be. To his surprise, he sees his son, out of his wheelchair, laughing and frolicking in the garden. He is so overcome with surprise and joy that he bursts into tears and embraces his son for the first time in years. The beauty and magic of the garden brought this family together again.

WELL, I GUESS
IT'S TIME TO
RENEW MYSELF.

MYSELF

YOUR
SUBSCRIPTION
HAS EXPIRED

We all need a place we can escape to, a sanctuary of some sort, where we can renew our spirits. And it doesn't have to be a rose garden, mountaintop or beachfront. It can be a bedroom or even a bathroom, just a place to be alone. Theo had his hideout:

> Whenever I would get too stressed out, or when I was not getting along with my parents, I would just go into the basement. There I had a hockey stick, a ball and a bare concrete wall on which I could take out my frustrations. I would just shoot the ball for half an hour and go back upstairs refreshed. It did wonders for my hockey game, but it was even better for my family relationships.

Adrian told me about his refuge. Whenever he got too stressed out, he would slip into his school's large sports hall through a back door. All alone in the quiet, dark and spacious hall, he could get away from all the bustle, have a good cry or just relax.

Allison found a garden all her own:

> My dad died in an industrial accident at work when I was little. I really don't know the details because I have always been afraid to ask my mother very many questions about it. Maybe it's because I have created this perfect picture of him in my mind that I don't want to change. To me he is this perfect human being who would protect me if he was here. He is with me all the time in my thoughts, and I imagine how he would act and help me if he was here.
>
> When I really need him I go to the top of the slide at the local primary school playground. I have this silly feeling that if I can go to the highest place I will be able to feel him. So I climb up to the top of the slide and just lie there. I talk to him in my thoughts and I can feel him talking

*to my mind. I want him to touch me, but of course know that he cannot.
I go there every time something really is bothering me and I just share my
burdens with him.*

Besides finding a place of refuge, there are so many other ways to
renew yourself and build your PBA. Exercise can do it, like going for
a walk, running, dancing or punching a bag. Some teenagers have
suggested watching old movies, playing a musical instrument, finger
painting or talking to friends who uplift you. Numerous others have
found that writing in their journals does wonders to help them cope.

Habit 7, Sharpen the Saw, is all about taking time to renew your
body, heart, mind, and soul. We'll talk more about it when we get
there. So hold your horses.

TAP INTO YOUR TALENTS

Finding and then developing a talent, hobby
or special interest can be one of the single
greatest deposits you can make into your PBA.

Why is it that when we think of talents we
think in terms of the 'traditional' high-profile
talents, such as the athlete, dancer or award-
winning scholar? The truth is, talents come in a
variety of packages. Don't think small. You may have a
knack for reading, writing or speaking. You may have a gift
for being creative, being a fast learner or being accepting of
others. You may have organizational, music or leadership skills. It
doesn't matter where your talent may lie, whether it's in chess,
drama or butterfly collecting, when you do something you
like doing and have a talent for – it's exhilarating. It's a form of
self-expression. And as this girl attests, it builds esteem.

*You might die laughing when I tell you that I have a real talent and
love for weeds. And I'm not talking about the kind you smoke but
weeds and flowers that grow everywhere. I realized that I always noticed them, while others just wanted them cut down.*

*So I started picking them and pressing them – and eventually mak-
ing beautiful pictures and postcards and art objects with them. I have
been able to cheer up many a sad soul with one of my personalized
cards. I am often asked to do arrangements of flowers for others and
to share my knowledge of preserving pressed plants. It's given me so
much joy and confidence – just knowing I have the special gift
and appreciation for something most people ignore. But it even*

goes beyond that – it's taught me that if there is so much to just simple weeds, how much more is there to almost everything else in life? It's made me look deeper. It makes me an explorer. And I actually am just a normal young girl.

My brother-in-law, Bryce, told me how developing a talent helped build his self-confidence and find a career in which he could make a difference. He grew up in America and his story is set in the Teton mountain range that stretches high above the plains of Idaho and Wyoming. The Grand Teton, the tallest of the Teton peaks, juts 13,776 feet above sea level.

As a young boy, Bryce had the picture-perfect baseball swing. Until his tragic accident. While playing with a gun one day, Bryce accidentally shot himself in the eye. Fearing that surgery might permanently impair his vision, the doctors left the shot in his eye.

Months later, when Bryce returned to baseball, he began striking out each time at bat. He had lost his depth perception and much of his vision in one eye and could no longer judge the ball. Said Bryce, 'I was an all-star player the year before and now I couldn't hit the ball. I was convinced that I would never be able to do anything again. It was a big blow to my confidence.'

Bryce's two older brothers were good at so many things, and he wondered what he could do now, given his new handicap. Since he lived near the Tetons he decided to give climbing a try. So he dropped by the local Army store and bought nylon rope, carabiners, chalks, pitons, and other climbing necessities. He checked out climbing books and studied how to tie knots, hook up a harness, and rappel. His first real climbing experience was rappelling off his friend's chimney. Soon he began climbing some of the smaller peaks surrounding the Grand Teton.

Bryce soon realized that he had a knack for it. Unlike many of his climbing partners, his body was strong and lightweight and seemed to be perfectly built for rock climbing.

After training for several months, Bryce finally climbed the Grand Teton all by himself. It took him two days. Reaching this goal was a great confidence builder.

Climbing partners were hard to come by, so Bryce began training on his own. He would drive to the Tetons, run up to the base of the climb, do the climb, and run back down. He did this so often he became very good at it. One day a friend of his, Kim, said, 'Hey, you ought to go after the record on the Grand Teton'.

He told Bryce all about it. A climbing ranger named Jock Glidden had set a record on the Grand by running to the top and back in four hours and eleven minutes. 'That's absolutely impossible,' thought Bryce. 'I'd like to meet this guy someday.' But as Bryce continued to do these types of runs, his times became faster and Kim kept saying, 'You must go after the record. I know you could do it'.

On one occasion, Bryce finally met Jock, the superhuman with the insurmountable record. Bryce and Kim were sitting in Jock's tent when Kim, a well-known climber himself, said to Jock, 'This guy here is thinking about going after your record'. Jock gazed at Bryce's 125-pound frame and laughed aloud, as if to say, 'Get a clue, you little runt'. Bryce felt devastated but quickly gathered himself. And Kim kept affirming him: 'You can do it. I know you can do it'.

Early in the morning on 26 August 1981, carrying a small orange backpack and a light jacket, Bryce ran to the top of the Grand and back in three hours, forty-seven minutes and four seconds. He stopped only twice: once to take rocks out of his shoes and once to sign the register at the summit to prove he had been there. He felt marvellous! He had actually broken the record!

A few years later, Bryce received a surprise call from Kim. 'Bryce, have you heard? Your record has just been broken'. Of course, he added, 'You need to get it back. I know you can do it!' A man named Creighton King, who had recently won the heralded Pike's Peak Marathon in Colorado, dashed to the top and back in three hours, thirty minutes and nine seconds.

On 26 August 1983, two years after his last assault on the mountain, and ten days after his record had been broken, Bryce stood in the Lupine Meadows parking lot at the base of the Grand Teton in brand-new running shoes, ready and eager to break King's record. With him were friends, family, Kim and a crew from the local television station to film his run.

As before, he knew the hardest part of the climb would be the mental aspect. He didn't want to become one of the two or three who die each year while attempting to scale the Grand.

Sportswriter Russell Weeks describes running the Grand as follows: 'From the parking lot you face a run of about nine or ten miles up switchback trails, through a canyon, up two glacial moraines, two saddles, a gap between two peaks and a 700-foot climb up the west wall of the Grand to the top. The rise and fall in altitude from Lupine Meadows to the top and back is about 15,000 feet. Leigh Ortenburger's *Climber's Guide to the Teton Range* lists the last 700 feet alone as a three-hour climb.'

Bryce took off running. As he ascended up, up, up the mountain, his heart pounded and his legs burned. Concentration was intense. Scaling the last 700 feet in twelve minutes, he reached the summit in one hour and fifty-three minutes and placed his verification card under a rock. He knew that if he were to break King's record he would have to do it coming down. The descent became so steep at times that he was taking ten- to fifteen-foot strides. He passed some friends who later told him his face had turned purple from oxygen depletion. Another climbing party apparently knew he was going for the record because, as he passed, they yelled, 'Go! Go!'

Amid cheers, Bryce returned to Lupine Meadows with bleeding knees, thrashed tennis shoes, and one horrific headache, three hours, six minutes and twenty-five seconds after he had left. He had done the impossible!

Word spread fast and Bryce became known as the best mountain climber around. 'It gave me an identity,' said Bryce. 'Everyone wants to be known for something, and so did I. My ability to climb gave me something to work for and was a great source of self-esteem. It was my way of expressing myself.'

Today, Bryce is founder and president of a very successful company that makes high-performance backpacks for climbers and mountain runners. Most important, Bryce is making a living doing what he loves to do and what he is good at and has used his talent to bless his life and the lives of many others.

Oh, by the way, the record still stands. (Now, don't get any wild ideas.) And Bryce still has that shot in his eye.

So, my friends, if you need a shot of confidence, start making some deposits into your PBA starting today. You'll feel the results instantly. And, remember, you don't have to climb a mountain to make a deposit. There are a million and one safer ways.

★ ★ ★

COMING ATTRACTIONS
Up ahead we'll talk about the many ways in which you and your dog are different. Read on and you'll see what I mean!

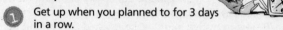

BABY STEPS

Keep Promises to Yourself

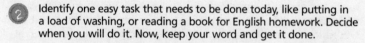

1. Get up when you planned to for 3 days in a row.

2. Identify one easy task that needs to be done today, like putting in a load of washing, or reading a book for English homework. Decide when you will do it. Now, keep your word and get it done.

Do Random Acts of Service

3. Sometime today, do a kind anonymous deed, like writing a thank-you note, taking out the rubbish, or making someone's bed.

4. Look around and find something you can do to make a difference, like cleaning up a park in your neighbourhood, volunteering in an old people's home or reading to someone who can't.

Tap Into Your Talents

5. List a talent you would like to develop this year. Write down specific steps to get there.

   Talent I want to develop this year: _____

   How do I get there: _____

   _____

   _____

   _____

6. Make a list of the talents you most admire in other people.

   Person: Talents I admire:

BABY STEPS

Be Gentle with Yourself

7 Think about an area of life you feel inferior in. Now breathe deeply and tell yourself, 'It's not the end of the world'.

8  Try to go an entire day without negative self talk. Each time you catch yourself putting yourself down, you have to replace it with three positive thoughts about yourself.

Renew Yourself

9 Decide on a fun activity that will lift your spirits and do it today. For example, turn up the music and dance.

10 Feeling lethargic? Get up right now and go for a fast walk around the block.

Be Honest

11 The next time your parents ask you about what you're doing, share the complete story. Don't leave out information meant to mislead or deceive.

12 For one day, try not to exaggerate or embellish!

HABIT ①

Be Proactive

– I Am
the Force

Growing up in my home was at times a big pain. Why? Because my dad always made me take responsibility for everything in my life.

Whenever I said something like 'Dad, my girlfriend makes me so mad', without fail Dad would come back with: 'Now come on, Sean, no one can make you mad unless you let them. It's your choice. You choose to be mad.'

> People are just about as happy as they make up their mind to be.
>
> ABRAHAM LINCOLN
> US PRESIDENT

Or if I said, 'My new biology teacher stinks. I'm never going to learn a thing', Dad would say, 'Why don't you go to your teacher and give him some suggestions? Change teachers. Get a tutor if you have to. If you don't learn biology, Sean, it's your own fault, not your teacher's.'

He never let me off the hook. He was always challenging me, making sure that I never blamed someone else for the way I acted. Luckily my mum let me blame other people and things for my problems or I might have turned out psycho.

I often screamed back, 'You're wrong, Dad! I didn't choose to be mad. She MADE, MADE, *MADE* me mad. Just get off my back and leave me alone.'

You see, Dad's idea that you are responsible for your life was hard medicine for me to swallow as a teenager. But, with hindsight, I see the wisdom in what he was doing. He wanted me to learn that there are two types of people in this world – the proactive and the reactive – those who take responsibility for their lives and those who blame; those who make it happen and those who get happened to.

Habit 1, Be Proactive, is the key to unlocking all the other habits and that's why it comes first. Habit 1 says 'I am the force. I am the captain of my life. I can choose my attitude. I'm responsible for my own happiness or unhappiness. I am in the driver's seat of my destiny, not just a passenger.'

Being proactive is the first step toward achieving the private victory. Can you imagine doing algebra before learning addition and subtraction? Not gonna happen. The same goes for the 7 Habits. You can't do habits 2, 3, 4, 5, 6 and 7 before doing Habit 1. That's because until you feel you are in charge of your own life, nothing else is really possible, now, is it? Hmmmm . . .

Proactive or Reactive ... the Choice Is Yours

Each day you and I have about 100 chances to choose whether to be proactive or reactive. In any given day, the weather is bad, you can't find a job, your sister steals your blouse, you lose an election at school, your friend talks behind your back, someone calls you names, your parents don't let you take the car (for no reason), you get a parking ticket and you fail a test. So what are you going to do about it? Are you in the habit of reacting to these kinds of everyday things, or are you proactive? The choice is yours. It really is. You don't have to respond the way everyone else does or the way people think you should.

How many times have you been driving down the road when suddenly somebody cuts in front of you, making you slam on your brakes? What do you do? Do you fly off at the mouth? Abuse them? Let it ruin your day? Lose bladder control?

Or do you just let it go? Laugh about it. Move on.

The choice is yours.

Reactive people make choices based on impulse. They are like a can of fizzy drink. If life shakes them up a bit, the pressure builds and they suddenly explode.

Reactive ▼

▲ Proactive

'Hey, you stupid idiot! Get out of my lane!'

Proactive people make choices based on values. They *think* before they act. They recognize they can't control everything that happens to them, but they can control *what they do about it*. Unlike reactive people who are full of carbonation, proactive people are like water. Shake them up all you want, take off the lid, and nothing. No fizzing, no bubbling, no pressure. They are calm, cool and in control.

'I'm not going to let that guy get me upset and ruin my day.'

A great way to understand the proactive mind-set is to compare proactive and reactive responses to situations that happen all the time.

Scene One:

You overhear your best friend bad-mouthing you in front of a group. She doesn't know you overheard the conversation. Just five minutes ago, this same friend was sweet-talking you to your face. You feel hurt and betrayed.

Reactive choices

- Tell her off. Then hit her.
- Go into a deep depression because you feel so bad about what she said.
- Decide that she's a two-faced liar and give her the silent treatment for two months.
- Spread vicious rumours about her. After all, she did it to you.

Proactive choices

- Forgive her.
- Confront her and calmly share how you feel.
- Ignore it and give her a second chance. Realize that she has weaknesses just like you and that occasionally you talk behind her back without really meaning any harm.

Scene Two:

You've been working at your job in the shop for over a year now and have been extremely committed and dependable. Three months ago, a new employee joined. Recently, he was given the coveted Saturday afternoon shift, the shift you were hoping for.

Reactive choices

- Spend half your waking hours complaining to everyone and their dog about how unfair this decision was.
- Scrutinize the new employee and find his every weakness.
- Become convinced your supervisor has formed a conspiracy and is out to get you.
- Begin to slack off while working your shift.

Proactive choices

- Talk with your supervisor about why the new employee got the better shift.
- Continue to be a hard-working employee.
- Learn what you can do to improve your performance.
- If you determine you are in a dead-end job, begin looking for a new one.

LISTEN TO YOUR LANGUAGE

You can usually hear the difference between proactive and reactive people by the type of language they use. Reactive language usually sounds like this:

'That's me. That's just the way I am.' What they're really saying is, *I'm not responsible for the way I act. I can't change. I was predetermined to be this way.*

'If my boss wasn't such a jerk, things would be different.' What they're really saying is, *My boss is the cause of all my problems, not me.*

'Thanks a lot. You just ruined my day.' What they're really saying is, *I'm not in control of my own moods. You are.*

'If only I attended a different school, had better friends, made more money, lived in a different flat, had a boyfriend . . . then I'd be happy.' What they're really saying is, *I'm not in control of my own happiness, 'things' are. I must have things to be happy.*

Notice that reactive language takes power away from you and gives it to something or someone else. As my friend John Bytheway explains in his book *What I Wish I'd Known in High School*, when you're reactive it's like giving someone else the remote control to your life and saying, 'Here, change my mood anytime you wish'. Proactive language, on the other hand, puts the remote control back into your own hands. You are then free to choose which channel you want to be on.

REACTIVE LANGUAGE	PROACTIVE LANGUAGE
I'll try	*I'll do it*
That's just the way I am	*I can do better than that*
There's nothing I can do	*Let's look at all our options*
I have to	*I choose to*
I can't	*There's got to be a way*
You ruined my day	*I'm not going to let your bad mood rub off on me*

● THE VICTIMITIS VIRUS

Some people suffer from a contagious virus I call 'victimitis'. Perhaps you've seen it. People infected with victimitis believe that everyone has it in for them and that the world owes them something . . . which isn't the case at all. I like the way author Mark Twain put it: 'Don't go around saying the world owes you a living. The world owes you nothing. It was here first.'

I played football with a guy who, unfortunately, became infected. His comments drove me crazy:

'I would be starting, but the coaches have something against me.'

'I was about to intercept the ball, but somebody cut me off.'

'Yeah, sure,' I always felt like saying. 'And I'd be President if my dad weren't bald.' To me, it was little wonder that he never played. In his mind, the problem was always 'out there'. He never considered that perhaps *his* attitude was the problem.

Rachel, a straight A student, grew up in a home plagued by victimitis:

I am black and proud of it. Colour has not stood in my way and I learn so much from white and black teachers and counsellors alike. But in my own home it's a different thing. My mother, who dominates the family, sees my doing good in school as a threat, as if I am joining the 'white folks'. She still uses language like 'the man is keeping us from doing this and that. He is keeping us boxed up and won't let us do anything'.

I always rebut with 'No man is keeping you from doing anything, only yourself, because you keep thinking the way you think.' Even my boyfriend falls into the white-man-is-holding-me-back attitude. When he was recently trying to purchase a car and the sale didn't go through, he remarked with frustration, 'The white man doesn't want us to get anything.' I almost lost it and confronted him with how silly that kind of thinking was. But it only resulted in him feeling that I was taking the side of the white man.

I remain convinced that the only person who can hold you back is yourself.

Besides feeling like victims, reactive people:
- Are easily offended
- Blame others
- Get angry and say things they later regret
- Whine and complain

- Wait for things to happen to them
- Change only when they have to

IT PAYS TO BE PROACTIVE

Proactive people are a different breed. Proactive people:
- Are not easily offended
- Take responsibility for their choices
- Think before they act
- Bounce back when something bad happens
- Always find a way to make it happen
- Focus on things they can do something about, and don't worry about things they can't

I remember starting a new job and working with a guy named Andrew. I don't know what his problem was, but for some reason Andrew didn't like me, and he wanted me to know it. He'd say rude and insulting things to me. He was constantly talking behind my back and getting others to side with him against me. I remember returning from a vacation one time and a friend telling me, 'Boy, Sean, if you only knew what Andrew has been saying about you. You'd better watch your back.'

There were times I wanted to pound the guy, but I somehow managed to keep my cool and ignore his silly attacks. Whenever he insulted me, I made it a personal challenge to treat him well in return. I had faith that things would work out in the end if I acted this way.

In a matter of a few months things began to change. Andrew could see that I wasn't going to play his game and began to lighten up. He even told me one time, 'I've tried to offend you, but you won't take offence.' After being at the company for about a year, we became friends and gained respect for each other. Had I reacted to his attacks, which was my feline instinct, I'm certain we wouldn't be friends today. Often all it takes is one person to create a friendship.

Beth discovered for herself the benefits of being proactive:

I had taken a subject at school where we had talked about proactivity, and I had wondered about how to really apply it. One day as I was on the checkout, a bloke suddenly told me that the shopping I had just rung up wasn't his. My first reaction was to say, 'You idiot', then put the bar down between the other customer's shopping. 'Why

didn't you stop me sooner?' So I have to delete it all and call to get the changes approved by a manager while he just stands there and thinks it's funny. Meanwhile the air is rising and I'm getting real irritated. To top it off he then has the nerve to question the price I charged him for the broccoli.

To my horror, I discovered that he was right. I had put the wrong code numbers in the register for the broccoli. Now I was extra irritated and so tempted to lash out at him to cover for my own mistake. But then this idea popped into my mind: 'Be Proactive.'

So I said, 'You are right, sir. It's completely my fault. I will correct the pricing. It will just take a couple of seconds.' I also remembered that being proactive doesn't mean you're a doormat, so I reminded him nicely that to avoid this kind of thing in the future he would need to always put the bar down that separates orders.

It felt so good. I had apologized, but I had also said what I wanted to say. It was such a simple little thing, but it gave me such inner conversion and confidence in this habit.

At this point you're probably ready to shoot me and say, 'Now come on, Sean. It's not that easy'. I won't argue with you. Being reactive is so much easier. It's easy to lose your cool. That doesn't take any control. And it's easy to whine and complain. Without question, being proactive is the higher road.

But, remember, you don't have to be perfect. In reality, you and I aren't either completely proactive or reactive but probably somewhere in between. The key then is to get in the habit of being proactive so you can run on autopilot and not even have to think about it. If you're choosing to be proactive 20 out of 100 times on average each day, try doing it 30 out of 100 times. Then 40. Never underestimate the huge difference small changes can make.

● WE CAN CONTROL ONLY ONE THING

The fact is, we can't control everything that happens to us. We can't control the colour of our skin, who will win the FA Cup, where we were born, who our parents are or how others might treat us. But there is one thing we *can* control: *how we respond to what happens to us.* And that is what counts! This is why we need to stop worrying about things we can't control and start worrying about things we *can.*

Picture two circles. The inner circle is our circle of control. It includes things we have control over, such as ourselves, our attitudes, our choices, our response to whatever happens to us.

Surrounding the circle of control is the circle of no control. It includes the thousands of things we can't do anything about.

Now, what will happen if we spend our time and energy worrying about things we can't control, like a rude comment, a past mistake or the weather? You guessed it! We'll feel even more out of control, as if we were victims. For instance, if your sister bugs you and you're always complaining about her weaknesses (something you have no control over), that won't do anything to fix the problem. It'll only cause you to blame your problems on her and lose power yourself.

Laura told me a story that illustrates this point. A week before her upcoming netball game, Laura learned that the mother of a player on the opposing team had made fun of Laura's netball skills. Instead of ignoring the comments, Laura became angry and spent the rest of the week stewing. When the game arrived, her only goal was to prove to this mother that she was a good player. To make a long story short, Laura played poorly, spent much of her time on the bench and her team lost the game. She was so focused on something she couldn't control (what was said about her) that she lost control of the only thing she could, herself.

Proactive people, on the other hand, focus elsewhere . . . on the things they *can* control. By doing so they experience inner peace and gain more control of their lives. They learn to smile about and live with the many things they can't do anything about. They may not like them, but they know it's no use worrying.

● TURNING SETBACKS INTO TRIUMPHS

Life often deals us a bad hand and it is up to us to control how we respond. Every time we have a setback, it's an opportunity for us to turn it into a triumph, as this account by Brad Lemley from *Parade* magazine illustrates:

'It's not what happens to you in life, it's what you do about it,' or so says W. Mitchell, a self-made millionaire, a sought-after speaker, a former mayor, a river rafter and sky-diver. And he accomplished all this after his accidents.

If you saw Mitchell you'd find this hard to believe. You see, this guy's face is a patchwork of multi-coloured skin grafts, the fingers of both his hands are either missing or mere stubs, and his paralyzed legs lie thin and useless under his trousers. Mitchell says sometimes people try to guess how he was injured. A car crash? A fire? The real story is more astounding than one could ever imagine. On 19 June 1971, he was on top of the world. The day before, he had bought a beautiful new motorcycle. That morning, he soloed in an airplane for the first time. He was young, healthy and popular.

'That afternoon, I got on that motorcycle to ride to work,' he recalls, 'and at a crossroads, a truck and I collided. The bike went down, crushed my elbow and fractured my pelvis, and the petrol cap popped open on the motorcycle. The petrol poured out, the heat of the engine ignited it and I got burned over 65 per cent of my body.' Fortunately, a quick-thinking man in a nearby car park doused Mitchell with a fire extinguisher and saved his life.

Even so, Mitchell's face had been burned off, his fingers were black, charred and twisted, his legs were nothing but raw, red flesh. It was common for first-time visitors to look at him and faint. He was unconscious for two weeks, and then he awakened.

Over four months, he had 13 transfusions, 16 skin-graft operations and several other surgeries. Four years later, after spending months in rehabilitation and years learning to adapt to his new handicaps, the unthinkable happened. Mitchell was involved in a freak airplane crash, and was paralyzed from the waist down. 'When I tell people there were two separate accidents,' he says, 'they can hardly stand it.'

After his paralyzing plane crash accident, Mitchell recalls meeting a nineteen-year-old patient in the hospital's gym. 'This guy had also been paralyzed. He had been a mountain climber, a skier, an active outdoors person, and he was convinced his life was over. Finally, I went over to this guy and said, "You know something? Before all this happened to me, there were 10,000 things I could do. Now there are 9,000. I could spend the rest of my life dwelling on the 1,000 that I lost, but I choose to focus on the 9,000 that are left."'

Mitchell says his secret is twofold. First is the love and encouragement of friends and family, and second is a personal philosophy he has gleaned from various sources. He realized he did not have to buy society's notion that one must be handsome and healthy to be happy. 'I am in charge of my own spaceship,' he states emphatically. 'It is my up, my down. I could choose to see this situation as a setback or a starting point.'

I like how Helen Keller put it, 'So much has been given to me. I have no time to ponder that which has been denied.'

Although most of our setbacks won't be as severe as Mitchell's, all of us will have our fair share. You might get dumped by a girlfriend, you may fail an exam, you may get beaten up by a gang, you may not get accepted to the university of your choice, you may become seriously ill. I hope and believe that you will be proactive and strong in these defining moments.

LOOK AT THIS AS AN OPPORTUNITY TO GROW.

I remember a major setback of my own. Two years after I had become the captain of my university football team, I seriously injured my knee, fell behind, and subsequently lost my position. I vividly recall my coach calling me into his office just before the season began and telling me they were handing the captain's position to someone else.

I felt sick. I had worked my whole life to get to this position. It was my final year. This *wasn't* supposed to happen.

As a backup, I had a choice to make. I could complain, bad-mouth the new guy, and feel sorry for myself. Or . . . I could make the most of the situation.

Luckily, I decided to deal with it. I was no longer winning matches, but I could help in other ways. So I swallowed my pride and began supporting the new guy and the rest of the team. I worked hard and prepared myself for each game as if I were the captain. And, more significant, I chose to keep my chin up.

Was it easy? Not at all. I often felt like a failure. Sitting out every game after being the captain was humiliating. And keeping a good attitude was a constant struggle.

Was it the right choice? Definitely. Even though I wore out my bum on the bench all year, I contributed to the team in other ways. Most important, I took responsibility for my attitude. I cannot begin to tell you what a positive difference this singular decision made in my life.

● RISING ABOVE ABUSE

One of the hardest setbacks of all is coping with abuse. I'll never forget the morning I spent with a group of teenagers who had been sexually abused as children, were victims of date rape or were otherwise abused emotionally or physically.

Heather told me this story:

I was sexually abused at fourteen. It happened when I was at a fair. A boy from school came up to me and said, 'I really need to talk to you, come with me for a few minutes'. I never suspected anything because this kid was my friend and had always been really nice to me. He took me on a long walk and we ended up on the school playing field. That was where he forced and raped me.

He kept telling me, 'If you tell anyone, no one will believe you. You wanted this to happen to you anyway'. He also told me that my parents would be so ashamed of me. I kept quiet about it for two years.

Finally, I was attending a help session where people who were abused told their stories and this one girl got up and told a story similar to mine. When she said the name of the boy that abused her, I started to cry because it was the same one who had raped me. It turned out that there were six of us who were victimized by him.

Fortunately, Heather is now on the road to recovery and has found tremendous strength in being part of a teen group that is trying to help other abuse victims. By coming forward, she has also put a stop to more people being hurt by the same boy.

Bridgett's story, unfortunately, is very common:

At the age of five I was sexually abused by a family member. Too afraid to tell anyone I tried to bury my hurt and anger. Now that I have come to terms with what happened, I look back on my life and can see how it has affected everything. In trying to hide something terrible I ended up hiding myself. It wasn't until thirteen years later that I finally confronted my childhood nightmare.

Many people have been through the same experience as I have or something that is related. Most hide it. Why? Some are afraid for their lives. Others want to protect themselves or someone else. But whatever the reason, hiding it isn't the answer. It only leaves a cut so deep in the soul that it seems that there's no way of healing it. Confronting it is the only way to sew up that bleeding gash. Find someone to talk to, someone you feel comfortable with, someone you can trust. It is a long and difficult process, but once you come to terms with it, it's only then that you can start to live.

If you have been abused, it's not your fault. And the truth has to be told. Abuse thrives in secrecy. By telling another person, you immediately divide your problem in half. Talk with a loved one or friend you can trust, take part in a help session, or visit a professional therapist. If the first person you share your troubles with isn't receptive, don't give up – keep sharing until you find someone who is. Sharing your secret with another is an important step in the healing and forgiving process. Be proactive. Take the initiative to do it. You don't need to live with this burden for one day longer. (Please refer to the abuse helplines listed at the back of the book for help or information.)

● BECOMING A CHANGE AGENT

I once asked a group of teenagers, *Who are your role models?* One girl mentioned her mother. Another kid talked about his brother. And so on. One guy was noticeably silent. I asked him whom he admired. He said quietly, 'I don't have a role model'. All he wanted to do was make sure he didn't turn out like the people who should have been his role models. Unfortunately, this is the case with many teenagers. They come from messed-up families and may not have anyone to pattern their lives after.

The scary thing is that bad habits such as abuse, alcoholism and welfare dependency are often passed down from parents to kids, and, as a result, dysfunctional families keep repeating themselves.

For example, if you have been abused as a child, the statistics show that you are likely to become an abuser as well. Sometimes these problems go back for generations. You may come from a long line of alcohol or drug abusers. You may come from a long line of dependency on welfare. Perhaps no one in your family has ever gone on to further education.

The good news is that you can stop the cycle. Because you are proactive, you can stop these bad habits from being passed on. You can become a 'change agent' and pass on good habits to future generations, starting with your own kids.

A tenacious young girl named Hilda from America shared with me how she has become a change agent in her family. Education was never valued in her home, and Hilda could see the consequences of it. Says Hilda: 'My mum worked in a factory sewing, for very little money, and my father worked for slightly over the minimum wage. I would hear them arguing over the money and how they were going to pay the rent. My parents left school at fifteen.'

Whether I fail
or succeed shall be
no man's doing
but my own.
I am the force.
ELAINE MAXWELL

As a young girl, Hilda vividly remembers her dad being unable to help her with her homework because he couldn't read English. This was hard on her.

When Hilda was in secondary school, her family moved from California back to Mexico. Hilda soon realized that there were limited educational options for her there, so she asked if she could move back to the States to live with her aunt. For the next several years Hilda made great sacrifices to stay in school.

'It was hard to be crowded into a room with my cousin,' she says, 'and have to share a bed and work to pay them rent as well as go to school, but it was worth it.

'Even though I had a kid and got married in school, I kept going to school and working towards finishing my education. I wanted to prove to my dad that no matter what, he was wrong when he said no one in our family could become a professional.'

Hilda will soon be graduating with a university degree in finance. She wants her educational values to be passed on to her kids: 'Today, every time I can, when I am not in school, I sit on the sofa and I read to my son. I am teaching him how to speak English and Spanish. I'm trying to save money for his education. One day he will need help with his homework, and I will be there to help him read it.'

I interviewed another sixteen-year-old kid named Shane who is also becoming a change agent in his family. Shane lives with his parents and two siblings on a fairly rough council estate. Although his parents are still together, they're constantly fighting and accusing each other of having affairs. His dad drives a lorry and is never home. His mum smokes weed with his twelve-year-old sister. His older brother left school with no qualifications. At one point Shane had lost hope.

Just when he'd thought he had hit rock bottom, he got involved in a character development class at school (that taught the 7 Habits), and he began to see that there were things he could do to seize control of his life and create a future for himself.

Fortunately, Shane's grandfather owned the upstairs flat where Shane's family lived, so Shane paid him £100 a month rent, and he moved to that flat. He now has his own sanctuary and is able to block out everything he doesn't want to be part of on the floor below. Says Shane: 'Things have gotten better now for me. I treat myself better and I show myself respect. My family doesn't have very much respect for themselves. Although nobody in my family has ever gone to college, I have been accepted to three different universities. Everything I do now is for my future. My future is going to be different. I know I won't sit down with my twelve-year-old daughter and smoke weed.'

You have the power within you to rise above whatever may have been passed down to you. You may not have the option of moving upstairs to escape from it all as Shane did, but you can figuratively move upstairs in your mind. No matter how bad your predicament is, you can become a change agent and create a new life for yourself and whatever may follow.

GROWING YOUR PROACTIVE MUSCLES

The following poem is a great summary of what it means to take responsibility for one's life and how a person can gradually move from a reactive to a proactive frame of mind.

AUTOBIOGRAPHY IN
FIVE SHORT CHAPTERS

From *There's a Hole in My Sidewalk*
by Portia Nelson

I

I walk down the street.
There is a deep hole in the sidewalk.
I fall in.
I am lost . . . I am helpless.
It isn't my fault.
It takes forever to find a way out.

II

I walk down the same street.
There is a deep hole in the sidewalk.
I pretend I don't see it.
I fall in again.
I can't believe I am in the same place.
But, it isn't my fault.
It still takes a long time to get out.

III

I walk down the same street.
There is a deep hole in the sidewalk.
I see it is there.
I still fall in. It's a habit.
My eyes are open.
I know where I am.
It is my fault. I get out immediately.

IV

I walk down the same street.
There is a deep hole in the sidewalk.
I walk around it.

V

I walk down another street.

You, too, can take responsibility for your life and stay away from potholes by flexing your proactive muscles. It's a 'breakthrough' habit that will save your bacon more often than you could ever imagine!

NOTHING CAN HURT 'PROACTIVE MAN'!

CAN-DO

Being proactive really means two things. First, you take responsibility for your life. Second, you have a 'can-do' attitude. Can-do is very different from 'no-can-do'. Just take a peek.

CAN-DO PEOPLE	NO-CAN-DO PEOPLE
Take initiative to make it happen	Wait for something to happen to them
Think about solutions and options	Think about problems and barriers
Act	Are acted upon

If you think can-do, and you're creative and persistent, it's amazing what you can accomplish. During university, I remember being told that to fulfill my language requirement, I would 'have to' take a course that I had no interest in and was meaningless to me. Instead of taking it, however, I decided to create my own. So I put together a list of books I would read and the coursework I would do and found a teacher to sponsor me. I then went to the head of the department and presented my case. He bought into my idea and I completed my language requirement by taking my self-built course.

American aviator Elinor Smith once said, 'It has long since come to my attention that people of accomplishment rarely sat back and let things happen to them. They went out and happened to things.'

It's so true. To reach your goals in life, you must seize the initiative. If you're feeling bad about not being asked out on dates, don't just sit around and sulk, do something about it. Find ways to meet people. Be friendly and try smiling a lot. Ask *them* out. They may not know how great you are.

Don't wait for that perfect job to fall in your lap, go after it. Send out your résumé, network, volunteer to work for free.

If you're at a shop and need assistance, don't wait for the salesperson to find you, you find them.

Some people mistake can-do for being pushy, aggressive or obnoxious. Wrong. Can-do is courageous, persistent and smart. Others think can-do people stretch the rules and make their own laws. Not so. Can-do thinkers are creative, enterprising and extremely resourceful.

Pia, a work associate of mine, shared the following story. Although it took place a long time ago, the principle of can-do is the same:

I was a young journalist in a big city in Europe, working full-time as a reporter for United Press International. I was inexperienced and always nervous that I wouldn't be able to live up to the expectations of a tough and much older male press crew. The Beatles were coming to town, and to my amazement I was appointed to cover their stay. (My editor didn't know how big they were.) They were the hottest thing in Europe in those days. Girls fainted by the hundreds just by their presence, and here I was going to cover their press conference.

The press conference was exciting and I was elated to be there, but I realized that everyone would have the same story – I needed something more, something meaty, something that really would make front page. I just couldn't waste this opportunity. One by one, all the experienced reporters went back to their papers to report and the Beatles went up to their rooms. I stayed behind. I've got to figure out a way to get to these guys, I thought. And there's no time to lose.

I walked to the hotel lobby, picked up the house phone and dialed the penthouse. I guessed they would be staying there. Their manager answered. 'This is Pia Jensen from United Press International. I would like to come talk to the Beatles,' I said confidently. (What did I have to lose?)

To my amazement he said, 'Come on up.'

Trembling and feeling like I had hit the jackpot, I entered the elevator and went up to the royal suites of the hotel. I was led into an area as big as an entire floor – and here they all sat, Ringo, Paul, John and George. I gulped down my nervousness and inexperience and tried to act like a world-class reporter.

I spent the next two hours laughing, listening, talking, writing and having the best time of my life. They treated me royally and gave me all the attention in the world!

My story was splashed on the front page of the leading newspaper in the country the next morning. And my more extended interviews with each of the Beatles appeared as a feature in most of the newspapers of the world within the next few days. When the Rolling Stones came to town after that – guess who they sent? Me, a young, female, inexperienced reporter. I used the same approach with them and it worked again. I soon realized what I could accomplish by being pleasantly persistent. A pattern was set in my mind, and I was convinced anything was possible. With this approach, I usually got the best story, and my news career took on a new dimension.

George Bernard Shaw, the playwright, knew all about can-do. Listen to how he said it: 'People are always blaming their circumstances for what they are. I don't believe in circumstances. The people who get on in this world are the people who get up and look for the circumstances they want, and if they can't find them, make them.'

Pay attention to how Denise was able to create the circumstances she wanted:

I know it's strange for a teenager to want to work in a library, but I really wanted that job – more than I had ever wanted anything, but they weren't hiring. I would go to the library every day and read, hang out with my friends and just get away from home – what better place to work than someplace I already hung out at? Although I didn't have a job there, I got to know the office staff, and I volunteered for special events and pretty soon I was one of the regulars. It paid off. When they finally had an opening, I was their first choice, and I found one of the best jobs I ever had.

● JUST PUSH PAUSE

So when someone is rude to you, where do you get the power to resist being rude back? For starters, just push pause. Yep, just reach up and push the pause button to your life just as you would on your remote control. (If I remember right, the pause button is found somewhere in the middle of your forehead.) Sometimes life is moving so fast that we instantly react to everything out of sheer habit. If you can learn to pause, get control and think about how you want to respond, you'll make

smarter decisions. Yes, your childhood, your parents, your genes and your environment *influence you* to act in certain ways, but they can't *make you* do anything. You are not determined but are free to choose.

While your life is on pause, open up your tool-box (the one that you were born with) and use your four human tools to help you decide what to do. Animals don't have these tools and that's why you're smarter than your dog. These tools are self-awareness, conscience, imagination and willpower. You might want to call them your power tools.

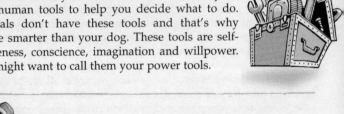

 SELF-AWARENESS: *I can stand apart from myself and observe my thoughts and actions.*

 CONSCIENCE: *I can listen to my inner voice to know right from wrong.*

IMAGINATION: *I can envision new possibilities.*

WILLPOWER: *I have the power to choose.*

Let's illustrate these tools by imagining a teenager named Rosa and her dog, Woof, as they go for a walk:

'Here, boy. What say we go outside,' says Rosa as Woof leaps up and down, wagging his tail.

It's been a rough week for Rosa. Not only has she just broken up with her boyfriend, Eric, but she and her mum are barely on speaking terms.

As she strolls down the sidewalk, Rosa begins thinking about the past week. 'You know what?' she muses to herself. 'Breaking up with Eric has really been tough on me. It's probably why I've been so rude to Mum and taking out all my frustrations on her.'

You see what Rosa is doing? She's standing apart from herself and evaluating and measuring her actions. This process is called **self-awareness.** *It's a tool that is native to all humanoids. By using her self-awareness, Rosa is able to recognize that she's allowing her breakup with Eric to affect her relationship with her mum. This observation is the first step to changing the way she has been treating her mother.*

Meanwhile, Woof sees a cat up ahead and instinctively takes off in a frenzy after it.

Although Woof is a loyal dog, he is completely unaware of himself. He doesn't even know that he is a dog. He is incapable of standing apart from himself and saying, 'You know what? Ever since Suzy (his dog friend next door) moved, I've been taking out my anger on all the neighbourhood cats.'

As she continues her stroll, Rosa's thoughts begin to wander. She can hardly wait for the school concert tomorrow, when she will be performing a solo. Music is her life. Rosa imagines herself singing at the concert. She sees herself dazzling the audience, then bowing to receive a rousing standing ovation from all of her friends and teachers . . . and, of course, all the cute guys.

*In this scene, Rosa is using another one of her human tools, **imagination.** It is a remarkable gift. It allows us to escape our present circumstances and create new possibilities in our heads. It gives us a chance to visualize our futures and dream up what we would like to become.*

While Rosa is imagining visions of grandeur, Woof is busily digging up the earth trying to get at a worm.

Woof's imagination is about as alive as a rock. Zilch. He can't think beyond the moment. He can't envision new possibilities. Can you imagine Woof thinking, 'Someday, I'm going to make Lassie look like chopped liver'?

'Hi, Rosa, whatcha doin'?' says Heide, pulling up alongside Rosa in her car.

'Oh, hello, Heide,' replies a startled Rosa, as she brings her thoughts back to earth. 'You surprised me. I'm just taking Woof for a walk.'

'Hey, I heard about you and Eric. What a bummer.'

Rosa is bothered by Heide's reference to Eric. It's none of her business. Although she is tempted to be curt with Heide, she knows Heide is new at school and desperately in need of friends. Rosa feels that being warm and friendly is the right thing to do.

'Yeah, breaking up with Eric has been tough. So how are things with you, Heide?'

*Rosa has just used her human tool called **conscience**. A conscience is an 'inner voice' that will always teach us right from wrong. Each of us has a conscience. And it will either grow or shrink depending upon whether or not we follow its promptings.*

Meanwhile, Woof is relieving himself on Mr Newman's newly painted fence.

Woof has absolutely no moral sense of right and wrong. After all, he is just a dog. And dogs will do whatever their instincts compel them to do.

Rosa's walk with Woof comes to an end. As she opens the front door to her house, she hears her mum yell from the other room, 'Rosa, just where have you been? I've been looking all over for you.'

Rosa had already made up her mind to not lose her cool with her mum, so, despite wanting to yell back 'Get out of my face,' she responds calmly,

'Just out for a walk with Woof, Mum . . .'

'Woof! Woof! Come back here,' screams Rosa as Woof darts out the open door to chase the local paper boy on his bike.

*While Rosa is using her fourth human tool of **willpower** to control her anger, Woof, who has been told not to chase the paper boy, is overcome by his instincts. Willpower is the power to act. It says that we have the power to choose, to control our emotions, and to overcome our habits and instincts.*

As you can see in the above example, we either use or fail to use our four human tools every day of our lives. The more we use them, the stronger they become and the more power we have to be proactive. However, if we fail to use them, we tend to *react* by instinct like a dog and not *act* by choice like a human.

HUMAN TOOLS IN ACTION

Mark Reed once told me how his proactive response to a family crisis changed his life forever. Mark was raised in a really rough area, the fourth in a family of seven kids. No one in the Reed family had ever gone on to further education, and Mark wasn't about to be the first. Mark was unsure about his future. His family was struggling. His street was filled with gangs and drug dealers. Could he ever get out? While in his house, on a still summer night before his final year at school, Mark heard a series of gunshots.

'It's becoming more and more common to hear gunshots, and I didn't pay it no mind,' said Mark.

Suddenly one of his friends, who'd been shot in the leg, burst through the door and began hollering that Mark's little brother, Kevin, had just been shot and killed.

'I was upset and I was angry and I was hurt and I lost somebody I ain't never going to see again in my life,' Mark told me. 'He was only thirteen years old. And he was shot over a petty little street scuffle. I can't explain how life went after that. It was just straight downhill for the whole family.'

Mark's natural reaction was to kill the murderer. After all, Mark was raised in the streets and this was the only real way he could pay back his dead brother. The police were still trying to figure out who did it, but Mark knew. On a muggy August night, a few weeks after Kevin's death, Mark got hold of a gun and went out in the streets to get revenge on Tony 'Fat Tone' Davis, the crack dealer who had killed his brother.

'It was dark. Davis and his friends couldn't see me. There he was sitting, talking, laughing, having fun, and here I am within fifty feet of him, crouched behind a car with a loaded gun. I was sitting there thinking, "I could just pull this little trigger and kill the guy who killed my brother."'

Big decision.

At this point, Mark pushed pause and caught hold of himself. Using his *imagination*, he thought about his past and his future. 'I thought about my life in a matter of seconds. I weighed my options. I weighed the chances of me escaping, not getting caught, the police trying to figure out who I was. I thought about the times Kevin would come watch me play football. He always told me I was going to be a professional football player. I thought about my future, about going to university. About what I wanted to make of my life.'

Pausing, Mark listened to his *conscience*. 'I'm holding a gun, I'm shaking and I think the good side of me told me to get up and go home and go to school. If I took revenge, I'd be throwing away my future. I'd be no better than the guy who shot my brother.'

Using raw *willpower*, Mark, instead of giving in to his anger and throwing away his life, got up, walked home, and vowed that he would finish college for his dead brother.

Nine months later Reed had got good grades in his A-levels. People in his school couldn't believe it. Five years later, he had become a university football star and a graduate.

Like Mark, each of us will face an extraordinary challenge or two along the way, and we can *choose* whether to rise to those challenges or to be conquered by them.

Elaine Maxwell sums up the entire matter quite well: 'Whether I fail or succeed shall be no man's doing but my own. I am the force; I can clear any obstacle before me or I can be lost in the maze. My choice; my responsibility; win or lose, only I hold the key to my destiny.'

It's kind of like the old Volkswagen commercials. 'On the road of life, there are passengers and there are drivers . . . Drivers wanted!'

So let me ask you, are you in the driver's seat of your life or are you merely a passenger? Are you conducting your symphony or simply being played? Are you acting like a can of fizzy drink or a bottle of water?

After all that's been said and done, *the choice is yours!*

COMING ATTRACTIONS

In the chapter that follows, I'll take you on a ride you'll never forget called The Great Discovery. Come along. It's a thrill a minute!

BABY STEPS

1. The next time someone sticks two fingers up at you, give them the peace sign back.

2. Listen carefully to your words today. Count how many times you use reactive language, such as 'You make me . . .' 'I have to . . .' 'Why can't they . . .' 'I can't . . .'

Reactive language I use most: _____

_____

_____

3. Do something today that you have wanted to do but never dared. Leave your comfort zone and go for it. Ask someone out on a date, raise your hand in class or join a team.

4. Write yourself a Post-it note: 'I will not let _____ decide how I'm going to feel.' Place it by your mirror or in your diary and refer to it often.

5. At the next party, don't just sit against the wall and wait for excitement to find you, you find it. Walk up and introduce yourself to someone new.

6. The next time you receive a mark that you think is unfair, don't cry about it, make an appointment with the teacher to discuss it and then see what you can learn.

7. If you get in a fight with a parent or a friend, be the first to apologize.

HABIT 1

BABY STEPS

8 Identify something in your circle of no control that you are always worrying about. Decide now to drop it.

Thing that I can't control that I always worry about:

_____

_____

9 Push the pause button before you react to someone who bumps into you in the corridor, calls you a name or jumps the queue.

10 Use your tool of self-awareness right now by asking yourself, 'What is my most unhealthy habit?' Make up your mind to do something about it.

Most unhealthy habit: _____

_____

What I'm going to do about it: _____

_____

_____

_____

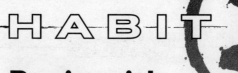

HABIT 2

Begin with the End in Mind

Control Your Own Destiny

OR SOMEONE ELSE WILL

'**Would** you tell me please which way I ought to walk from here?'
'That depends a good deal on where you want to get to,' said the Cat.
'I don't much care where—' said Alice.
'Then it doesn't matter which way to walk,' said the Cat.
FROM *ALICE'S ADVENTURES IN WONDERLAND*

You've just been asked to put together a jigsaw puzzle. Having done many such puzzles before, you're excited to get started. You pour out all 1,000 pieces, spreading them out across a large table. You then pick up the lid to the box to look at what you're putting together. But there's no picture! It's blank! How will you ever be able to finish the puzzle without knowing what it looks like, you wonder? If you only had a one-second glimpse of what it's supposed to be. That's all you'd need. What a difference it would make! Without it, you don't have a clue where to even start.

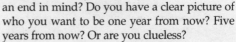

Now think about your own life and your 1,000 pieces. Do you have

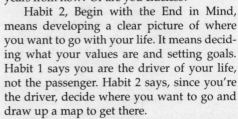

an end in mind? Do you have a clear picture of who you want to be one year from now? Five years from now? Or are you clueless?

Habit 2, Begin with the End in Mind, means developing a clear picture of where you want to go with your life. It means deciding what your values are and setting goals. Habit 1 says you are the driver of your life, not the passenger. Habit 2 says, since you're the driver, decide where you want to go and draw up a map to get there.

'Now just wait a minute, Sean,' you might be thinking. 'I don't know what my end in mind is. I don't know what I want to be when I grow up.' If it makes you feel any better, I'm grown up and I still don't know what I want to be. By saying begin with the end in mind, I'm not talking about deciding every little detail of your future, like choosing your career or deciding whom you'll marry. I'm simply talking about thinking beyond today and deciding what direction you want to take with your life, so that each step you take is always in the right direction.

Begin with the End in Mind — What It Means $\widehat{Y}$ou may not realize it, but you do it all the time. Beginning with the end in mind, that is. You draw up a blueprint before you build a house. You read a recipe before you bake a cake. You create an outline before you write an essay (at least I hope you do). It's part of life.

Let's have a begin-with-the-end-in-mind experience right now using your tool of imagination. Find a place where you can be alone without interruption.

There. Now, clear your mind of everything. Don't worry about school, your friends, your family, or that zit on your forehead. Just focus with me, breathe deeply and open your mind.

In your mind's eye, visualize someone walking toward you about half a block away. At first you can't see who it is. As this person gets closer and closer, you suddenly realize, believe it or not, that it's you. But it's not you today, it's you as you would *like to be* one year from now.

Now think deeply.

What have you done with your life over the past year?

How do you feel inside?

What do you look like?

What characteristics do you possess? (Remember, this is you as you would *like to be* one year from now.)

You can float back to reality now. If you were a good sport and actually tried this experiment, you probably got in touch with your deeper self. You got a feel for what's important to you and what you'd like to accomplish this next year. That's called beginning with the end in mind. And it doesn't even hurt.

As Jim discovered, beginning with the end in mind is a powerful way to help turn your dreams into realities:

When I feel frustrated or get depressed, I have found something that really helps me. I go someplace where I can be alone, and then I close my eyes and I visualize mentally where I want to be and where I want to go when I am an adult. I try to see the whole picture of my dream life – and then I automatically begin to think about what it's going to take to get there, what I need to change. This technique started when I was fifteen, and today I am on my way to making some of those visualizations become a reality.

In fact, thinking beyond today can really be quite exciting and, as this A-level student attests, can help you take charge of your life:

HABIT 2

I have never planned a thing in my life. I just do things as they pop up. The thought that one should have an end in mind never, ever entered my mind. It has been so exciting to learn, because I suddenly find myself thinking beyond the now. I am now not only planning my education but also thinking about how I want to raise my kids, how I want to teach my family and what kind of home life we should have. I am taking charge of me – and not blowing in the wind anymore!

Why is it so important to have an end in mind? I'll give you two good reasons. The first is that you are at a critical crossroads in life, and the paths you choose now can affect you forever. The second is that if you don't decide your own future, someone else will do it for you.

THE CROSSROADS OF LIFE

Let's take a look at the first important reason. So here you are. You're young. You're free. You have your whole life before you. You're standing at the crossroads of life and you have to choose which paths to take:

Do you want to go to university?

What will your attitude toward life be?

Should you try out for that team?

What type of friends do you want to have?

Will you join a gang?

Who will you date?

Will you have sex before marriage?

Will you drink, smoke, do drugs?

What values will you choose?

What kind of relationships do you want with your family?

What will you stand for?

How will you contribute to your community?

The paths you choose today can shape you forever. It's both frightening and exciting that we have to make so many vital decisions when we're so young and full of hormones, but such is life. Imagine an eighty-foot rope stretched out before you. Each foot represents one year of your life. Teenagehood is only seven years, such a short span of rope, but those seven affect the remaining sixty-one, for good or bad, in such a powerful way.

What About Friends?

Take your choice of friends as an example. What a powerful influence they can have on your attitude, reputation and direction! The need to be accepted and be part of a group is powerful. But too often we choose our friends based on whoever will accept us. And that's not always good. For example, to be accepted by the kids who do drugs, all you have to do is do drugs yourself.

It's hard, but sometimes it is better to have no friends for a time than to have the wrong friends. The wrong group can lead you down all kinds of paths you really don't want to be on. And retracing your steps can be a long and hard journey. I have a close friend who fortunately had enough common sense to drop his old friends for some new ones, and he shared the following:

The summer before my last year at school, I had a really good friend named Jack. The month before school started, he went to Europe and to my surprise came back with a powerful drug called hashish. Neither of us had ever experimented with drugs before. He began to invite me to join him in using this drug with a group of his 'new' friends. He also started the '24 club', where you would sit in a circle and drink twenty-four tall bottles of beer, one after another, until they were gone. I knew there was no future in any of it and that eventually he would self-destruct if he continued using these drugs. However, he had been my best friend since primary school, and I didn't have a lot of other close friends. I didn't want to be a loner, but I also didn't want to end up where I thought Jack was going.

I remember finally deciding (sadly) that it was just too risky to hang out with him anymore. And so in my final year I had to start over making friends. At first I felt awkward, didn't fit in and felt stupid being alone. But after a few months I made friends with guys who had similar values and were also a lot of fun.

My old friend Jack turned into a druggie, barely passed his exams, and eventually drowned in a swimming pool while intoxicated. It was very sad, but I was grateful I had the guts to stick with the right decision and think long-term at a crucial time in my life.

If you're having trouble making good friends, remember that your friends don't always have to be your age. I once spoke to a guy who seemed to have very few friends at school, but he did have a grandpa who listened to him and was a great friend. This seemed to fill the friendship void he had in his life. The long and short of it is, just be wise when choosing friends, because much of your future hangs on who you hang out with.

What About Sex?

And what about sex? Talk about an important decision with huge consequences! If you wait until the 'heat of the moment' to choose which path to take, it's too late. Your decision has already been made. You need to decide now. The path you choose will affect your health, your self-image, how fast you grow up, your reputation, whom you marry, your future children and so much more. Think this decision through . . . carefully. One way to do this is to imagine how you hope to feel on your wedding day. How do you hope your future mate is leading his or her life right now?

In a recent poll, going to movies was ranked as the favourite pastime of teenagers. I love movies, so I'm right there with you. But I'd be careful about the values they promote. The movies lie, especially when it comes to issues like sex. They glamorize sleeping around and having one-night stands without acknowledging the potential risks and consequences. The movies don't show you the life-altering reality of contracting a sexually transmitted disease like Aids or becoming pregnant and having to deal with everything that brings with it. They don't tell you what it's like living on minimum wage because you had to drop out of school (and the father of the child is long gone and sends no money) or what it's like spending your weekends changing nappies and caring for a baby instead of cheering on your football team, going to clubs and just being a kid.

We are free to choose our paths, but we can't choose the consequences that come with them. Have you ever gone on a water slide? You can choose which slide you want to go down, but once you're sliding, you can't very well stop. You must live with the consequences . . . to the end. A teenage girl shared this story:

I had one bad year when I did everything from drinking, drugs, older guys, bad crowds, etc., mostly because I was frustrated and unhappy. It just lasted a year, but I am still paying for those past mistakes. No one forgets and it's hard to have to deal with a past you aren't too proud of. I feel as though it will haunt me forever. All kinds of people still come up to my boyfriend and say, 'I hear your girlfriend drinks, and smokes, and is easy.' And things like that. But the worst is probably the fact that every time I have a problem of any kind, I immediately think, 'Maybe if I hadn't done that, everything would be okay.'

What About School?

What you do about your schooling can also shape your future in a major way. Jane's experience goes to show how beginning with the end in mind in your educational pursuits pays off:

In the Lower Sixth, I decided to take an AS level in history.

Throughout the school year the teacher bombarded us with homework. It was difficult to keep up, but I was determined to do well in the class as well as pass the exam. With this end in mind, it was easy to put forth my full effort on each assignment.

One assignment was particularly time consuming. The teacher asked each student to watch a documentary on the Civil War and write an essay on each segment. The series lasted ten days and each segment was two hours long. As an active student, it was difficult to find the time, but I did. I submitted the essays and discovered I was one of only a handful of students who watched the series.

The day of the exam finally arrived. The students were nervous and the air was thick. The test administrator announced, 'Begin'. I took a deep breath and broke the seal on the first section – multiple choice. With each question, I gained confidence. I KNEW the answers! I completed the section several minutes before I heard, 'Pencils down'.

Next we would each write an essay. I nervously opened the seal of the essay book and scanned the questions quickly. I answered a question

related to the Civil War using references from my reading as well as the
documentary. I felt calm and confident as I completed the exam.
Several weeks later I received my score in the post – I had passed!

WHO'S IN THE LEAD?

The other reason to create a vision is that if you don't, someone else
will do it for you. As Jack Welch, former teenager and current business
executive, put it, 'Control your own destiny or someone else will.'

'Who will?' you may ask.

Perhaps your friends or parents or the media. Do you want your
friends to tell you what you stand for? You may have fine parents,
but do you want them to draw up the blueprint for your life? Their
interests may be far different from yours. Do you want to adopt the
values portrayed in soaps, magazines and on the big screen?

By now you might be thinking, 'But I don't like to think about
the future so much. I like to live in the moment and go with the
flow.' I agree with the *live in the moment* part. We ought to enjoy the
moment and not have our heads too far in the clouds. But I disagree with the *go with the flow* part. If you decide to just go with the
flow, you'll end up where the flow goes, which is usually downhill,
often leading to a big pile of sludge and a life of unhappiness.
You'll end up doing what everyone else is doing, which may not be
your end in mind at all. 'The road to anywhere is really a life to
nowhere.'

Without an end in mind of our own we are often so quick to follow anyone who is willing to lead, even into things that won't get
us far. It reminds me of an experience I once had at a 10K road race.
Some other runners and I were waiting for the race to start, but no
one knew where the starting line was. Then a few runners began
walking down the road as if they knew. Everyone, including me,
began following. We just assumed they knew where they were
going. After walking for about a mile, we all suddenly realized, that
like a herd of stupid sheep, we were following some idiot who had
no idea where he was going. It turned out that the starting line was
back right where we had begun.

Never assume that the herd must know where they are going,
because they usually don't.

A Personal Mission Statement

So if it is so important to have an end in mind, how do you do it? The best way I have found is to write a personal mission statement. A personal mission statement is like a personal credo or motto that states what your life is about. It is like the blueprint to your life. Countries have constitutions, which function just like a mission statement. And most companies, like Microsoft and Coca-Cola, have mission statements. But I think they work best with people.

So why not write your own personal mission statement? Many teenagers have. As you'll see, they come in all types and varieties. Some are long and some are short. Some are poems and some are songs. Some teenagers have used their favourite quote as a mission statement. Others have used a picture or a photograph.

Let me share a few teenage mission statements with you.

This first one was contributed by a teenager named Beth Haire:

First and foremost, I will remain faithful
always to my God.

I will not underestimate the power of family unity.

I will not neglect a true friend, but I will set aside
time for myself as well.

I will cross my bridges as I come to them
(divide and conquer).

I will begin all challenges with optimism,
rather than doubt.

I will always maintain a positive self-image
and high self-esteem, knowing that all my intentions begin
with self-evaluation.

Mary Sylvester took her mission statement from the Sinéad O'Connor song 'Emperor's New Clothes'. It reads:

I will live by my own policies.
I will sleep with a clear conscience.
I will sleep in peace.

HABIT 2

Steven Strong shared this one:

R eligion
  E ducation
    S ucceeding
      P roductive
        E xercise
          C aring
            T ruthful

I met a teen named Adam Sosne who was familiar with the 7 Habits and was 'on fire' about his future plans. Not surprisingly, he had a mission statement, which he volunteered:

MISSION STATEMENT

- Have confidence in yourself and everyone else around you.
- Be kind, courteous and respectful to all people.
- Set reachable goals.
- Never lose sight of these goals.
- Never take the simple things in life for granted.
- Appreciate other people's differences and see their differences as a great advantage.

- Ask questions.
- Strive each day to reach interdependence.
- Remember that before you can change someone else, you must first change yourself.
- Speak with your actions, not with your words.
- Make the time to help those less fortunate than yourself or those who are having a bad day.
- Read the 7 Habits every day.

Read this mission statement every day.

So what can writing a mission statement do for you? Tons. The most important thing it will do is open your eyes to what's really important to you and help you make decisions accordingly. An eighteen year old shared how writing a mission statement made such a difference in her life:

During the Lower Sixth I couldn't concentrate on anything because I had a boyfriend. I wanted to do everything for him to make him happy, and then, naturally, the subject of sex came up – and I wasn't at all prepared for it, and it became a nagging constant thing on my mind. I felt like I wasn't ready and that I didn't want to have sex – but everyone else kept saying, 'Just do it'.

Then I participated in a personal development class at school where they taught me to write a mission statement. I started to write and kept on writing and writing, and kept adding things to it. It gave me direction and a focus and I felt like I had a plan and a reason for doing what I was doing. It really helped me to stick to my standards and not do something I wasn't ready for.

A personal mission statement is like a tree with deep roots. It is stable and isn't going anywhere, but it is also alive and continually growing.

You need a tree with deep roots to help you survive all of the storms of life that beat you up. As you've probably noticed already, life is anything but stable. Think about it. People are fickle. Your boyfriend loves you one minute and then dumps you the next. You're someone's best friend one day, and they're talking behind your back the next.

Think about all of the events you can't control. You have to move. You lose your job. The country is at war. Your parents are getting divorced.

Fads come and go. Sweaters are popular one year and on their way out the next. Rap music is the thing. Rap music stinks.

While everything about you changes, a personal mission statement can be your deep-rooted tree that never moves. You can deal with change if you have an immovable trunk to hang on to.

UNCOVERING YOUR TALENTS

An important part of developing a personal mission statement is discovering what you're good at. One thing I know for sure is that everyone has a talent, a gift, something they do well. Some talents, like having the singing voice of an angel, attract a lot of attention. But there are many other talents, maybe not as attention grabbing but every bit as important if not more – things like being skilled at listening, making people laugh, giving, forgiving, drawing or just being nice.

Another truth is that we all blossom at different times. So if you're a late bloomer, relax. It may take you a while to uncover your talents.

After carving a beautiful sculpture, Michelangelo was asked how he was able to do it. He replied by saying that the sculpture was already in the block of granite from the very beginning; he just had to chisel off everything else around it.

Likewise, Victor Frankl, a famous Jewish-Austrian psychiatrist who survived the death camps of Nazi Germany, taught that we don't *invent* our talents in life but rather we *detect* them. In other words, you are already born with your talents, you just need to uncover them.

I'll never forget my experience with finding a talent I never thought I had. To fulfill Mr Williams' creative writing for one of my first year modules, I excitedly turned in my first homework, entitled 'The Old Man and the Fish'. It was the same story my father had often told me at night while I was growing up. I just assumed he had made it up. He didn't bother telling me he had stolen the plot directly from Ernest Hemingway's award-winning novel *The Old Man and the Sea*. I was shocked when my paper was returned with the remarks, 'Sounds a bit trite. Like Hemingway's *Old Man and the Sea*.' 'Who's this guy Hemingway?' I thought. 'And how come he copied my dad?' That was my poor start to four years of rather boring English classes, which were about as exciting to me as a clump of dirt.

It wasn't until university, when I took a short story class from a remarkable professor, that I began to detect my passion for writing. If you can believe it, I even got a first in English. Mr Williams would have died.

The Great Discovery

The Great Discovery* is a fun activity designed to help you get in touch with your deeper self as you prepare to write a mission statement. As you walk through it, answer the questions honestly. You can write your answers in the book, if you'd like. If you don't feel like writing your answers down, just think them through. When you're finished, I think you'll have a much better idea of what inspires you, what you enjoy doing, whom you admire and where you want to take your life.

---

*For additional worksheets of The Great Discovery, please call www.franklincovey.com
*www.7Habits4teens.com

THE
GREAT
DISCOVERY!

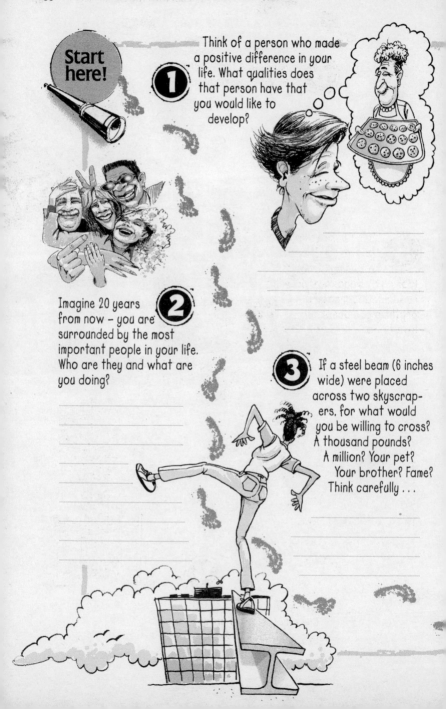

Start here!

1 Think of a person who made a positive difference in your life. What qualities does that person have that you would like to develop?

2 Imagine 20 years from now – you are surrounded by the most important people in your life. Who are they and what are you doing?

3 If a steel beam (6 inches wide) were placed across two skyscrapers, for what would you be willing to cross? A thousand pounds? A million? Your pet? Your brother? Fame? Think carefully . . .

6 Describe a time when you were deeply inspired.

_____

_____

_____

_____

5 List 10 things you love to do. It could be singing, dancing, looking at magazines, drawing, reading, daydreaming . . . anything you absolutely love to do!

1 _____

2 _____

3 _____

4 _____

5 _____

6 _____

7 _____

8 _____

9 _____

10 _____

4

If you could spend one day in a great library studying anything you wanted, what would you study?

_____

_____

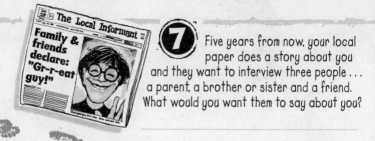

7 Five years from now, your local paper does a story about you and they want to interview three people . . . a parent, a brother or sister and a friend. What would you want them to say about you?

_____

_____

_____

8 Think of something that represents you . . . a rose, a song, an animal . . . Why does it represent you?

_____

_____

_____

9 If you could spend an hour with any person who ever lived, who would that be? Why that person? What would you ask?

_____

_____

_____

Good with numbers
Good with words
Creative thinking
Sport
Making things happen
Sensing needs
Mechanical
Artistic
Working well with people
Memorizing things
Decision making
Building things
Accepting others
Predicting what will happen

Speaking
Writing
Dancing
Listening
Singing
Humorous
Sharing
Music
Trivia

10 Everyone has one or more talents. Which of the ones above are you good at? Or write down ones not listed.

Getting Started on Your Mission Statement Now that you've taken the time to walk through The Great Discovery, you've got a good jump-start on developing a mission statement. Below, I've listed four easy methods to help you get started writing your own mission statement. You may want to try one of them or combine all four of them in any way you see fit. These are just suggestions, so feel free to find your own method.

Method #1: The Quote Collection. Collect one to five of your very favourite quotes onto one sheet of paper. The sum of these quotes then becomes your mission statement. For some, great quotes are very inspiring, and this method works well for them.

Method #2: The Brain Dump. Speed write about your mission for fifteen minutes. Don't worry about what's coming out. Don't edit what you're writing. Just keep writing and don't stop writing. Get all of your ideas down on paper. If you get stuck, reflect upon your answers to The Great Discovery. That should get your imagination in gear. When your brain has been sufficiently purged, take another fifteen minutes to edit, arrange and make sense of your brain dump.

The result is that in just thirty minutes, you'll have a rough draft of your mission statement. Then over the next several weeks you can revise it, add to it, clarify it or do whatever else you need to make it inspire you.

Method #3: The Retreat. Plan a large chunk of time, like an entire afternoon, and go to a place you adore and where you can be alone. Think deeply about your life and what you want to make of it. Review your answers to The Great Discovery. Look to the mission statement examples in this book for ideas. Take your time and construct your own mission statement using any method you see fit.

Method #4: The Big Lazy. If you're really lazy, use the US Army's slogan 'Be All That You Can Be' as your personal mission statement. (Hey, I'm only joking.)

A big mistake teenagers make when writing a mission statement is that they spend so much time thinking about making it perfect they never get started. You are much better off writing an imperfect rough draft and then improving it later.

Another big mistake is that teenagers try to make their mission statements look like everyone else's. That doesn't work. Mission statements come in many forms – a poem, a song, a quote, a picture, many words, a single word, a collage of magazine pictures. There is no single right way to do it. You're not writing it for anyone else but you. You're not writing it for your English teacher and it's not going to be marked by anyone. It is *your* secret document. So make it sing! The most important question to ask yourself is, 'Does it inspire me?' If you can answer yes, you did it right.

Once you have it written, put it in a place where you can easily access it, like inside your diary or on your mirror. Or you could reduce it, laminate it and put it in your purse or wallet. Then refer to it often, or, even better, memorize it.

Here are two more examples of teen mission statements, each very different in style and length:

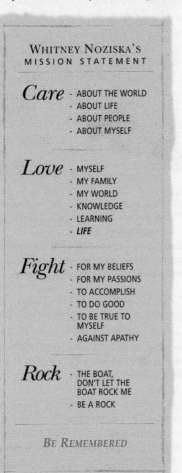

WHITNEY NOZISKA'S
MISSION STATEMENT

Care - ABOUT THE WORLD
- ABOUT LIFE
- ABOUT PEOPLE
- ABOUT MYSELF

Love - MYSELF
- MY FAMILY
- MY WORLD
- KNOWLEDGE
- LEARNING
- *LIFE*

Fight - FOR MY BELIEFS
- FOR MY PASSIONS
- TO ACCOMPLISH
- TO DO GOOD
- TO BE TRUE TO MYSELF
- AGAINST APATHY

Rock - THE BOAT, DON'T LET THE BOAT ROCK ME
- BE A ROCK

BE REMEMBERED

This one was written by Katie Hall. It is short, but to her it means everything:

MY
MISSION
STATEMENT

**NOTHING
LESS.**

HABIT 2

❋ THREE WATCH-OUTS

As you strive to begin with the end in mind and develop a personal mission statement, watch out for dangerous roadblocks!

Watch-Out #1: Negative Labels. Have you ever felt labelled by others in a negative way? By your family, teachers or friends?

'You guys from the East End are all the same. Always gettin' into trouble.'

'You're the laziest kid I know. Why don't you get off your back-side and do something for a change?'

'There goes Suzy. I hear she's a total tease.'

I'm sure your school has its own labels. Labels are an ugly form of prejudice. Break down the word prejudice and what do you get? Ta da! Pre-judge. Isn't that interesting? When you label someone you are pre-judging them; that means making conclusions about someone without knowing them. I don't know about you, but I can't stand it when I am unfairly judged by someone who doesn't know a thing about me.

You and I are much too complex to be neatly shelved into a category like clothing in a department store, as if there were only a handful of different types of people in the world instead of millions of unique individuals.

If you've been falsely labelled, you can live with it. The real danger comes when you start to believe the labels yourself, because labels are just like paradigms. What you see is what you get. For instance, if you've been labelled as being lazy, and you begin to believe it yourself, it will become a self-fulfilling belief. You'll act out the label. Just remember, you are not your labels.

Watch-Out #2: 'It's All Over' Syndrome. Another thing to watch out for is when you've made a mistake or three and feel so bad about what you've done that you say to yourself, 'It's all over. I've blown it. Who cares what happens now?' At this point you'll often begin to self-destruct and let it all hang out.

Let me just say this. It's never over. It seems that many teenagers go through a time where they lose it and experiment and do a whole bunch of things they aren't proud of . . . almost as if they are testing the boundaries of life. If you have made mistakes, you're normal. Every teenager has. Every adult has. Just get your head screwed on straight as quickly as you can and you'll be okay.

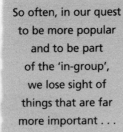

So often, in our quest to be more popular and to be part of the 'in-group', we lose sight of things that are far more important . . .

Watch-Out #3: Wrong Wall. Have you ever worked really hard to get something you wanted only to find that when you got it you felt empty inside? So often, in our quest to be more popular and to be part of the 'in-group', we lose sight of things that are far more important, like self-respect, true friendships and peace of mind. We are often so busy climbing the ladder of success that we never take time to see if our ladder is leaning against the right wall. Having no end in mind is a problem. But having an end in mind that leads us in the wrong direction can be an even bigger problem.

I once played football with a guy who was an incredible player. He had everything going for him, including being the team captain and being really fit. Each game he would excite fans with heroic efforts and spectacular athletic feats. Fans praised his name, young boys worshipped him and women adored him. He had it all.

Or so it appeared.

You see, even though he was shining on the field, he wasn't doing right off the field. And he knew it. And so did I, because I had grown up with him. As his fame increased, I watched him turn away from his principles and lose his direction. He gained the respect of the crowd but compromised something else far more meaningful, his character. It doesn't really matter how fast you're going or how good you're lookin' if you're headed in the wrong direction.

How can you tell if your ladder is leaning against the right wall? Stop, take a moment right now and ask yourself: 'Is the life I'm living leading me in the right direction?' Be brutally honest as you pause and listen to your conscience, that inner voice. What is it telling you?

Our lives don't always require 180-degree shifts in direction. More often, we need only small shifts. But small changes can make huge destination differences. Imagine this: If you wanted to fly from New York to Tel Aviv in Israel but made a one degree change north, you would end up in Moscow instead of Tel Aviv.

● GO FOR THE GOAL

Once you have your mission in place you will want to set goals. Goals are more specific than a mission statement and can help you break down your mission into bite-sized pieces. If your personal mission was to eat a whole pizza, your goal would be how to slice it up.

Sometimes when we hear the word *goals* we go on a guilt trip. It reminds us of all the goals we should be setting and the ones we have blown. Forget about any mistakes you may have made in the past. Follow the advice of George Bernard Shaw, who said: 'When I was a young man I observed that nine out of ten things I did were failures. I didn't want to be a failure, so I did ten times more work.'

Here are five keys to goal setting.

KEY NO. 1: *Count the Cost*

How many times do we set goals when we are in the mood but then later find we don't have the strength to follow through? Why does this happen? It's because we haven't counted the cost.

Let's pretend you set a goal to get better marks in school this year. Good and fine. But now, before you begin, count the cost. What will it require? For instance, you will have to spend more time doing maths and grammar and less time hanging out with your friends. You will have to stay up late some nights. Finding more time for school-work might mean giving up watching TV or reading your favourite magazine.

Now, having counted the cost, consider the benefits. What could good marks bring you? A feeling of accomplishment? A place at a good university? A good job? Now ask yourself, 'Am I willing to make the sacrifice?' If not, then don't do it. Don't make commitments to yourself you know you're going to break because you'll take withdrawals from your personal bank account.

A better way is to make the goal more bite-sized. Instead of setting a goal to get better marks in all your subjects, you might set a goal to get better marks in just two subjects. Then, next term, take another bite. Counting the cost will always add a touch of needed realism to your goals.

KEY NO. 2: *Put It in Pen*

It's been said, 'A goal not written is only a wish'. There are no ifs and buts about it, a written goal carries ten times the power.

A young woman named Louise told me how writing down her goals helped her eventually choose the right marriage partner. Louise had been in an emotionally abusive relationship with a guy named Tom for several years and felt trapped. She had become dependent on him and was miserable. A visit from a special friend one day finally gave her the inner spark she needed to make a change. This is an excerpt from Louise's journal when she was eighteen:

Just yesterday I found enough strength and strong will to leave Tom and the environment I was a part of for the past 2½ years. I needed to make a 180-degree change in order to find inner strength enough to succeed. I drew up a mental picture of where I wanted to be in five years and how I wanted to feel. I had a vision of being my own person, of having the strength to make good decisions for my life and most of all being with someone in a good, healthy relationship. I came up with a list of qualities I wanted in a relationship, and I think I will write them down now for future reference.

Qualities for a Relationship/Future Spouse:

1. Respect
2. Unconditional love
3. Honesty
4. Loyalty
5. Will support me in my pursuits/goals in life
6. Righteous (spiritual nature)
7. Fun/good sense of humour
8. Makes me laugh every day
9. Will make me feel whole—not torn apart
10. Good father/good with children
11. Good listener
12. Will make time for me and will want the best for me in life

Now that I have this list documented I have someplace to turn to get a glimpse of what the future can hold. It gives me hope when I read it, and it reminds me of a better way to live life.

Louise later met and married a great guy who fulfilled her requirements. Happy endings do happen.

As Louise discovered, there is something magical about writing down your goals. Writing forces you to be specific, which is very important in goal setting. As actress Lily Tomlin has said, 'I always wanted to be somebody. But I should have been more specific.'

KEY NO. 3: *Just Do It!*

I once read a story about Cortés and his expedition to Mexico. With over five hundred men and eleven ships, Cortés sailed from Cuba to the coast of the Yucatán in 1519. On the mainland he did something no other expedition leader had thought of: He burned his ships. By cutting off all means of retreat, Cortés committed his entire force and himself to the cause. It was conquest or bust.

'To every thing there is a season,' says the Bible. A time to say, 'I'll try', and a time to say, 'I will'. A time to make excuses, and a time to burn your ships. Of course, there are times when trying our best is all we can do. But I also believe there is a time for doing. Would you lend two thousand pounds to a business partner who said, 'I'll try to return it'? Would you get married if your partner, when asked to take you as the lawfully wedded husband or wife, said, 'I'll try'?

Get the point?

I once heard a story about a captain and a lieutenant:

'Lieutenant, would you please deliver this letter for me.'

'I'll do my best, sir.'

'No, I don't want you to do your best. I want you to deliver this letter.'

'I'll do it or I'll die, sir.'

'You misunderstand, lieutenant. I don't want you to die. I want you to deliver this letter.'

Finally the lieutenant caught on and said, 'I will do it, sir.'

Once we are fully committed to doing a task, our power to complete it will increase. 'If you do the thing,' said Ralph Waldo Emerson, 'you will have the power.' Each time I have committed myself to a goal, I seem to dig up gold mines of willpower, skill and creativity I never thought I possessed. Those who are committed always find a way.

The following passage by W. H. Murray is one of my all-time favourites. It describes what happens inside when we say 'I will'.

Until one is committed, there is hesitancy, the chance to draw back, always ineffectiveness. There is one elementary truth, the ignorance of which kills countless ideas and splendid plans, that the moment one definitely commits oneself then providence moves too. All sorts of things begin to occur which would never otherwise have occurred, and a whole stream of events issues from the decision, raising in one's favour all manner of unforeseen incidents and material assistance which no man could have dreamt would have come his way. I have learned a deep respect for one of Goethe's couplets:

Whatever you can do or dream you can begin it.
Boldness has genius, power, and magic in it.

In the words of Yoda, the great Jedi master: 'Do or do not. There is no try.'

KEY NO. 4: *Use Momentous Moments*

Certain moments in life contain momentum and power. The key is to harness these moments for goal setting.

Things with starts and finishes or beginnings and ends carry momentum. For example, a new year represents a start. Breaking up, on the other hand, represents an end. I remember how sick I felt after breaking up with my girlfriend after two years of dating. But I also remember the excitement of creating a new list of girls to date.

The following is a list of moments that can provide momentum for you as you set out to make new goals:

- A new school year
- A life-changing experience
- Breaking up
- A new job
- A new relationship
- A second chance
- Birth
- Death
- An anniversary
- A triumph
- A setback
- Moving to a new city
- A new season
- Graduation
- Marriage
- Divorce
- A new home
- A promotion
- A demotion
- A new look
- A new day

Often, tough experiences can carry momentum. Are you familiar with the myth of the phoenix bird? After every lifespan of 500 to 600 years, the beautiful phoenix would burn itself at the stake. Out of the ashes, it would later arise, reborn. In like manner, we can regenerate ourselves out of the ashes of a bad experience. Setbacks and tragedies can often serve as a springboard for change.

Learn to harness the power of key moments, to set goals and make commitments when you are in the mood to do it. Be assured, as well, that the mood to do it will pass. Sticking with it when you don't feel like it is the true test of your character. As someone once put it:

Character is the discipline to follow through with resolutions long after the spirit in which they were made has passed.

KEY NO. 5: *Rope Up*

My brother-in-law, the mountain climber, once escorted me and a friend up the 13,776-foot Grand Teton. It was terrifying! As we ascended, the mountain turned vertical. At that point, we 'roped up', or tied ourselves together with ropes to aid us in climbing and to save our lives if one of us fell. On two occasions that rope kept me from taking thousand-foot falls to my death. Believe me, I loved that rope as I've never loved a rope before. By assisting each other and relying on the ropes, we finally reached the summit safely.

You'll accomplish much more in life if you'll rope up and borrow strength from others. Let's suppose you set a goal to get in great shape. Now think. How could you rope up? Well, maybe you could find a friend who has the same goal and the two of you could work out together and become each other's cheerleaders. Or maybe you could tell your parents about your goal and get their buy in. Or maybe you could share your goal with an athletic trainer or your gym coach and ask him or her for advice. Get creative. Rope up with friends, brothers, sisters, girlfriends, parents, counsellors, grandparents or whomever else you can. The more ropes you have out, the greater your chances for success.

● GOALS IN ACTION

When I was sixteen, I was twice the size of my brother even though we were only one year apart. But David had a mountain of a spirit and did incredible things to get to where he wanted to go. This is his story:

I will never forget when, aged fourteen, I tried out for the American football team. At five feet two inches and weighing only 40 kilos, I was the stereotypical weakling. I couldn't find any football equipment to fit me; it was all too big. I was issued the smallest helmet they had but still had to tape three ear pads together on each side of it to make it fit my head. I looked like a mosquito with a balloon on its head.

I used to dread football practice, especially when we had to crack heads with the year above. We used to line up facing each other about ten yards apart with us on one side and them on the opposite side. When coach blew the whistle, you were supposed to hit your opponent until the whistle blew again.

I used to count the players in my line to see when my turn would come up, and then count the players in the other line to see who would have the privilege of teaching me how to fly. It seemed that I always ended up getting the biggest, meanest kid as my opponent. 'I'm dead meat', was my constant thought. I would line up, wait for the whistle, and in a moment find myself flying backwards and upwards through the air.

That winter I tried out for the wrestling team. I wrestled in the 45 kilo division. Even though I weighed in with all my clothes on after eating a big meal, I still couldn't tip the scales at 45 kilos. In fact I was the only guy on the team who didn't have to lose weight to wrestle. My brothers thought I would be a good wrestler because, unlike football, wrestling allowed me to compete with guys about my own weight. But to make a long story short, I got pinned almost every match.

In the spring I tried out for athletics. But as luck would have it, I was one of the slowest guys on the team. Little wonder – you should have seen my pencil-thin legs.

One day after workouts I just couldn't stand it anymore. 'That's it,' I said to myself. 'I am sick of this.' That night, in the privacy of my room, I wrote down some goals I wanted to achieve during school. To be successful in my athletics, I knew I had to get bigger and stronger, so I set goals in these areas first. By my final year I set a goal to be six feet tall, to weigh 80 kilos and to bench-press 110 kilos. In football, I set a goal to be the starting wide receiver on the football team. And in athletics I set a goal to be a county sprinter. I also envisioned myself being captain on both the football team and the athletics team.

A lot of nice dreams, wouldn't you say? At that moment, however, I was staring reality in the face. All 40 kilos of it. But I stuck with my plan from then until my final year.

Let me illustrate. As part of my weight-gaining process, I made a rule that my stomach would never be empty. So I ate constantly. Breakfast, lunch and dinner were merely three meals in an eight-meal day. I made a secret agreement with Cary, one of the best players in the football team, who stood six feet three inches tall and weighed 105 kilos. He promised me that if I helped him with his algebra homework, he would allow me to eat lunch with him every day for weight gain and protection purposes.

I was determined to eat the same amount he ate, so each day at lunch I bought two lunches, three cartons of milk, and four rolls. We must have been a hilarious sight together! I was also taking my Gain Weight Fast protein powder along with my lunch. I would mix the sickening powder in each of my milks and nearly vomit each time I drank it.

During my next school year I began working out with my good friend Eddie who was also yearning to get big. He added another requirement to my food list: ten full teaspoons of straight peanut butter and three glasses of milk each night before bed. Each week we were required to gain two pounds. If we didn't 'make weight' on the official weigh-in day, we were required to eat or drink water until we did.

My mum read an article that said if a young kid slept ten hours a night in a completely dark room and drank two to three extra glasses of milk a day, he could grow one to two inches more than he normally would. I believed this and followed it rigidly. After all, I needed to reach my goal of six feet, and my dad's height of five feet ten inches wasn't going to help me. 'Dad,' I said, 'I want the darkest room in the house.' I got it. Then I put towels under the door crack and over the window. No light was going to shine on me!

Next I set a sleeping timetable: I went to bed around 8:45 P.M. and got up around 7:15 A.M. This ensured me 10½ hours of sleep. Finally, I drank all the milk I could.

I also began lifting weights, running, and catching the football. Each day I would work out at least two hours. When Eddie and I lifted at the weight room, we would check out the XL shirts in hopes that one day we would fill them. At first I could only bench-press 35 kilos, slightly more than the bar.

As the months passed I began to see results. Small results. Slow results. But results. By the time I was sixteen I was five feet five inches and about 55 kilos. I had grown three inches and gained 15 kilos. And I was much stronger.

Some days I felt like a lone man against the whole world. I especially hated it when people would ask me, 'How come you're so skinny? Why don't you just eat more?' I felt like saying back, 'You idiot. Do you have any idea of the price I've been paying?'

By the lower sixth I was five feet eight inches and 65 kilos. I continued with my weight-gain programme, the running, the lifting and the skill development. In my track workouts, I made it a goal never to loaf, not even for one sprint. And I never missed a practice, even when I was sick. Then suddenly the sacrifice really started paying off. I got real big, real fast. In fact I grew so fast that I have stretch marks across my chest, as if I was mauled by a bear.

As I approached my final year, I had reached my goal of becoming six feet tall and fell only a couple of kilos short of my goal of 80 kilos. I became a starting wide receiver on the football team and was also elected as a team captain.

My senior year in athletics was even more rewarding. Again I was selected as a team captain, became the fastest sprinter on the team, and one of the fastest sprinters in the county.

At the end of the year, weighing 80 kilos and bench-pressing 150 kilos, I was awarded 'Best Body' by the senior girls of the high school, the award that I loved most of all.

I did it! I really did it! I accomplished most of the goals I had set that night in my room years ago. Truly, as Napoleon Hill wrote, 'Whatever the mind of man can conceive and believe, the hand of man can achieve.'

TURNING WEAKNESSES INTO STRENGTHS

Notice how David used the five keys to goal setting. He counted the cost, he put his goals in pen, he roped up with his friend Eddie and others, he set his goals during a momentous moment (when he was sick of being a punk), and he had the raw tenacity to 'just do it'. Now, I'm not endorsing being body-centred, as David was for a period. And I can't promise you that you can will your way into growing taller. I'm only trying to demonstrate the power that goals can play in your life.

As David told me his story, it became clear that being a 50 kilo punk may have been a blessing in disguise. His apparent weakness (skinny body) actually became his strength (forced him to develop discipline and perseverance). People who lack the native physical, social or mental gifts they desire must fight just that much harder. And that uphill battle can produce qualities and strengths they couldn't develop any other way. That is how a weakness can become a strength.

So if you're not endowed with all the beauty, biceps or brains that you covet – congratulations! You just may have the better draw. This poem by Douglas Malloch says it well:

> *The tree that never had to fight*
> *For sun and sky and air and light,*
> *But stood out in the open plain*
> *And always got its share of rain,*
> *Never became a forest king*
> *But lived and died a scrubby thing . . .*
> *Good timber does not grow with ease,*
> *The stronger wind, the stronger trees.*

Make Your Life Extraordinary   Life is short. This point is emphasized in Tom Schulman's screenplay for the classic movie *Dead Poets Society*. On the first day of class at Welton Academy, a boarding school steeped in tradition, Mr Keating, the new English teacher, takes his class of twenty-five boys out into the hall to look at old black-and-white photos of the young men who attended Welton more than half a century earlier.

'We are food for worms, lads,' he tells his class, as they look at the old photos. 'Believe it or not each and every one of us in this room is one day going to stop breathing, turn cold and die. I would like you to . . . peruse some of the faces from the past. You've walked by them many times but I don't think you've really looked at them.

'They're not that different from you, are they? Same haircuts. Full of hormones, just like you. Invincible, just like you feel. The world is their oyster. They believe they are destined for great things, just like many of you. Their eyes are full of hope, just like you. Did they wait until it was too late to make from their lives even one iota of what they were capable? Because you see, gentlemen, these boys are now fertilizing daffodils. If you listen real close you can hear them whisper their legacy to you. Go on, lean in. Listen. Do you hear it?'

As the boys curiously lean in toward the glass enclosure, Professor Keating whispers in their ears, 'Car-pe. Car-pe. Carpe diem. Seize the day, boys! *Make your lives extraordinary!*'

Since your destiny is yet to be determined, why not make it extraordinary and leave a lasting legacy?

As you do this, remember, life is a mission, not a career. A career is a profession. A mission is a cause. A career asks, 'What's in it for me?' A mission asks, 'How can I make a difference?' Martin Luther King's mission was to ensure civil rights for all people. Gandhi's mission was to liberate 300 million Indians. Mother Teresa's mission was to clothe the naked and feed the hungry.

These are extreme examples. You don't have to change the world to have a mission. As educator Maren Mouritsen says, 'Most of us will never do great things. But we can do small things in a great way.'

COMING ATTRACTIONS
You've heard of willpower. But have you ever heard of won't power? That's up next!

HABIT 2

BABY STEPS

1. Determine the three most important skills you'll need to succeed in your career. Do you need to be more organized, be more confident speaking in front of other people, have stronger writing skills?

The three most important skills I need for my career:

_____

2. 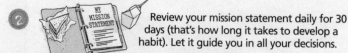 Review your mission statement daily for 30 days (that's how long it takes to develop a habit). Let it guide you in all your decisions.

3. Look in the mirror and ask, 'Would I want to marry someone like me?' If not, work to develop the qualities you're lacking.

4. Go to your school guidance or employment counsellor and talk about career opportunities. Take an aptitude test that will help you evaluate your talents, abilities and interests.

5. What is the key crossroad you are facing in your life right now? In the long run, what is the best path to take?

Key crossroad I am facing: _____

_____

The best path to take: _____

_____

6. Make a copy of The Great Discovery. Then take a friend or family member through it step by step.

7. Think about your goals. Have you put them in pen and written them down? If not, take time to do it. Remember, a goal not written is only a wish.

8. Identify a negative label others may have given you. Think up a few things you can do to change that label.

Negative label: _____

How to change it: _____

Put **First Things** First

Will and Won't **Power**

I watched the Indy 500, and I was thinking that if they left earlier they wouldn't have to go so fast.
STEVEN WRIGHT, COMEDIAN

I was listening to a speech on tape when the speaker began comparing the challenges faced by today's teenagers to those of teenagers who lived 150 years ago. I listened with interest. I agreed with most of what he said until this: 'The challenge that teenagers faced 150 years ago was hard work. The challenge that teenagers face today is a lack of hard work.'

Ex-squeeze me! I mumbled to myself. *A lack of hard work? What are you smokin'?* I think teenagers are busier today and working harder than ever. I see it with my own eyes every day. Between school, extracurricular activities, teams, sport, parttime jobs, helping to raise a younger brother or sister and on and on, there's barely time to breathe. A lack of hard work? Ha! Milking cows and mending fences doesn't sound any more difficult than juggling the multi-faceted life of a modern teen.

Let's face it. You've got a lot to do and there just isn't enough time. After school you have rehearsal, followed by work. You've also gotta study for that biology test tomorrow. And don't forget to give your friend a call. On top of that, you should exercise. The dog needs a walk. And your room is a wreck. What will you do?

Habit 3, Put First Things First, can help. It's all about learning to prioritize and manage your time so that your first things come first, not last. But there's more to this habit than just time management. Putting first things first also deals with learning to overcome your fears and being strong during hard moments.

In Habit 2, you decided what your first things are. Habit 3, then, is putting them *first* in your life.

Sure we can have a nice list of goals and good intentions, but doing them, putting them first is the hard part. That's why I call Habit 3 the habit of *will-power* (the strength to say yes to your most important things) and *won't-power* (the strength to say no to less important things and to peer pressure).

The first three habits build upon each other. Habit 1 says, 'You are the driver, not the passenger'. Habit 2 says, 'Decide where you want to go and draw up a map to get you there'. Habit 3 says, 'Get there! Don't let roadblocks knock you off course'.

PACKING MORE INTO YOUR LIFE

Have you ever packed a suitcase and noticed how much more you can fit inside when you neatly fold and organize your clothes instead of just throwing them in? It's really quite surprising. The same goes for your life. The better you organize yourself, the more you'll be able to pack in – more time for family and friends, more time for school, more time for yourself, more time for your first things.

I'd like to show you an amazing model called the Time Quadrants that can help you pack more in (especially important things). It's made up of two primary ingredients, 'important' and 'urgent'.

Important – your most important things, your first things, activities that contribute to your mission and your goals.

Urgent – pressing things, in-your-face things, activities that demand immediate attention.

In general, we spend our time in four different time quadrants, as shown below. Each quadrant contains different kinds of activities and is represented by a type of person.

The Time Quadrants

	URGENT	NOT URGENT
IMPORTANT	**1 THE PROCRASTINATOR** • EXAM TOMORROW • FRIEND GETS INJURED • LATE FOR WORK • PROJECT DUE TODAY • CAR BREAKS DOWN	**2 THE PRIORITIZER** • PLANNING, GOAL SETTING • ESSAY DUE IN A WEEK • EXERCISE • RELATIONSHIPS • RELAXATION
NOT IMPORTANT	**3 THE YES-MAN** • UNIMPORTANT PHONE CALLS • INTERRUPTIONS • OTHER PEOPLE'S SMALL PROBLEMS • PEER PRESSURE	**4 THE SLACKER** • TOO MUCH TV • ENDLESS PHONE CALLS • EXCESSIVE COMPUTER GAMES • SHOPPING MARATHONS • TIME WASTERS

HABIT 3

If you haven't already noticed, we live in a society that is addicted to urgency. It's the NOW generation. That's why we have instant pudding, crash diets, fast food, pay-per-view, pagers, mobile phones and so on. It reminds me of the spoiled rich girl in *Willie Wonka and the Chocolate Factory*, who keeps saying, 'Now, Daddy! Now! I want an Umpalumpa now!'

Urgent things aren't bad, necessarily. The problem comes when we become so focused on *urgent* things that we put off *important* things that aren't urgent, like working on that essay in advance, going for a walk in the mountains or writing an important letter to a friend. All these *important* things get pushed aside by *urgent* things, like phone calls, interruptions, drop-ins, deadlines, other people's problems and other 'in-your-face-do-it-now' things.

As we dig a little deeper into each quadrant, ask yourself, 'What quadrant am I spending most of my time in?'

QUADRANT 1: *The Procrastinator*

Let's start with Q1, things that are both urgent and important. There will always be Q1 things that we can't control and that must get done, like helping a sick child or meeting an important deadline. But we also cause many Q1 headaches because we procrastinate, like when we put off doing our homework and then have to cram all night for an exam or when we neglect our car for too long and then have to take it in to get repaired. Q1 is part of life, but if you're spending too much time in Q1, believe me, you'll be a 'stress case' and you'll seldom be performing to your potential.

Meet the Procrastinator, who hangs out in Q1. Perhaps you know her. Her motto is, 'I'm going to stop procrastinating – sometime soon'. Don't expect her to work on an essay or study for a test until the night before. And don't expect her to take time to get petrol; she's usually too busy driving.

The Procrastinator is addicted to urgency. She likes to put things off and put things off and put things off . . . until it becomes a crisis. But she likes it that way because, you see, doing everything at the last minute gives her a rush. In fact, her mind won't kick into gear until there's an emergency. She thrives under pressure.

Planning ahead is simply out of the question for the Procrastinator because it would ruin the excitement of doing everything at the last possible moment.

The Procrastinator reminds me of the comedian who said:

'My mum always told me that I would be a procrastinator.'

I replied, 'Just you wait.'

I can relate to the Procrastinator because I was a cram artist in school. I used to think I was pretty cool not studying all term and then cramming the night before and pulling out a good grade. How stupid! Sure I got the grade, but I didn't learn a thing and I paid for it in university, and in many ways I'm still paying for it.

One procrastinating teenager said it this way:

'What I do is I slack off until the end of the term and kill myself for the last two weeks. I get really high marks but I don't feel I have earned it because everyone else turned stuff in on time and does what they're supposed to. They're not stressed. That's how I want to be.'

The results of too much time in Q1 are:
- Stress and anxiety
- Burnout
- Mediocre performance

QUADRANT 2: *The Prioritizer*

We'll save the best for last.

QUADRANT 3: *The Yes-man*

Q3 represents things that are urgent but not important. It is characterized by trying to please other people and responding to their every desire. This quadrant is deceptive because urgent things have the appearance of being important. In truth, they're often not. For example, a ringing phone is urgent, but often the conversation is so unimportant, or worse, it's a telemarketer! Q3 is loaded with activities that are important to other people but not important to you – things that you would like to say no to but can't because you're afraid you might offend someone.

Meet the Yes-man of Q3, who has a real hard time saying no to anything or anyone. He

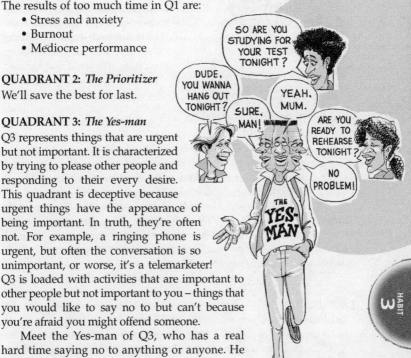

HABIT 3

tries so hard to please everyone that he usually ends up pleasing no one, including himself. He often caves in to peer pressure because he likes to be popular and he wouldn't want to stand out. His motto is, 'Tomorrow, I'm going to be more assertive – if that's okay with you.'

When his friends dropped by unexpectedly one evening and wanted him to go cruising till dawn, he just couldn't muster up enough courage to turn them down. He didn't want to disappoint his buddies. It didn't matter that he was taking some gargantuan test the next morning and needed to study and get some sleep.

Although he told his sister that he'd help her with maths, he couldn't resist taking that urgent phone call that took most of the night but wasn't really that important.

He didn't really want to join the swimming team. He preferred art. But his dad was a swimmer and, of course, he didn't want to let him down.

I think all of us, myself included, have a little Q3 inside of us. But we won't accomplish much if we say yes to everything and never learn to focus on what's important. Comedian Bill Cosby has said it well: 'I don't know the key to success, but the key to failure is to try to please everyone.' Q3 is one of the worst quadrants to be in because it has no backbone. It's fickle and will blow whichever way the wind is blowing.

The results of spending too much time in Q3 are:
- Reputation for being a 'pleaser'
- Lack of discipline
- Feeling like a doormat for others to wipe their feet on

QUADRANT 4: *The Slacker*

Q4 is the category of waste and excess. These activities are neither urgent nor important.

Meet the Slacker who loafs about in Q4. He loves anything in excess, like too much TV, too much sleep, too many video games or too much time on the internet. Two of his favourite pastimes include regular three-hour phone calls and shopping marathons each weekend.

He is a professional loafer. Sleeping in until noon takes real skill, after all. He absolutely loves comic books. In fact, he reads several dozen a week. He's never had a job. But he's young and has his health, so why would he want to work? School, of course, is the last thing on his mind. He'd rather, you know, just hang out.

Going to movies, chatting on the internet or just hanging out are part of a healthy lifestyle. It's only when they're done in excess that they become a waste of time. You'll know when you cross that line. Watching that first TV show might be just what you need to relax, and that's okay. But then watching the second, third, or even fourth show (a rerun that you've seen six times) until 2 A.M. turns a relaxing evening into a wasted one.

The results of living in Q4 are:
- Lack of responsibility
- Guilt
- Flakiness

QUADRANT 2: *The Prioritizer*

Now back to Q2. Q2 is made of things that are important but not urgent, like relaxation, building friendships, exercising, planning ahead and doing homework . . . on time! It's the quadrant of excellence – the place we want to be. Q2 activities are important. But are Q2 activities urgent? No! And that's why we have trouble doing them. For example, getting a good summer job may be very important to you. But since it's weeks away and not urgent, you may put off looking for that job until it's too late and suddenly all the good jobs are filled.

Had you been in Q2, you would have planned ahead and found a better job. It wouldn't take more time, just a little more planning.

Meet the Prioritizer. Although she's by no means perfect, she's basically got it together. She takes a look at everything she has to do and then prioritizes, making sure her first things get done first and her last things last. Because she has the simple but powerful habit of planning ahead, she's usually on top of things. By doing her homework on time and writing her essays in advance, she does her best work and avoids the stress and burnout that come from cramming. She makes time to exercise and renew herself, even if it means pushing aside other things. The people who matter most in her life, like her friends and her family, come first. Although it's a struggle, staying balanced is important to her.

She changes the oil in her car regularly. And

she doesn't wait until she's running on fumes to fill up with petrol. She loves going to the cinema, surfing the internet, and reading suspense novels but never lets those activities go too far.

She's learned how to say no with a smile. When her friends dropped by unexpectedly one evening to go to a party, she said, 'No thanks. I have a huge test tomorrow. But how about Friday night? Let's get together then.' Her friends were okay with that and secretly wished they had had the courage to say no as well. She's learned that resisting peer pressure appears unpopular at first, but that people come to respect her for it.

The results of living in Q2 are:
- Control of your life
- Balance
- High performance

So in which quadrant are you spending the majority of your time? 1, 2, 3 or 4? Since, in reality, we all spend some time in each quadrant, the key is to shift as much time as possible into Q2. And the only way you'll find more time for Q2 is to reduce the amount of time you spend in the other quadrants. Here is how to do that:

Shrink Q1 by procrastinating less. You're always going to have lots to do in Q1. That's guaranteed. But if you can cut your procrastination in half by doing important things early, you'll be in Q1 far less often. And less Q1 time means less stress!

Say no to Q3 activities. Learn to say no to unimportant things that pull you away from more important ones. Don't be so interruptible. Trying to please everyone is like a dog trying to catch its tail. Remember, when you're saying no you're really saying yes to more important things.

Cut down on Q4, slacker activities. Don't stop doing these things, just do them less often. You don't have time to waste. Shift this time to Q2. You need to relax and kick back, but remember relaxation is Q2. Excessive relaxation is Q4.

In addition to spending more time in Q2, consider two other suggestions to help you better manage your time and put first things first: Pick up a planner and plan weekly.

PICK UP A PLANNER

To start with, I highly recommend using a planner of some sort that has a calendar and space to write down appointments, assignments, to-do lists and goals. If you want, you can even make your own planner out of a spiral-bound notebook. Upon hearing the word 'planner', some of you may be thinking, 'Hey, I don't want to haul another book around with me'. If this is your hang-up, remember that planners come in all sizes.

Others may be thinking, 'I don't want my life to be tied to a planner. I like my freedom.' If this is you, keep in mind that a planner wasn't designed to tie you down but to free you up. With a planner you'll no longer have to worry about forgetting things or double-booking yourself. It will remind you when your essays are due and tests are to be taken. You can keep all of your important information (like telephone numbers, internet addresses, birthdays) in one place instead of on fifty scraps of paper. A planner is not meant to be your master but a tool to help you live your life.

Plan Weekly

Take fifteen minutes each week to plan your week and just watch what a difference it can make. Why weekly? Because we think in weeks and because daily planning is too narrow a focus and monthly planning is too broad a focus. Once you have a planner of some sort, follow this three-step weekly planning process.

Step 1: Identify Your Big Rocks. At the end or beginning of each week, sit down and think about what you want to accomplish for the upcoming week. Ask yourself, 'What are the most important things I need to do this week?' I call these your big rocks. They are sort of like minigoals and should be tied into your mission statement and longer-term goals. Not surprisingly, you'll find that most of them will be Q2's.

You might come up with a list of big rocks that looks something like this:

<u>My Big Rocks for the Week</u>
- Study for science test
- Finish reading book
- Attend Megan's game
- Complete employment application
- Party at Isabella's
- Exercise 3 times

Another way to identify your big rocks is to think through the key roles of your life, such as your role as a student, friend, family member, worker, individual and whatever else you do and then come up with the one or two most important things you want to get done in each role. Planning your life around roles will help you stay balanced.

ROLE	MY BIG ROCKS FOR THE WEEK
Student	Get started on history essay
Friend	Mario's birthday Be more complimentary
Family	Take Colleen to shops Call Grandma
Job	Get to work on time
Me	Go to concert Write in diary every night

As you're identifying your big rocks for the week, don't get carried away. Although you may feel you have forty big rocks that must get done, be realistic and narrow your focus to no more than ten to fifteen.

<u>*Step 2: Block Out Time for Your Big Rocks.*</u> Have you ever seen

the big-rock experiment? You get a bucket and fill it half full of small pebbles. You then try to put several big rocks in the bucket, on top of the pebbles. But they don't all fit. So you empty the bucket and start over. This time you put the big rocks in the bucket first, followed by the pebbles. The pebbles neatly fill in the spaces around the big rocks. This time it all fits! The difference is the order in which the rocks and pebbles were placed in the

bucket. If you put the pebbles in first, the big rocks don't all fit. But if you put the big rocks in first, everything fits, big rocks *and* pebbles. Big rocks represent your most important things. Pebbles represent all the little everyday things that suck up your time, such as chores, busy work, phone calls and interruptions. The moral of the story is, if you don't schedule your big rocks in first, they won't get done.

During your weekly planning, block out time for your big rocks by booking them in your planner. For example, you might decide that the best time to get started on your history essay is Tuesday night and the best time to call your grandma is Sunday afternoon. Now block out those times. It's like making a reservation. If your big rock such as 'give out three compliments each day this week' doesn't have a specific time attached to it, write it somewhere in your planner where it can be seen.

If you block out time for your big rocks first, the other everyday activities will fit in as well. And even if they don't, who cares? You'd rather push aside pebbles than big rocks.

Step 3: Schedule Everything Else. Once you have your big rocks booked, schedule in all of your other little to-dos, daily tasks, and appointments. Here's where the pebbles go. You may also want to look ahead on your calendar and record upcoming events and activities, like a holiday, concert or birthday.

Adapt Daily

With your weekly plan in place, adapt each day as needed. You'll probably need to rearrange some big rocks and pebbles now and then. Try your best to follow your plan, but if you don't accomplish everything you set out to do, no big deal. Even if you only get a third of your big rocks accomplished, that's a third more than you might have accomplished without planning ahead.

If this weekly planning method feels too rigid or complicated, don't scrap it entirely, just do weekly planning *light*. For example, you may find you only want to schedule two or three big rocks for the week and that's about it.

The point is: The simple act of planning ahead each week will help you focus on your big rocks and consequently accomplish so much more.

Does It Really Work?

Does this time-management stuff really work? You bet it does. I have personally read numerous letters from teenagers who have had great success with the above suggestions. Here are comments from two teenagers who were taught about the Time Quadrants and began using a planner and doing weekly planning:

Jacob:

I remember looking at the diagram of the Time Quadrants and saying, 'This is true. I do a lot of last-minute things.' Like homework. If an essay was due, I'd do it Sunday night to hand in Monday, or if there was a test on Friday, I'd skip school on Thursday to study for my test. I was pretty much in crisis.

Once I figured out what was important to me, I started to prioritize and started using a planner. If I wanted to go fishing I would say, 'Well, this other thing is more important. I'll do that first, and then maybe tomorrow I will have the whole day to fish.' Eventually I started studying more effectively, got top marks in my tests and everything just fell into place. My life would have been less stressful if I only had used my time more effectively earlier.

Philippa:

My stress level has decreased because I am no longer constantly trying to remember what I have to do a few days ahead. Now I can just pull out my schedule and I'm all set. When I get in a bad mood and stressed out, I look at my schedule and realize that I still have time to do everything, especially the things just for me.

One of the few things that can't be recycled is wasted time. So make sure you treasure each moment. In the words of Queen Elizabeth I on her deathbed: 'All my possessions for one moment of time.'

• THE OTHER HALF

Time management isn't all there is to Habit 3. It's only half of it. The other half is learning to overcome fear and peer pressure. It takes courage and guts to stay true to your first things, like your values and standards, when the pressure is on. I once asked a group of kids, 'What are your first things?' to which they answered, among other things: 'family', 'friends', 'freedom', 'excitement', 'growth', 'trust', 'God', 'stability', 'belonging', 'looks'. I then asked, 'What keeps you from putting these things first in your life?' Not surprisingly, 'fear' and 'peer pressure' were two of the top responses. So we're going to talk about how to deal with these.

The Comfort Zone and the Courage Zone

Putting your first things first takes courage and will often cause you to stretch outside your comfort zone. Take a peek at the Courage and Comfort Zone diagram.

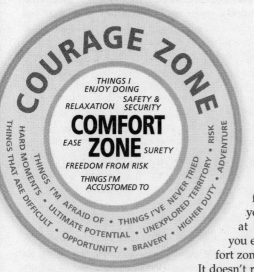

Your comfort zone represents things you're familiar with, places you know, friends you're at ease with, activities you enjoy doing. Your comfort zone is risk free. It's easy. It doesn't require any stretching. Within these boundaries we feel safe and secure.

On the other hand, things like making new friends, speaking before a large audience or sticking up for your values makes your hair stand on end. Welcome to the courage zone! Adventure, risk and challenge included! Everything that makes us feel uncomfortable is found here. In this territory waits uncertainty, pressure, change, the possibility of failure. But it's also the place to go for opportunity and the only place in which you'll ever reach your full potential. You'll never reach it by hanging out in your comfort zone. That's for sure.

What's that you asked? *'What's so wrong about enjoying your comfort zone?'*

Nothing. In fact, much of our time should be spent there. But there is something absolutely wrong with never venturing into unknown waters. You know as well as I do that people who seldom try new things or spread their wings live safe but boring lives! And who wants that? 'You miss 100 percent of the shots you never take,' said hockey great Wayne Gretzky. Why not show some faith in yourself, take a risk, and parachute into your courage zone from time to time? Remember, the risk of riskless living is the greatest risk of all.

Never Let Your Fears Make Your Decisions

> It's not the mountain we conquer, but ourselves.
>
> EDMUND HILLARY
> *(first person to climb Mount Everest)*

There are a lot of sick emotions is this world, but perhaps one of the worst is *fear*. When I think about all I failed to do in my life because my fears got the best of me I ache inside. In high school I had a crush on a beautiful girl named Sarah but I never asked her out because my fears whispered, 'She may not like you'. I remember quitting my school football team after one practice because I was afraid of competition. I'll never forget contemplating running for prefect but chickening out because I was too scared of speaking in front of the whole school.

Throughout my life there have been classes I never took, friends I never made and teams I never played for – all because of these ugly, yet very real, fears. I like how Shakespeare put it in *Measure for Measure:*

> *Our doubts are traitors,*
> *And make us lose the good we oft might win*
> *By fearing to attempt.*

My dad once told me something I've never forgotten. 'Sean,' he said, 'never let your fears make your decisions. You make them.' Isn't that a great idea? Think of all the heroic acts that have been accomplished by people who acted in the face of fear. Think of Nelson Mandela, who was instrumental in ending the oppressive apartheid system in South Africa. Mandela was imprisoned for twenty-seven years (imagine that) for speaking out against apartheid before being elected as the first non-white president of South Africa. What if, because of his fears, he had never dared to fight the system? Or consider the unyielding courage of Susan B. Anthony as she led the long struggle that finally won women the right to vote under the US Constitution. Or think of Winston

Churchill, prime minister during World War II, who led the free world in its fight against Nazi Germany. What if, because of self-doubt, he had been fainthearted during the war? Surely all great deeds, whether by famous people or by everyday people, were accomplished in the face of fear.

Acting in the face of fear will never be easy, but afterward you'll always be glad you did it. During my year of school I needed to choose an extra module so I skimmed through the class schedule looking for something to fill the hours. When I came across 'Private Voice Instruction,' as in singing lessons, I thought, 'Why not step outside my comfort zone and give it a try?'

I was careful to sign up for private lessons instead of group lessons because I didn't want to make a fool of myself by singing in front of other students.

> TO BE OR NOT TO BE.

Things went fine until the end of term when my singing teacher brought the shocking news. 'By the way, Sean, have you decided which song you want to sing before the other students?'

'What do you mean?' I asked in horror.

'Well, the class requirements state that you have to sing at least one time in front of the other private voice students.'

"Acting in the face of fear"

'That would not be a good idea,' I said emphatically.

'Oh, it's no big deal. You'll do fine.'

Well, to me it *was* a huge deal. The thought of singing in front of a group made me physically sick. 'How am I going to get out of this one?' I thought. But I couldn't allow myself to do that because I had been speaking to various groups over the past year advising them to never let fears make their decisions. Now . . . I was up to bat.

'Courage, Sean.' I kept rehearsing in my mind. 'You've got to at least try.'

That dreaded day finally arrived. As I entered the 'room of doom' where I was to make my debut, I kept trying to convince myself, 'Settle down, Sean. This can't be that bad.'

But it kept getting worse. I became increasingly intimidated as I discovered that nearly everyone in the room was either a music or drama student. I mean, these people really knew how to sing. Since childhood they'd been performing in musicals and choruses. My fear only increased when the first student called upon sang a song from the play *Les Misérables* that sounded better than in the original production. The guy was incredible. Yet the class had the audacity to critique him. 'I think that your tonality was a little flat,' someone said. 'Oh, no! What will they think of me?'

'Sean, you're up.'

Now it was my turn.

As I stood in front of the class, three million light years outside my comfort zone, I kept repeating to myself, 'Courage! I can't believe I'm doing this. Courage! I can't believe I'm doing this.'

'I will be singing "On the Street Where You Live" from *My Fair Lady*,' I quivered.

As the accompanist began playing the prelude and all eyes fell upon me, I couldn't help but think, 'How? How in the world did I get myself into this situation?' And from the smiles on everyone's faces it looked as if they were actually going to take me seriously.

'I have often walked down this street before . . .' I rang out.

Even before I reached the second line, the expressions of excitement on the students' faces turned to anguish. I was so nervous that my body felt as tight as jeans just pulled from the dryer. I had to squeeze each word out.

Near the end of the song is a really high note. It had always been difficult for me to reach, even in practice. Now I anticipated it with terror. But as that note approached I thought, 'What the hell. Go for it!'

I don't recall if I hit that note or missed it. All I remember is that a few students were so embarrassed that despite their best efforts they could no longer bear to look at me.

I finished and sat down quickly. Silence. No one knew what to say.

'That was great, Sean.'

'Thanks a lot,' I shrugged, as if I believed them. But do you know what? Although that experience nearly killed me, when I left that classroom and walked alone through the empty car park to my car I was so proud of myself. I felt a great sense of personal accomplishment, and I frankly didn't care what anyone else thought about my high note. I had survived and I was proud of it. As Edmund Hillary, the first person to climb Mount Everest, put it,

'It's not the mountain we conquer, but ourselves.' So the next time you want to:

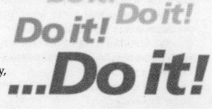

- make a new friend,
- resist peer pressure,
- break an old habit,
- develop a new skill,
- try out for a team,
- audition for a play,
- ask out the one and only,
- change your job,
- get involved,
- be yourself,

or even if you want to sing in public . . . Do it! . . . even when all your fears and doubts scream out, 'You stink', 'You'll fail', 'Don't try'. Never let your fears make your decisions. You make them.

Winning Means Rising Each Time You Fall

We all feel fear from time to time, and that's okay. 'Feel the fear and do it anyway' goes the saying. One way I've learned to overcome fear is to keep this thought always in the back of my mind: *Winning is nothing more than rising each time you fall.* We should worry less about failing and more about the chances we miss when we don't even try. After all, many of the people we most admire failed many times.

For instance, Babe Ruth struck out 1,330 times. Albert Einstein didn't talk until he was four. Beethoven's music teacher said, 'As a composer he is hopeless'. Louis Pasteur was marked 'mediocre' in chemistry. Rocket scientist Wernher von Braun failed algebra as a teenager. Chemist Madame Marie Curie experienced near financial ruin before creating the field of nuclear chemistry and forever changing the course of science. Michael Jordan was dropped from his school basketball team.

Below are events in the life history of a man who failed many times but kept fighting back. See if you can guess who it is. This man:

- failed in business at age twenty-two
- was defeated for the state legislature at age twenty-three
- failed in business at age twenty-five
- coped with the death of his sweetheart at age twenty-six
- suffered a nervous breakdown at age twenty-seven
- was defeated for speaker at age twenty-nine
- was defeated for congressional nomination at age thirty-four
- was elected to Congress at age thirty-seven
- lost renomination for Congress at age thirty-nine

- was defeated for the Senate at age forty-six
- was defeated for the vice-presidency of the United States at age forty-seven
- and was defeated for the Senate at age forty-nine

This person was none other than Abraham Lincoln, elected president of the United States at age fifty-one. He rose each time he fell and eventually reached his destination, gaining the respect and admiration of all nations and peoples.

Be Strong in the Hard Moments

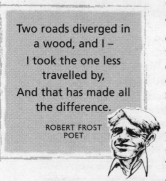

Two roads diverged in a wood, and I –
I took the one less travelled by,
And that has made all the difference.

ROBERT FROST
POET

The poet Robert Frost wrote, 'Two roads diverged in a wood, and I – I took the one less travelled by, And that has made all the difference.' I have come to believe that there are certain hard moments, diverging-road moments, that, if we are strong in them, will make 'all the difference' down the road of life.

So what exactly are hard moments? Hard moments are conflicts between doing the right thing and doing the easier thing. They are the key tests, the defining moments of life – and how we handle them can literally shape our forevers. They come in two sizes, small and large.

Small hard moments occur daily and include things like getting up when your alarm rings, controlling your temper or disciplining yourself to do your homework. If you can conquer yourself and be strong in these moments your days will run so much more smoothly. For example, if I'm weak in a hard moment and sleep in (mattress over mind), it often snowballs and becomes the first of many little failures throughout the day. But if I get up when planned (mind over mattress), it often becomes the first of many little successes.

In contrast to small hard moments, larger ones occur every so often in life and include things like choosing good friends, resisting negative peer pressure and rebounding after a major setback: You may get dropped from a team or dumped by your lover, your parents may get divorced or you may have a death in the family. These moments have huge consequences and often strike when you're least expecting them. If you recognize that these moments will come (and they will), then you can prepare for them and meet them head on like a warrior and come out victorious.

Be courageous at these key junctures! Don't sacrifice your future happiness for one night of pleasure, a weekend of excitement or a thrilling moment of revenge. If you are ever thinking about doing something really stupid, remember these lines from Shakespeare (Wow! Shakespeare twice in one chapter):

What win I, if I gain the thing I seek?
A dream, a breath, a froth of fleeting joy.
Who buys a minute's mirth to wail a week?
Or sells eternity to get a toy?
For one sweet grape who will the vine destroy?

These lines are about sacrificing your future for a brief moment of joy. Who would want to give up the rest of his or her life for a toy? Or who would want to buy a minute of happiness (mirth) for a week's worth of pain? Or who would destroy an entire vine for just one grape? Only a stupid person would.

Overcoming Peer Pressure

Some of the hardest moments come when facing peer pressure. Saying no when all your friends are saying yes takes raw courage. However, standing up to peer pressure, what I call 'won't power', is a massive deposit into your PBA.

A counsellor at a school shared this:

A girl rushed into my office before school with tears streaming down her face. 'They hate me! They hate me!'

She had just been dumped by her group of friends who told her to get lost because she had been 'too good' the day before to ditch school and ride up to Chicago for the day. She said at first she wanted to go but then thought how much it would hurt her mum when the school called home and told her that her daughter wasn't in school. She felt she just couldn't do that to her mum because she had made so many sacrifices for her. She couldn't let her down!

She stood up and said no I can't do it, and everyone just blew her off. She thought the next day that everything would be okay, but it wasn't – they all told her to find new friends because she was too good for them.

Through the tears and pain she began to see that she felt good inside, but lonely, as her friends didn't accept her. But she accepted herself and gained self-respect and inner peace despite outside rejection. A life lesson learned and a moment of standing up for herself.

Sometimes peer pressure can be so strong that the only way to resist it is to remove yourself entirely from the environment you're in. This is especially the case if you're involved with a gang or a tight group of friends. For Heather, changing her environment was the best solution:

Even though I knew for a long time that I needed to change my friends, I just didn't know how. My 'best friend' would encourage me to do the things she was, like sleeping around and doing drugs. Before long people at school started to call me a slut.

I still wanted to be friends with her, and my other friends, because I would think about all the good times we'd had together. Yet when I went out with them at night we would get into stuff we weren't supposed to. I knew I was holding on to things that I shouldn't be.

I decided I needed to change my whole environment and get away from it all. I asked my mum if I could go and stay with my aunt to get a new start and find a better group of friends. She agreed, and since then I've moved in with my aunt.

Now, around my new friends, I say whatever I feel is right, and I am being more myself. I don't care what people say about me, and if they don't like me, then oh well! This is me, and I am not going to change just to fit in with them. I am going to change for me.

To overcome peer pressure, you've got to care more about what *you* think of you than what *your peers* think of you, as this short poem by Portia Nelson reminds us:

Any day of the week
I would choose to be 'out'
with others
and in touch
with myself . . .
than to be 'in' with others
and out of touch
with myself.

Why is peer pressure so hard to resist? It's because you are dying to belong. That's why teenagers are often willing to go through brutal initiation rituals or get heavy into drugs and violence to become a member of a gang. Sometimes we simply need a wake-up call to snap us out of it, as was the case with Ryan:

Peer pressure and wearing the latest styles in clothes was really important to me. Then I got really sick with a kidney disease, and it just kind of seemed silly to buy a bunch of clothes when in a few months they were not the cool thing anymore. I decided that I was going to do what was most important. I started spending more time with my family, instead of being out with my friends so much, and I stopped worrying about what they thought about me, and started being myself.

Not all peer pressure is bad. In fact, much of it can be very good. If you can find a friend who puts positive pressure on you to be your best, then hang on to him or her for dear life, because you've got something very special.

If you find yourself wanting to stand up but instead you are continually caving in to peer pressure, here are two things you can do.

First, build your personal bank account. If your self-confidence and self-respect are low, how can you expect to have the strength to resist? What can you do? You can begin today to build your PBA, little by little. Make a promise to yourself and keep it. Help someone in need. Develop a talent. Renew yourself. Eventually you'll have sufficient strength to forge your own path instead of following the beaten ones. (You may want to review the chapter on the personal bank account.)

Second, write your mission statement and set goals. If you haven't decided what your values are, how can you expect to stick up for them? It will be a whole lot easier to say no if you know what goals you're saying yes to. For example, it's easier to say no to bunking off when you are saying yes to your goal of getting good marks and making it to university. (You may want to review the chapter on Habit 2, Begin with the End in Mind.)

● THE COMMON INGREDIENT OF SUCCESS

In the final analysis, putting first things first takes discipline. It takes discipline to manage your time. It takes discipline to overcome your fears. It takes discipline to be strong in the hard moments and resist peer pressure. A man by the name of Albert E. Gray spent years studying successful people in an attempt to figure out that special ingredient that made them all successful. What do you think he found? Well, it wasn't dressing for success, or eating bran or having a positive mental attitude. Instead, this is what he found. Read it carefully.

Albert E. Gray's Common Denominator of Success:

All successful people have the habit of doing the things failures don't like to do. They don't like doing them either necessarily. But their disliking is subordinated to the strength of their purpose.

What does this mean? It means that successful people are willing to grit their teeth from time to time and do things they don't like doing. Why do they do them? Because they know these things will lead them to their goals.

In other words, sometimes you've just got to exercise your special human tool called *willpower* to get things done, whether you feel like it or not. Do you think a concert pianist always enjoys hours of practice each day? Does a person who is committed to earning her own way through university enjoy taking on a second job?

I remember reading a story about an American collegiate wrestler who was asked what the most memorable day of his career had been. He replied that it was the one day during his career when practice had been cancelled. He hated practice, but was willing to endure it for a greater purpose, his love of being the best he could be.

A FINAL WORD

We've surveyed thousands of people on the 7 Habits and guess which habit is the hardest one to live? You guessed it! It's Habit 3. So don't get discouraged if you struggle with it. You've got company.

If you don't know where to start with Habit 3, go to the baby steps. That's what they are there for – to help you get started.

Your teen years can be some of the most exciting and adventurous years of life. So value each moment, as this poem so beautifully communicates:

> *To realize the value of One Year,*
> *Ask a student who failed his or her exams.*
>
> *To realize the value of One Month,*
> *Ask a mother who gave birth to a premature baby.*
>
> *To realize the value of One Week,*
> *Ask an editor of a weekly magazine.*
>
> *To realize the value of One Day,*
> *Ask a daily wage labourer who has six kids to feed.*
>
> *To realize the value of One Hour,*
> *Ask the lovers who are waiting to meet.*
>
> *To realize the value of One Minute,*
> *Ask a person who missed their train.*
>
> *To realize the value of One Second,*
> *Ask the person who survived an accident.*
>
> *To realize the value of One Millisecond,*
> *Ask the person who won a silver medal in the Olympics.*

★★★

COMING ATTRACTIONS

Just up ahead we'll talk about the stuff that life is made of. I think you'll be surprised what that stuff is. So keep moving! By the way, you're halfway done with the book. Congratulations!

HABIT 3

BABY STEPS

1. Set a goal to use a planner for one month. Stick to your plan.

2. Identify your biggest time-wasters. Do you really need to spend two hours on the phone, surf the internet all night or watch that sitcom rerun?

   My biggest time-wasters: _____

3. Are you a 'pleaser,' someone who says yes to everything and everyone? If so, have the courage to say no today when it's the right thing to do.

4. If you have an important test in one week, don't procrastinate and wait until the day before to study. Buckle down and study a little each day.

5. Think of something you've procrastinated for a long time but that's very important to you. Block out time this week to get it done.

   Item I've procrastinated forever: _____

6. Note your ten most important big rocks for the upcoming week. Now, block out time on your schedule to accomplish each one.

7. Identify a fear that is holding you back from reaching your goals. Decide right now to jump outside your comfort zone and stop letting that fear get the best of you.

   Fear that's holding me back: _____

8. How much impact does peer pressure have on you? Identify the person or people who have the most influence upon you. Ask yourself, 'Am I doing what I want to do or what they want me to do?'

   Person or people who most influence me: _____

PART III

The Public Victory

The Relationship Bank Account
The Stuff That Life Is Made Of

Habit 4 – Think Win-Win
Life Is an All-You-Can-Eat Buffet

Habit 5 – Seek First to Understand, Then to Be Understood
You Have Two Ears and One Mouth . . . Hel-lo!

Habit 6 – Synergize
The 'High' Way

The Relationship Bank Account

THE STUFF THAT LIFE IS MADE OF

One of my favourite quotes, which, by the way, always makes me feel guilty, is 'On their deathbed nobody has ever wished they had spent more time at the office.'

I've often asked myself, 'What *do* they wish they had spent more time doing?' I think the answer might be 'Spent more time with the people they love'. You see, it's all about relationships, the stuff that life is made of.

What's it like to be in a relationship with you? If you had to rate how well you're doing in your most important relationships, how would you score?

HOW ARE YOUR RELATIONSHIPS WITH . . .	LOUSY ◀──▶ EXCELLENT				
Your friends?	1	2	3	4	5
Your siblings?	1	2	3	4	5
Your parents or guardian?	1	2	3	4	5
Your girlfriend or boyfriend?	1	2	3	4	5
Your teachers?	1	2	3	4	5

Maybe you're doing pretty well. Maybe not. Either way, this chapter is designed to help you improve these key relationships. But before we go there, let's quickly review where we've just come from.

In the Private Victory, we learned about the personal bank account and Habits 1, 2 and 3. In the Public Victory section, we'll learn about the relationship bank account and Habits 4, 5 and 6. As we've already discussed, the key to mastering relationships is first mastering yourself, at least to some degree. You don't have to be perfect; you just need to be making progress.

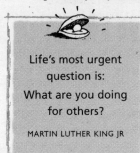

Life's most urgent question is:

What are you doing for others?

MARTIN LUTHER KING JR

Why is success with self so important to success with others? It's because the most important ingredient in any relationship is *what you are.* As the essayist and philosopher Ralph Waldo Emerson put it, 'Who you are speaks so loudly I can't hear what you're saying.' If you're struggling in your relationships, you probably don't have to look any further than yourself for the answer.

The Private Victory will help you become independent so that you can say, 'I am responsible for myself and I can create my own destiny.' This is a huge accomplishment. The Public Victory will help you become interdependent, that is, help you learn to work cooperatively with others, so that you can say, 'I am a team player and I have power and influence with people.' This is an even greater accomplishment. The long and short of it is, your ability to get along with others will largely determine how successful you are in your career and your level of personal happiness.

Now back to talking about relationships. Here's a practical way to think about them. I call it the relationship bank account (RBA). In an earlier chapter we spoke about your personal bank account (PBA), which represents the amount of trust and confidence you have in yourself. Similarly, the RBA represents the amount of trust and confidence you have in each of your relationships.

The RBA is very much like a current account at a bank. You can make deposits and improve the relationship, or take withdrawals and weaken it. A strong and healthy relationship is always the result of steady deposits made over a long period.

Although there are similarities, the RBA is different from a financial account in three ways, as a colleague of mine, Judy Henrichs, once pointed out to me:

1. Unlike a bank where you may have only one or two accounts, you have an RBA with everyone you meet. Suppose you come across a new kid in the neighbourhood. If you smile and say

hello, you've just opened an account with him. If you ignore him, you've just opened an account as well, although a negative one. There's no getting around it.

2. Unlike a current account, once you open an RBA with another person, you can never close it. That's why you can run into a friend you haven't seen in years and pick up right where you left off. Not a pound is lost. It's also why people hang on to grudges for years.

3. In a current account, ten pounds is ten pounds. In an RBA, deposits tend to evaporate and withdrawals tend to turn to stone. This means that you need to continually make small deposits into your most important relationships just to keep them in the positive.

So how can you build a rich relationship or repair a broken one? It's simple. One deposit at a time. It's the same way you'd eat an elephant if you had to. One bite at a time. There is no quick fix. If my relationship with you is £5,000 in the hole, I'll need to make £5,001 worth of deposits to get it back in the positive.

I once asked a group of teenagers, 'What is the most powerful deposit someone has made into your RBA?' These are some of their responses:

- 'The steady stream of deposits my family makes that strengthen me.'
- 'When a friend, teacher, loved one or employer takes the time to say "You look nice" or "Great job". A few words go a long way.'
- 'My friends made me a banner on my birthday.'
- 'Bragging about me to others.'
- 'When I have made mistakes, they forgive, forget and help and love.'
- 'My friend told me, after I read some poems I wrote, that I was brilliant and I should write a book. It was hard to share some of those in the first place.'
- 'My mother called from California, as well as both of my sisters, to wish me a happy birthday, before I left for school.'
- 'My brother would always take me to hockey games with his friends.'
- 'Little things.'

- 'I have four really good friends, and just being together as friends and knowing that we're all doing good and are happy keeps me going.'
- 'Whenever Chris says "Hi, how are you, Ryan?" it makes me feel so uplifted the way he does it.'
- 'I had a friend who told me he believed I was very sincere and always myself. It meant a lot that someone would recognize that.'

As you can see, there are many kinds of deposits, but here are six that seem to work every time. Of course, with every deposit, there is an opposite withdrawal.

RBA DEPOSITS	RBA WITHDRAWALS
Keep promises	Break promises
Do small acts of kindness	Keep to yourself
Be loyal	Gossip and break confidences
Listen	Don't listen
Say you're sorry	Be arrogant
Set clear expectations	Set false expectations

● KEEPING PROMISES

'Sean, I don't want to ask you again. There are rubbish bags in the trunk of my car from the party the other night. Please throw them away.'

'Okay, Dad.'

As a carefree teenager, I somehow forgot to empty the rubbish bags in Dad's Ford, as I said I would, because I had a hot date that Saturday afternoon. I had asked my dad if I could use the Ford, but he said no because it wasn't his car. It was a loaner that his friend at the dealership had arranged for. But I took it anyway because he was busy and I was sure he wouldn't notice.

My date and I had a wonderful time. On the way home, however, I rammed into the back of a car doing thirty. No one was seriously hurt, but both cars were practically ruined. I'll never forget the most miserable phone call of my life.

'Dad.'

'What?'

'I had an accident.'

'YOU WHAT? ARE YOU OK?

'I got into a wreck. No one's hurt.'

'IN WHICH CAR?'

'Your car.'

'NOOOOOOOOOOO!!!' By this time I was holding the phone six inches away. And it still hurt.

I had the car towed to the Ford dealership to see if they could salvage it. Since it was Saturday, they told me they wouldn't be able to work on it until Monday. On Monday my dad received a call from the repair shop. The manager said that when his people opened the boot to repair the car, the smell of rotting rubbish (the rubbish I forgot to empty) was so disgusting that they refused to work on the car. If you thought my dad was mad before, you should have seen him then.

For the next several weeks I lived in the dog house. It wasn't the crash he was so mad about. He was angry because I had broken two promises: 'I won't take your car, Dad', and 'Don't worry, Dad. I'll take the rubbish out of the boot'. It was a huge withdrawal, and it took me a long time to rebuild my RBA with my dad again.

Keeping small commitments and promises is vital to building trust. You must do what you say you're going to do. If you tell your mum you're going to be home at 11:00 or that you will do the dishes tonight, then do it and make a deposit. Give out promises sparingly, and then do everything you can to keep them. If you find you can't keep a commitment for some reason (it happens), then let the other person know why. 'Little sister, I'm really sorry I can't come to your play tonight. I didn't realize I had a rugby match. But I'll be there tomorrow.' If you're genuine and try to keep your promises, people will understand when something interferes.

If your RBA with your parents is low, try building it by keeping your commitments, because when your parents trust you, everything goes so much better. But I don't need to tell you what you already know.

DO SMALL ACTS OF KINDNESS

Have you ever had a day where everything is going wrong and you feel totally depressed . . . and then suddenly, out of nowhere, someone says something nice to you and it turns your whole day around? Sometimes the smallest things – a hello, a kind note, a smile, a compliment, a hug – can make such a big difference. If you want to build friendships, try doing the little things, because in relationships the little things *are* the big things. As Mark Twain put it, 'I can live three months on a good compliment.'

A friend of mine, Karen, once told me about a £1,000 deposit her brother made into her RBA:

One kind word
can warm three
winter months.

JAPANESE SAYING

When I was fifteen, my big brother Mike, who was in the sixth form at school, seemed to me to be the epitome of popularity. He was good in sports and dated a lot. Our house was always filled with his cool friends, guys I dreamed would someday think of me as more than just 'Mike's dumb little kid sister.'

Mike asked Rebecca Knight, the most popular girl in the school, to go with him to the summer ball. She accepted. He rented the dinner suit, bought the flowers, and, along with the rest of his popular crowd, hired a limo and made reservations at a fancy restaurant. Then, disaster struck. On the afternoon of the ball, Rebecca came down with a terrible strain of flu. Mike was without a date, and it was too late to ask another girl.

There were a number of ways Mike could have reacted, including getting angry, feeling sorry for himself, blaming Rebecca, even choosing to believe that she really wasn't sick and just didn't want to go with him, in which case he would have had to believe that he was a loser. But Mike chose not only to be proactive but to give someone else the night of her life.

He asked me – me! his little sister! – to go with him to his summer ball.

Can you imagine my ecstasy? Mum and I flew about the house getting me ready. But when the limo pulled up with all of his friends, I almost chickened out. What would they think? But Mike just grinned, gave me his arm, and proudly escorted me out to the car like I was the queen of the ball. He didn't warn me not to act like a kid; he didn't apologize to the others; he ignored the fact that I was dressed in a simple short-skirted evening dress while all of the other girls were in elegant dresses.

I was bedazzled at the dance. Of course, I spilled punch on my dress. I'm sure Mike bribed every one of his friends to dance at least one dance with me, because I never sat out once. Some of them even pretended to fight over who got to dance with me. I had the greatest time. And so did Mike. While the guys were dancing with me, he was dancing with their dates! The truth is, everyone was wonderful to me the whole night, and I think part of the reason was because Mike chose to be proud of me. It was the dream night of my life, and I think every girl in the school fell in love with my brother, who was cool enough, kind enough and self-confident enough to take his little sister to his summer ball.

If, as the Japanese saying goes, 'one kind word can warm three winter months', think how many winter months were warmed by this single act of kindness.

You don't have to look far to find opportunities for small acts of kindness. A young man named Lee, who was taught about the RBA, related this:

I am the head boy at my school. I decided to try the small kindness deposit I learned about by putting a simple note in the pigeon holes of the prefects I didn't know well. I told them that I appreciated the work they did. They took me about five minutes to write up.

The next day one of the girls I had written a note to came up to me and abruptly gave me a big hug. She thanked me for the note, and handed me a letter and a chocolate bar. The note said she had had a terrible day. She had a great deal of stress and was very depressed. My small note had turned her whole day around, helping her to happily accomplish the things that had caused her so much grief. The strange thing was that I had hardly known her when I gave her the note, and I was sure that she didn't like me anyway because she never really paid any attention to me. What a surprise! I couldn't believe how much a simple note meant to her.

Small acts of kindness don't always have to be one on one. You can also join with others to make a deposit. I remember reading about a deposit the kids at one school in America made in the life of an unsuspecting teenage girl named Lori when they crowned her homecoming queen.

You see, unlike most of the students, Lori was special ed and made her way around the school in a motorized wheelchair. Because of cerebral palsy, her words were often difficult to understand and her movements awkward.

After being nominated for homecoming queen by students in one of her classes, Lori made the first cut when students narrowed the slate to ten. At a rally soon after, it was announced that she had won. The entire student body of twenty-five hundred started chanting, 'Lori! Lori!' A day later, she was still receiving visitors at her home and roses by the dozen.

When asked how long she intended to wear her crown, Lori answered, 'Forever'.

Follow the golden rule and treat others as you would want them to treat you. Think about what a deposit means to someone else, not what *you* would want as a deposit. A nice gift may be a deposit for you, but a listening ear may be a deposit for another person.

If you ever have something nice to say, don't let that thought just rot, *say it*. As Ken Blanchard wrote in his book *The One Minute Manager*, 'Unexpressed good thoughts aren't worth squat!' Don't wait until people are dead to give them flowers.

● BE LOYAL

One day at school, I'll never forget watching a football game with my friend Eric. I began making fun of one of the players who always sat on the bench. He was a nice guy and had always been good to me, but a lot of other people made fun of him so I thought I would too. It made Eric laugh. After I had ripped on this kid for several minutes, I happened to turn around and, to my horror, saw this kid's younger brother sitting right behind me. He had over-heard everything. I'll never forget the look of betrayal written all over his face. Quickly turning back around, I sat quietly for the rest of the game. I felt like a total idiot, about one foot tall. Did I ever learn an important lesson about loyalty that night!

One of the biggest RBA deposits you can make is to be loyal to other people, not only when they're in your presence but more especially when they're not present. When you talk behind people's backs, you're only hurting yourself, in two ways.

First, you make withdrawals from everyone who hears your comments. If you hear me trash Greg when Greg isn't there to defend himself, what do you think I'm going to be doing when you're not present? That's right. I'll be gossiping about you.

Second, when you bad-mouth or gossip you make what I call an 'invisible withdrawal' from the person you're attacking. Have you ever sensed that someone has been talking about you behind your back? You didn't hear it, but you can feel it. It's strange but true. If you sweet-talk people when they're facing you but bad mouth them when their backs are turned, don't think they won't feel it. It some-how gets communicated.

Gossiping is a huge problem among teenagers, especially girls. Guys usually prefer other ways of attacking people (we call them *fists*), but girls like *words*. Why is gossiping so popular? For one thing, you hold someone's reputation in the palms of your hands and that's a powerful feeling. For another, we gossip because we're insecure, afraid, or threatened. That's why gossipers usually like to pick on people who look different, think different, are self-confident or stand out in some way. But isn't it kind of silly to think that tearing someone else down builds you up?

Gossip and rumours probably have destroyed more reputations and relationships than every other bad habit combined. This story, told by my friend Annie, illustrates their venomous power:

The summer following GCSEs my best friend, Tara, and I were dating two really great blokes. They were best friends, we were best friends, and we often went out as a foursome. One weekend Tara and my boyfriend, Sam, both went out of town with their families. Tara's boyfriend, Will, called and said, 'Hey, let's do a movie since both Tara and Sam are out of town and we have nothing to do.'

We truly went out only as friends – Will knew that and I knew that. Of course, someone saw us at the movies and misinterpreted the situation. Well, in a small town, things have a tendency to grow. When Tara and Sam returned, and even before I had a chance to talk to my best friend or my boyfriend, the word was out. There was no pulling back the stories and rumours. As I called to say 'hi' to them, I got a frigid blast of arctic air. There was no explaining. There was no communication. My best friend and my boyfriend chose to believe the nasty rumours that were being spread, and in their anger added fuel to the fire. I learned a really tough lesson about loyalty that summer that I have never forgotten nor even gotten over. And to this day, my best friend still doesn't believe me.

In the above catastrophe, it seems to me that a little loyalty would have solved a lot of problem. So just what is it that makes a loyal person?

Loyal people keep secrets. When people share something with you and ask you to keep it 'just between you and me', then for goodness' sake, keep it 'just between you and them' instead of running out and telling every last soul every juicy detail as if you had no control of your bodily functions. If you enjoy being told secrets, then keep them secret, and you'll get more of 'em told to you.

Loyal people avoid gossip. Have you ever been hesitant to leave a group chat because you're afraid someone might start gossiping about you? Don't let others think that about you. Avoid gossip like rabies. Think well of others and give them the benefit of the doubt. This doesn't mean that you can't talk about other people, just try to do it in a constructive way. Remember, strong minds talk about ideas; weak minds talk about people.

Loyal people stick up for others. The next time a group starts gossiping about another person, refuse to participate in the gossip or stick up for that person. You can do so without sounding self-righteous. Katie shared this story:

> *One day in my English class, my friend Matt started talking about a girl I knew in my neighbourhood, although we had never been close friends. His friend had taken her out to a dance and so he started saying things like 'She is so snobby' and 'She's such a bimbo.'*
>
> *I turned around and said, 'Excuse me, but Kim and I have grown up together and I think she's one of the sweetest people I have ever met.' After I said it I was kind of surprised at myself. I had actually been struggling to get along with her. Even though Kim never knew what I said about her, my attitude toward her changed and we became really close friends.*
>
> *Matt and I still are good friends. I think he knows he can count on me to be a loyal friend.*

Cutting against the grain of gossip takes courage. But after the initial embarrassment it may cause you, people will admire you because they know you're loyal to the core. I'd make an extra effort to be loyal to your family members, since these relationships will last a lifetime.

As illustrated so well in the *Winnie-the-Pooh* classics, people need to feel safe and secure in relationships:

Piglet sidled up behind Pooh.

'Pooh,' he whispered.

'Yes, Piglet?'

'Nothing,' said Piglet, taking Pooh's paw. 'I just wanted to be sure of you.'

● LISTEN

Listening to someone can be one of the single greatest deposits you can make into another's RBA. Why? Because most people don't listen and, furthermore, listening can heal wounds, as it did in the case of this fifteen-year-old named Jessica:

At the beginning of the year I was having communication troubles with my parents. They were not listening and I was not listening. It was one of those 'I'm right and you're wrong' kind of things. I would come in late and just go to bed, and in the morning I would have breakfast and go to school and not say anything.

I went to see my cousin, who is older than me, and said, 'I need to talk to you.' We went for a drive across town so we could be alone. She listened to me freak out and cry and scream for two and a half hours. She really helped me a lot because she just listened to all of it. She was optimistic that it would be all right and suggested that it might help if I tried to win back my parents' trust.

I have been trying to see things from their point of view lately. We are not in a fight anymore, and things are getting back to normal.

People need to be listened to almost as much as they need food. And if you'll take time to feed them, you'll create some fabulous friendships. We'll talk about listening a lot more when we get to Habit 5: Seek First to Understand, Then to Be Understood. It's just up ahead.

SAY YOU'RE SORRY

Saying you're sorry when you yell, overreact or make a stupid mistake can quickly restore an overdrawn bank account. But it takes guts to go to a friend and say, 'I was wrong', 'I apologize', or 'I'm sorry'. It's especially hard to admit that you made a mistake to your parents, because, of course, you know so much more than they do. Seventeen-year-old Lena had this to say:

I know from experience how much an apology means to my parents. It's like they forgive me for almost anything and are ready to start over if I admit my mistakes and apologize. But that doesn't mean it's easy to do.

I recall one night recently when my mother confronted me with something she didn't approve of that I had done. I didn't confess to any of it; on the contrary I ended up acting like they were total jerks and slamming the door to my room right in front of my mother's nose.

As soon as I got inside my room I felt sick about it. I realized I probably had known all along I was wrong and that I had been extremely rude. Should I just stay in my room and go to bed and hope it would blow over, or should I go upstairs and apologize? I waited about two minutes and then took the high road and went straight to my mum, gave her a big hug, and told her how sorry I was for acting that way.

It was the best thing I ever could have done. Immediately it was as though it had never happened. I felt light and happy and ready to concentrate on something else.

Don't let your pride or a lack of courage stand in the way of saying you're sorry to people you may have offended, because it's never as scary as it seems, and it will make you feel so good afterward. In addition, apologies disarm people. When people get offended their tendency is to take up a sword, so to speak, to protect themselves in the future. But when you apologize, you take away their desire to fight you and they will drop their swords. *Clank!*

Seeing that you and I will continue to make mistakes the rest of our lives, saying you're sorry ain't too bad a habit to get hooked on.

● SET CLEAR EXPECTATIONS

'I think that we should be dating other people,' your partner might tell you.

'But I thought we were going out,' you might reply.

'Well, not really.'

'What about everything you told me about how you feel about me?'

'I didn't really mean it that way.'

How often have you seen someone get hurt because another person led them on? Our tendency is to want to flatter and please others, and, as a result, we often set unclear or unrealistic expectations.

To please your dad at the moment, you might say, 'Sure, Dad, I can help you fix up the car this weekend.' But, realistically, you're booked the entire weekend and don't have a second. In the end, you disappoint your dad. You would have been better off being realistic up front.

To develop trust we need to avoid sending vague messages or implying something that is not true or not likely to happen.

Jacqueline says, 'I had a great time, Jeff. Let's be sure to do something again next week!' What she really means is: 'I had a good time. Let's just be friends.' But since she's created false expectations, Jeff will continue to ask her out and Jacqueline will continue to turn him down saying, 'Maybe next week.' Everyone would have been better off if Jacqueline had been honest from the start.

Whenever you get into a new job, relationship or setting, you're better off taking the time to lay all expectations out on the table so that everyone is on the same page. So many withdrawals are made because one party assumes one thing and another party assumes something else.

Your boss might say, 'I need you to work this Tuesday evening.'

You might reply, 'I'm sorry, but I have to watch my baby brother on Tuesday nights for my mum.'

'You should have told me that when I hired you. Now what am I going to do?'

Build trust through telling it like it is and laying out clear expectations right up front.

A Personal Challenge   I would like to leave you with a personal challenge. Pick one important relationship in your life that is damaged. It may be with a parent or a sibling or a friend. Now commit yourself to rebuilding that relationship one deposit at a time. The other person may be suspicious at first and wonder what you're up to. 'What's up with you? Do you want something from me?' But be patient and stick with it. Remember, it may take months to build up what took months to tear down. But little by little, deposit by deposit, they'll begin to see that you are genuine and that you really want to be friends. I never said it would be easy, but I promise you it will be worth it.

★ ★ ★

COMING ATTRACTIONS

If you love a buffet (and who doesn't?), you're just going
to love the chapter that follows.

Keep Promises

1   The next time you go out for the night, tell your mum or dad what time you will be home and keep to

2   All day today, before giving out any commitments, pause and think about whether or not you can honour them. Don't say, 'I'll call tonight', or 'Let's have lunch today', unless you can follow through.

Do Small Acts of Kindness

3   Buy a burger for a homeless person this week.

4   Write a thank-you note to someone you've been wanting to thank for a long time.

Person I need to thank: _____

Be Loyal

5   Pinpoint when and where it is most difficult for you to refrain from gossip. Is it with a certain friend during lunch? Come up with a plan of action to avoid it.

6   Try to go one whole day saying only positive things about others.

Listen

7   Don't talk so much today. Spend the day listening.

8   Think of a family member you've never really taken the time to listen to, like a little sister, big brother or grandpa. Take the time.

Say You're Sorry

9   Before you go to bed tonight, write a simple note of apology to someone you may have offended.

Set Clear Expectations

10   Think of a situation where you and the other party have different expectations. Put together a plan for how to get on the same page.

Their expectation: _____

My expectation: _____

HABIT 4

Think
Win-Win

Life Is an All-You-Can-Eat Buffet

What do we live for, if it is not to make life less difficult for each other?
GEORGE ELIOT, AUTHOR

I did a business degree at a well-respected university that utilized the infamous 'forced curve' marking policy. Every class consisted of ninety students and in each class, 10 per cent, or nine people, would receive what was called a category III. A category III was a nice way of saying 'You failed!' In other words, no matter how well or poorly the class performed as a whole, nine people would fail the module. And if you failed too many modules, you were kicked out of university. The pressure was awful!

Pride gets no pleasure out of having something, only out of having more of it than the next man.

C. S. LEWIS
AUTHOR

The problem was, everyone in the class was smart. (I must have been an admissions error.) So the competition became very intense, which *influenced* me (notice I didn't say *made* me) and my classmates to act in funny ways.

Instead of aiming for good marks, as I did in school, I found myself aiming not to be one of the nine people that would fail. Instead of playing to win, I was playing not to lose. It reminds me of the story I once heard about two friends being chased by a bear, when one turned to the other and said, 'I just realized that I don't need to outrun the bear; I only need to outrun you.'

While sitting in class one day, I couldn't help but look around the room and try to count off nine people who were more stupid than me. When someone made a stupid comment, I caught myself thinking, 'Oh goody, he's guaranteed to fail. Only eight more to go.' Sometimes I found myself not wanting to share my best ideas with others during seminars because I was afraid they would steal my ideas and get credit for them instead of me. All these feelings were eating me up inside and making me feel real small, as if my heart were the size of a grape. The problem was, I was thinking Win-Lose. And Win-Lose thinking will always fill your heart with negative feelings. Luckily, there is a more excellent way. It's called Think Win-Win and it's Habit #4.

Think Win-Win is an attitude toward life, a mental frame of mind that says I can win, and so can you. It's not me or you, it's both of us.

Think Win-Win is the foundation for getting along well with other people. It begins with the belief that we are all equal, that no one is inferior or superior to anyone else, and no one really needs to be.

Now, you might say, 'Get real, Sean. That's not how it is. It's a cutthroat, competitive world out there. Everyone can't always win.'

I disagree. That's not how life really is. Life really isn't about competition, or getting ahead of others, or scoring in the 95th percentile. It may be that way in business, sports and school, but those are merely institutions that we've created. It's certainly not that way in relationships. And relationships, as we learned just a chapter ago, are the stuff life is made of. Think how silly it is to say, 'Whose winning in your relationship, you or your friend?'

So let's explore this strange idea called Think Win-Win. From my experience, the best way to do it is to see what Win-Win is not. Win-Win is not Win-Lose, Lose-Win, or Lose-Lose.

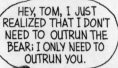

These are all common but poor attitudes toward life. Climb aboard, strap yourself in, and let's take a look at each one.

• WIN-LOSE – THE TOTEM POLE

'Mum, there's a big match tonight and I need to take the car.'

'I'm sorry, Marie, but I need to go to the supermarket tonight. Your friends will have to pick you up.'

'But, Mum. My friends always have to pick me up. It's embarrassing.'

'Listen, you've been complaining about not having any food in the house for a week. This is the only time I have to go shopping. I'm sorry.'

'You're not sorry. If you were sorry you'd let me take the car. You are so unfair. You could care less about me.'

'All right. All right. Go ahead. Take the car. But don't come complaining to me when there's nothing to eat tomorrow.'

Marie won and Mum lost. This is called Win-Lose. But has Marie really won? Maybe she has this time, but how does Mum feel? And what's she going to do the next time she has a chance to get even with Marie? That's why in the long run it never pays to think Win-Lose.

Win-Lose is an attitude toward life that says the pie of success is only so big, and if you get a big piece there is less for me. So I'm going to make sure I get my slice first or that I get a bigger piece than you. Win-Lose is competitive. I call it the totem pole syndrome. 'I don't care how good I am as long as I'm a notch higher than you on the totem pole.' Relationships, friendships and loyalty are all secondary to winning the game, being the best and having it your way.

Win-Lose is full of pride. In the words of C. S. Lewis, 'Pride gets no pleasure out of having something, only out of having more of it than the next man . . . It is the comparison that makes you proud, the pleasure of being above the rest.'

Don't feel too bad if you think Win-Lose at times, because we have been trained to do so from an early age, especially those of us who have been raised in the West. Asian countries tend to be much more cooperative in their attitudes.

To illustrate my point, let's follow Rodney, an ordinary boy, as he grows up. Rodney's first experience with competition begins when he is nine when he runs in the annual sports day and quickly discovers that prizes are given only to first, second and third place finishers. Rodney doesn't win any races but is excited to at least receive a prize for *participation*, until his best friend tells him that 'those ribbons don't really count 'cause everyone gets one'.

When Rodney starts at secondary school, his parents can't afford the latest-style jeans and shoes, so Rodney has to wear older, less trendy styles. He can't help but notice what his wealthier friends are wearing and feels as though he isn't quite measuring up.

In school, Rodney begins playing the violin and joins the orchestra. To his dismay, he learns that only one person can be first fiddle. Rodney is disappointed when he's assigned second fiddle but feels very good about the fact that he's not third.

At home, Rodney has been his mum's favourite child for several years. But now his younger brother, who happened to win a lot of prizes at his sports day, is taking over as mum's golden child. Rodney begins studying extra hard at school for he figures that if he can get better marks than his brother, he might become mum's chosen one again.

After four years of secondary school, Rodney is ready for sixth form college. So he takes his GCSEs and gets mostly Cs, which means that he is smarter than lots of his peers, but not as smart as those getting As and Bs. Unfortunately, his grades aren't enough to get into the college of his choice.

The college Rodney attends uses forced-curve marking. In his first chemistry class of thirty students, Rodney learns that there are only five A grades and five B grades available. The rest get C's and D's. Rodney works hard to avoid a C or D and luckily earns the last B grade available.

And the story continues . . .

After being raised in this kind of world, is it any wonder then that Rodney and the rest of us grow up seeing life as a competition and winning as everything? Is it any wonder that we often find ourselves looking around to see how we stack up on the totem pole? Fortunately, you and I are not victims. We have the strength to be proactive and rise above all of this Win-Lose conditioning.

A Win-Lose attitude wears many faces. The following are some of them:

- Using other people, emotionally or physically, for your own selfish purposes.
- Trying to get ahead at the expense of another.
- Spreading rumours about someone else (as if putting someone else down builds you up).
- Always insisting on getting your way without concerning yourself with the feelings of others.
- Becoming jealous and envious when something good happens to someone close to you.

In the end Win-Lose will usually backfire. You may end up on the top of the totem pole. But you'll be there alone and without friends. 'The trouble with the rat race,' said actress Lily Tomlin, 'is that even if you win, you're still a rat.'

LOSE-WIN – THE DOORMAT

One teen wrote:

'I, for one, am a big peacemaker. I would much rather take the blame for just about anything than get into an argument. I constantly find myself saying that I am stupid . . .'

Do you find yourself identifying with this statement? If so, you have fallen into the trap of Lose-Win. Lose-Win looks prettier on the surface, but it's just as dangerous as Win-Lose. It's the doormat syndrome. Lose-Win says, 'Have your way with me. Wipe your feet on me. Everyone else does.'

Lose-Win is weak. It's easy to get stepped on. It's easy to be the nice guy. It's easy to give in, all in the name of being a peace-maker. It's easy to let your parents have their way with you rather than try to share your feelings with them.

With a Lose-Win attitude you'll find yourself setting low expectations and compromising your standards again and again. Giving in to peer pressure is Lose-Win. Perhaps you don't want to ditch school, but the group wants you to. So you give in. What happened? Well, you lost and they won. That's called Lose-Win.

A girl named Jenny once told me about her wanderings in the world of Lose-Win during her fourteenth year before she finally broke free:

My problems with my mum all started one day when she said to me sarcastically, 'Wow, you're a bit cheeky today.' I took it so literally that then and there I decided to close off from her and to never talk back to her. I began faking the respect and authority she wanted. So every time she would say something, even if I disagreed with her, I would just say, 'Okay, whatever you want, Mum.' Half the time she didn't even know that things were bothering me because I wouldn't tell her.

When my mum would set rules about friends and times for getting home I would just be like, 'Whatever you say'. It was easier to just do whatever she asked because I never felt that my opinions or suggestions would be taken seriously.

But it really got old quickly. And my resentment began to build. One night I had just finished talking to my mum about some homework to which she said, 'Oh, that's nice', and then went back to mopping the floor.

'Don't you even care?' I thought. But I didn't say anything and stormed off. She had no idea I was even upset. She would have been willing to talk to me had I told her how important it was to me. But it seemed that I was eager to be a victim and to take whatever she dished out.

Eventually, I just blew up. 'Mum, this has got to change. I can't han-dle you anymore. You tell me everything you want me to do and I just do it because it's easier than fighting. Well, I'm sick of it.' I spilled my guts and let her know about all the feelings I had been harbouring inside. This all came as a surprise to her.

After my blowup, it was really rocky for a while. We felt like we were starting all over in our relationship. But it's getting better all the time. We discuss things now, and I always share my feelings with her.

If you adopt Lose-Win as your basic attitude toward life, then people will wipe their dirty feet on you. And that's a real shame. You'll also be hiding your true feelings deep inside. And that's not healthy.

There is a time to lose, of course. Lose-Win is just fine if the issue isn't that important to you, like if you and your sister can't agree on who gets which side of the wardrobe or if your mum doesn't like the way you hold your fork. Let others win the little issues, and it will be a deposit into their RBA. Just be sure you take a stand on the important things.

If you're trapped in an abusive relationship, you're deep into Lose-Win. Abuse is a never-ending cycle of hurt and reconciliation, hurt and reconciliation. It never gets better. There's no win in it for you whatsoever, and you need to get out. Don't think that somehow the abuse is your fault or that somehow you deserve to be abused. That's how a doormat thinks. No one deserves to be abused, ever. (Please see the Abuse Hotlines in the back of this book.)

LOSE-LOSE – THE DOWNWARD SPIRAL

Lose-Lose says, 'If I'm going down, then you're going down with me.' After all, misery enjoys company. War is a great example of Lose-Lose. Think about it. Whoever kills the most people wins the war. That doesn't sound like anyone ends up winning at all. Revenge is also Lose-Lose. By getting revenge, you may think you're winning, but you're really only hurting yourself.

Lose-Lose is usually what happens when two Win-Lose people get together. If you want to win at all costs, and the other person wants to win at all costs, you're both going to end up losing.

Lose-Lose can also occur when someone becomes obsessed with another person in a negative way. This is especially likely to happen with those closest to us.

'I don't care what happens to me as long as my brother fails.'

'If I can't have Jeff, I'm sure as heck not going to let my friend Sarah have him.'

If you're not careful, boyfriend-girlfriend relationships can sour into Lose-Lose. You've seen it. Two good people begin dating and things go well at first. It's Win-Win. But gradually they become emotionally glued and codependent. They begin to get possessive and jealous. They constantly need to be together, to touch, to feel secure, as if they own the other person. Eventually, this dependency brings out the worst in both of them. They begin to fight, argue, and 'get back at' each other, resulting in a downward spiral of Lose-Lose.

WIN-WIN – THE ALL-YOU-CAN-EAT BUFFET

Win-Win is a belief that everyone can win. It's both nice and tough all at once. I won't step on you, but I won't be your doormat either. You care about other people and you want them to succeed. But you also care about yourself, and you want to succeed as well. Win-Win is abundant. It is the belief that there's plenty of success to go around. It's not either you or me.
It's both of us. It's not a matter of who gets the biggest piece of pie. There's more than enough food for everyone. It's an all-you-can-eat buffet.

A friend of mine named Dawn Meeves shared how she discovered the power of thinking Win-Win:

At school, I played on the girls' basketball team. I was pretty good for my age and regularly made the first team. One of my classmates named Pam, a dear friend was also on the team.

I had a sweet little shot I could hit quite regularly from ten feet out. I began making four or five of those shots a game and began getting recognized for it. It soon became apparent that Pam didn't like all the attention I was getting and decided, consciously or not, to keep the ball from me. It didn't matter how open I was for the shot, Pam stopped passing the ball to me.

One night, after playing a terrible game in which Pam kept the ball from me most of the game, I was as mad as I had ever been. I spent many hours talking with my dad, going over everything, and expressing my anger toward my friend-turned-enemy, Pam. After a long discussion, my dad told me that the best thing he could think of would be to give Pam the ball every time I got it. Every time. I thought it was the most stupid suggestion he had ever given me. He simply told me it would work and left me at the kitchen table to think about it. But I didn't. I knew it wouldn't work and put it aside as silly fatherly advice.

The next game came quickly, and I was determined to beat Pam at her own game. I planned and plotted and came out with a mission to ruin Pam's game. On my first possession of the ball, I heard my dad above the crowd. He had a booming voice, and though I shut out everything around me while playing basketball, I could always hear Dad's deep voice. At the moment I caught the ball, he yelled out, 'Give her the ball!!' I hesitated for one second and then did what I knew was right. Although I was open for a shot, I found Pam and passed her the ball. She was shocked for a moment, then turned and shot, sinking the ball for two points. As I ran down the court to play defence, I felt a feeling I had never felt before: true joy for the success of another human being. And, even more, I realized that it put us ahead in the game. It felt good to be winning. I continued to give her the ball every time I got it in the first half. Every time. In the second half, I did the same, only shooting if it was a designated play or if I was wide open for a shot.

We won that game, and in the games that followed, Pam began to pass me the ball as much as I passed it to her. Our teamwork was getting stronger and stronger, and so was our friendship. We won the majority of our games that year and became a legendary small town duo. The local newspaper even did an article on our ability to pass to one another and sense each other's presence. Overall, I scored more points than ever before.

You see, Win-Win always creates more. An endless buffet. And as Dawn discovered, wanting another person to win fills you full of good feelings. By passing the ball, Dawn didn't score fewer points but eventually scored more. In fact, they both scored more points and won more games than if they had selfishly kept the ball from each other.

You probably do more Win-Win thinking than you give yourself credit for. The following are all examples of the Win-Win attitude:

- You recently got a promotion at the restaurant you work at. You share the praise and recognition with all of those who helped you get there.
- You were just elected to an important school office and make up your mind not to develop a 'superiority complex.' You treat everyone the same, including the friendless and the unpopular.

- Your best friend just got accepted at the university you wanted to get into. You didn't make it. Although you feel terrible about your own situation, you are genuinely happy for your friend.
- You want to go out for dinner. Your friend wants to see a movie. You jointly decide to rent a movie and pick up food to eat at home.

How to Think Win-Win   So how do you do it? How can you be happy for your friend when he just got accepted at university and you didn't? How can you avoid feeling inferior to the girl next door who has all those gorgeous clothes? How can you find solutions to problems so that both of you can win?

Might I suggest two clues: Win the private victory first and avoid the tumour twins.

WIN THE PRIVATE VICTORY FIRST

It all begins with you. If you are extremely insecure and haven't paid the price to win the private victory, it will be difficult to think Win-Win. You'll be threatened by other people. It'll be hard to be happy for their successes. It will be difficult to share recognition or praise. Insecure people get jealous very easily. This conversation between Doug and his girlfriend is typical of an insecure person:

'Amy, who was the guy you were talking to just now?' asks Doug.

'He's just a good friend I grew up with,' says Amy.

'I don't want you hangin' out with that guy,' rants Doug.

'Doug, he's just a friend I've known for a long time. We went to primary school together.'

'I don't care how long you've known him. You shouldn't be so friendly to him.'

'It's no big deal. He's having some problems and just needs a friend.'

'Are you committed to me or not?'

'OK, Doug. If that's what you want, I won't talk to him anymore.'

Can you see how hard it would be for Doug to be big-hearted in this situation as long as he is insecure and emotionally dependent upon his girlfriend? Doug needs to start with himself. As he makes deposits into his PBA, takes responsibility for his life, and gets a plan in place, his confidence and security will increase and he'll start enjoying other people instead of being threatened by them. Personal security is the foundation for thinking Win-Win.

• AVOID THE TUMOUR TWINS

There are two habits that, like tumours, can slowly eat you away from the inside. They are twins and their names are competing and comparing. It's virtually impossible to think Win-Win with them around.

Competing

Competition can be extremely healthy. It drives us to improve, to reach and stretch. Without it, we would never know how far we could push ourselves. In the business world, it makes our economy prosper. The glory of the Olympic Games is all about excellence and competition.

But there is another side to competition that isn't so nice. In the movie *Star Wars*, Luke Skywalker learns about a positive energy shield called 'the force', which gives life to all things. Later, Luke confronts the evil Darth Vader and learns about the 'dark side' of the force. As Darth puts it, 'You don't know the power of the dark side'. So it is with competition. There is a sunny side and a dark side, and both are powerful. The difference is this: Competition is healthy when you compete against yourself, or when it challenges you to reach and stretch and become your best. Competition becomes dark when you tie your self-worth into winning or when you use it as a way to place yourself above another.

LET'S FIND A **WIN-WIN** SOLUTION, DAD.

While reading a book called *The Inner Game of Tennis* by Tim Galwey, I found some words that say it perfectly. Wrote Tim:

When competition is used as a means of creating a self-image relative to others, the worst in a person comes out; then the ordinary fears and frustrations become greatly exaggerated. It is as if some believe that only by being the best, only by being a winner, will they be eligible for the love and respect they seek. Children who have been taught to measure themselves in this way often become adults driven by a compulsion to succeed which overshadows all else.

A famous coach once said that the two worst traits an athlete can have are a fear of failure and an inordinate desire to win, or a win-at-any-cost attitude.

I'll never forget an argument I had with my younger brother after his team beat mine in a game of beach volleyball.

'I can't believe you guys beat us,' I said.

'What's so unbelievable about that?' he replied. 'You think you're a better athlete than me, don't you?'

'I know I am. Look at the evidence. I went much further than you in sports.'

'But you're using your own narrow definition of what an athlete is. I frankly think that I'm a better athlete because I can jump higher and run faster.'

'Bull! You're not faster than me. And what does jumping and running have to do with it anyway? I can kick your butt in every sport.'

'Oh yeah?'

'Yeah!'

After we calmed down, we both felt like idiots. We had been seduced by the dark side. And the dark side never leaves you with a good aftertaste.

Let's use competition as a bench-mark to measure ourselves against, but let's stop competing over boyfriends, girlfriends, status, friends, popularity, positions, attention and the like and start enjoying life.

Comparing

Comparing is competition's twin. And just as cancerous. Comparing yourself to others is nothing but bad news. Why? Because we're all on different development timetables. Socially, mentally and physically. Since we all bake differently, we shouldn't keep opening the oven door to see how well our cake is rising compared to our neighbour's, or our own cake won't rise at all. Although some of us are like the poplar tree, which grows like a weed the moment it's planted, others are like the bamboo tree, which shows no growth for four years but then grows ninety feet in year five.

I once heard it described this way: Life is like a great obstacle course. Each person has their own course, separated from every other course by tall walls. Your course comes complete with customized obstacles designed specifically for your personal growth. So what good does it do to climb the wall to see how well your neighbour is doing or to check out his obstacles in comparison to your own?

Building your life based on how you stack up compared to others is never good footing. If I get my security from the fact that my exam results are higher than yours or my friends are more popular than yours, then what happens when someone comes along with higher marks or more popular friends? Comparing ourselves makes us feel

THE BAMBOO TREE

| YEAR 1 | YEAR 2 | YEAR 3 | YEAR 4 | YEAR 5 |

like a wave of the sea tossed to and fro by the wind. We go up and down, feeling inferior one moment and superior the next, confident one moment and intimidated the next. The only good comparison is comparing yourself against your own potential.

I love how noted author Paul H. Dunn put it in a speech entitled 'On Feeling Inferior':

I have noticed that daily we meet moments that steal our self-esteem. They are inevitable. Pick up any magazine; you see people who look healthier, skinnier or better dressed than you are. Look around. There is always someone who seems smarter, another more self-assured, still another more talented. In fact, each day we are reminded that we lack certain talents, that we make mistakes, that we do not excel in all things. And amidst all this, it is easy to believe that we do not quite measure up in the great scheme of things, but are inferior in some secret way.

If you base your self-esteem, your feeling of self-worth, on anything outside the quality of your heart, your mind or your soul, you have based it on a very shaky footing. So you and I are not perfect in form or physical figure. So you and I are not the richest, the wisest, the wittiest. So what?

I once interviewed a girl named Anne, who got caught in the web of comparisons for several years before managing to escape. She has a message for those who are caught:

My problems began when I moved and went to a new school before starting GCSEs. Most of the kids in my new school had money. And how you dressed was everything. The big question was: Who is wearing what today? There were even some unspoken rules about clothes, such as never wear the same thing twice and never wear the same thing as someone else. Brand names and expensive jeans were a must. You had to have every colour, every style.

During that first year, I had a boyfriend who was two years older and whom my parents didn't like. Our relationship was good at first, but after a while, he began to make me feel self-conscious. He would say things like, 'Why can't you look like her?' 'How come you're so fat?' 'If you just changed a little bit you'd be just right.'

I began to believe my boyfriend. I started looking at other girls and analyzing all the reasons I wasn't as good as them. Even though I had a wardrobe full of clothes, I remember having anxiety attacks because I couldn't decide what to wear. I even began shoplifting because I wanted to have the latest and best clothes. After a while, who I was hinged upon who I was with, what I looked like, and what kind of clothes I had on. I never felt good enough, for anyone.

To cope, I started to binge and purge. The eating gave me comfort and the purging gave me some strange form of control. Although I wasn't fat, I was so scared of being fat. It soon became a big part of my life. I started throwing up thirty to forty times a day. I would do it at school, in the bathrooms, and anywhere else I could find. It was my secret. I couldn't tell my parents because I didn't want to let them down.

I remember being asked by the popular group one time to go to the football game. They were sixteen, one year older than me. I was so excited! My mum and I worked and worked to find me the perfect outfit. I waited by the window for hours, but they never came to pick me up. I felt so worthless. I thought, 'I wasn't picked up because I wasn't cool enough or didn't have the right look'.

Finally, it all came to a head. While I was on stage performing in a play, I suddenly became totally disoriented and passed out. Waking up in the dressing room, I found my mum at my side. 'I need help,' I whispered.

Admitting that I had a problem was the first step to my recovery, which took several years. Looking back now, I can't believe I got myself into that state of mind. I had everything I needed to be happy yet I was so miserable. I was a cute, talented, skinny girl who got caught up in a world of comparisons and was made to feel not good enough. I want to shout out to the world: 'Don't ever do this to yourself. It's not worth it.'

The key to my recovery was meeting some really special friends who made me feel that I mattered because of who I was and not what I wore. They told me, 'You don't need this. You are better than that.' I began to change for myself, not because someone else told me that I had to change to be worthy of their love.

The pearl of wisdom from the story is: Stop doing it. Break the habit. Comparing yourself can become an addiction as strong as drugs or alcohol. You don't have to look like or dress like a model to be good enough. You know what really matters. Don't get caught up in the game and worry so much about being popular during your teen years, because most of life comes after. (Please see the Eating Disorder Helplines and websites in the back of this book.)

THE FRUITS OF THE WIN-WIN SPIRIT

I've learned never to underestimate what can happen when some-one thinks Win-Win. This was Andy's experience:

At first I could see no point to Win-Win. But I started applying it in my part-time job, and I was just blown away. I have used it now for two years and it's honestly scary how powerful this habit is – I wish I had known about it much sooner in my life. It's taught me to exercise my leadership ability and to approach my job with an attitude of 'let's make this job more fun. Let's make it a win for both me and my employer'. I now sit down with my manager monthly and tell her all the little things I can see in the company that aren't getting done that I am willing to do.

The last time we met she said to me, 'I have always wondered how we could get all these little loose ends done. I am so impressed with how you look for opportunities and are so willing to perform.' And then she gave me a raise.

Believe me, this Win-Win stuff is contagious. If you're big-hearted, committed to helping others succeed and willing to share recognition, you'll be a magnet for friends. Think about it. Don't you just love people who are interested in your success and want you to win? It makes you want to help them in return, doesn't it?

The Win-Win spirit can be applied to just about any situation, from working out major conflicts with your parents to deciding who walks the dog, as Jon shared below.

My sister and I are always arguing about who has to walk the dogs and do the dishes. We both would choose the dogs over the dishes any day. But someone has to do one or the other. So we decided that I would wash the dishes, she would dry them, and then we'd walk the dogs together. I'm glad it worked out like that, because now we get what needs to be done finished but also add a little fun to it by doing it together.

Sometimes, no matter how hard you try, you won't be able to find a Win-Win solution. Or the other party may be so bent on Win-Lose that you don't even want to approach him or her. That happens. In these situations, don't get ugly yourself (Win-Lose) or get stepped on (Lose-Win). Instead, go for Win-Win or No Deal. In other words, if you can't find a solution that works for both of you, decide not to play. No Deal. For example, if you and your friend can't decide what to do one night, instead of doing an activity that one of you might resent, split up that night and get together another

night. Or if you and your girlfriend or boyfriend can't develop a Win-Win relationship, it might be best to go for No Deal and part ways. It sure beats going for Win-Lose, Lose-Win, or, worst of all, Lose-Lose.

A fifteen-year-old named Bryan, who was taught Win-Win by his father, shared this interesting story:

> Last year, my friend Steve and I wanted to make some money during the summer holiday. So we started a window washing and lawn care business. We thought Green and Clean was kind of a cool name to use for our business.
>
> Steve's parents had a friend who needed his windows washed, and before too long the word spread and we got a few jobs.
>
> We used a programme on my dad's computer to make a little sheet we call a Win-Win agreement. When we get to the house we go around and get the window measurements and write down an estimate. We make it totally clear that they are going to get clean windows for a set price. There is a line for them to sign on. If we don't perform well, we know we won't get hired back. After we are done, we walk them around and show them our work. We want them to know we're accountable. It puts us on a better footing with the customer.
>
> We have a little Green and Clean fund. Once we started making money, we split the money and then put some aside to buy window washing equipment. As long as our customers are happy, and they get clean windows, they are winning. We win, because at fifteen, it's a way for us to make some extra money.

Watch How It Makes You Feel

Developing a Win-Win attitude is not easy. But you can do it. If you're thinking Win-Win only 10 per cent of the time right now, start thinking it 20 per cent of the time, then 30 per cent, and so on. Eventually, it will become a mental habit, and you won't even have to think about. It will become part of who you are.

Perhaps the most surprising benefit of thinking Win-Win is the good feelings it brings on. One of my favourite stories that illustrates the power of *thinking* Win-Win is the true story of Jacques Lusseyran as told in his autobiography *And There Was Light*. The editors of *PARABOLA* magazine, who wrote the book's foreword, summarize Lusseyran's story this way:

'Born in Paris in 1924, [Jacques] was fifteen at the time of the German occupation, and at sixteen he had formed and was heading an underground resistance movement . . . which from a beginning of fifty-two boys . . . within a year had grown to six hundred. This would seem remarkable enough, but add to it the fact that from the age of eight, Jacques had been totally blind.'

Although totally blind, Jacques could see, in a different way. As he put it: 'I saw light and went on seeing it though I was blind . . . I could feel light rising, spreading, resting on objects, giving them form, then leaving them . . . I lived in a stream of light.' He called this stream of light that he lived in 'my secret'.

Yet there were times when Jacques' light would leave him and he became cloudy. It was whenever he thought Win-Lose. As he put it:

'When I was playing with my small companions, if I suddenly grew anxious to win, to be the first at all costs, then all at once I could see nothing. Literally I went into fog or smoke.

'I could no longer afford to be jealous or unfriendly, because, as soon as I was, a bandage came down over my eyes, and I was bound hand and foot and cast aside. All at once a black hole opened, and I was helpless inside it. But when I was happy and serene, approached people with confidence and thought well of them, I was rewarded with light. So is it surprising that I learned to love friendship and harmony when I was very young.'

The true test of whether or not you are thinking Win-Win or one of the alternatives is how you feel. Win-Lose and Lose-Win thinking will cloud your judgment and fill you with negative feelings. You simply cannot afford to do it. On the other hand, just as Jacques discovered, thinking Win-Win will fill your heart with happy and serene thoughts. It will give you confidence. Even fill you with light.

★ ★ ★

COMING ATTRACTIONS

In the upcoming chapter, I'll share the secret to getting under your parents' skins in a positive way. So don't stop now!

1. Pinpoint the area of your life where you most struggle with comparisons. Perhaps it's with clothes, physical features, friends or talents.

Where I'm struggling most with comparisons: _____

_____

2. If you play sports, show sportsmanship. Compliment someone from the opposing team after the match or game.

3. If someone owes you money, don't be afraid to mention it in a friendly way. 'Did you forget about that ten pounds I loaned you last week? I could use it right now.' Think Win-Win, not Lose-Win.

4. Without caring whether you win or lose, play a card, board or computer game with others just for the fun of it.

5. Do you have an important exam coming up soon? If so, study with someone else and share your best ideas with them. You'll both do better.

6.  The next time someone close to you succeeds, be genuinely happy for them instead of feeling threatened.

7. Think about your general attitude toward life. Is it based on Win-Lose, Lose-Win, Lose-Lose, or Win-Win thinking? How is that attitude affecting you?

8. Think of a person who you feel is a model of Win-Win. What is it about this person you admire?

Person: _____

What I admire about them: _____

_____

Are you in a Lose-Win relationship with a member of the opposite sex? If you are, then decide what must happen to make it a Win for you or choose to go for No Deal and get out of the relationship.

HABIT ⑤

Seek **First** to
Understand,
Then to Be Understood

You Have
Two Ears
AND ONE MOUTH ...
Hel-lo!

Before I can walk in another's shoes, I must first remove my own.
UNKNOWN

Let's say you go into a shoe shop to buy a new pair of shoes. The sales assistant asks, 'What kind of shoes are you looking for?'

'Well, I'm looking for something that . . .'

'I think I know what you'd like,' he interrupts. 'Everyone is wearing these. Trust me.'

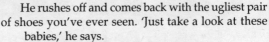

He rushes off and comes back with the ugliest pair of shoes you've ever seen. 'Just take a look at these babies,' he says.

'But I really don't like them.'

'Everyone likes them. They're the hottest thing going right now.'

'I'm looking for something different.'

'I promise you. You'll love them.'

'But I . . .'

'Listen. I've been selling shoes for ten years and I know a good shoe when I see it.'

After this experience, would you ever want to go to that shop again? Definitely not. You can't trust people who give you solutions before they understand what your needs are. But did you know that we often do the same thing when we communicate?

'Hey, Melissa, how's it goin'? You look really depressed. Is something the matter?'

'You wouldn't understand, Colleen. You'd think it was stupid.'

'No, I wouldn't. Tell me what's going on. I'm all ears.'

'Oh, I don't know.'

'C'mon. You can tell me.'

'Well, okay . . . uuhm . . . things just aren't the same between Tony and me anymore.'

'I told you not to get involved with him. I just knew this would happen.'

'Tony's not the problem.'

'Listen, Melissa, if I were you, I'd just forget about him and move on.'

'But, Colleen, that's not how I feel.'

'Believe me. I know how you feel. I went through the same thing last year. Don't you remember? It practically ruined my entire year.'

'Just forget it, Colleen.'

'Melissa, I'm only trying to help. I really want to understand. Now, go on. Tell me how you feel.'

It's our tendency to want to swoop out of the sky like Superman and solve everyone's problems before we even understand what the problem is. We simply don't listen. As the American Indian proverb goes, 'Listen, or thy tongue will make thee deaf.'

The key to communication and having power and influence with people can be summed up in one sentence: Seek first to understand, then to be understood. In other words, listen first, talk second. This is Habit 5, and it works. If you can learn this simple habit – to see things from another's point of view before sharing your own – a whole new world of understanding will be opened up to you.

OH, GOODY... HERE COMES 'ANSWER MAN.'

The Deepest Need of the Human Heart Why is this habit the key to communication? It's because the deepest need of the human heart is to be understood. Everyone wants to be respected and valued for who they are – a unique, one-of-a-kind, never-to-be-cloned (at least for now) individual.

People won't expose their soft middles unless they feel genuine love and understanding. Once they feel it, however, they will tell you more than you may want to hear. The following story about a girl with an eating disorder shows the power of understanding:

I was a professional anorexic by the time I met Julie, Pam and Liz, my university roommates in my first year. I had spent my last two years of school concentrating on exercising, dieting and triumphing in every ounce I lost. At eighteen years old and five foot eight, I weighed in at a breezy 43 kilos, a tall pile of bones.

I didn't have many friends. Constant deprivation had left me irritable, bitter and so tired I couldn't carry on casual conversations. School social events were out of the question too. I didn't feel like I had anything in common with any of the kids I knew. A handful of loyal friends really stuck it out with me and tried to help, but I tuned out their preachy lectures about my weight and chalked it up to jealousy.

My parents bribed me with new wardrobes. They badgered me and demanded that I eat in front of them. When I wouldn't, they dragged me off to a series of doctors, therapists and specialists. I was miserable and convinced my whole life was going to be that way.

Then I moved away to attend university. The luck of the draw settled me into a flat with Julie, Pam and Liz, the three girls who made my life worth living again.

We lived in a tiny flat where all my strange eating patterns and exercising neuroses were right out in the open. I know they must have thought I looked strange with my sallow complexion, bruises, thinning hair and jutting hips and collarbones. When I see pictures of myself at eighteen, I'm horrified at how terrible I looked.

But they weren't. They didn't treat me like a person with a problem. There were no lectures, no force feeding, no gossiping, no browbeating. I almost didn't know what to do.

Almost immediately, I felt like one of them, except that I didn't eat. We attended classes together, found jobs, jogged in the evenings, watched television and hung out on Saturdays. My anorexia, for once, was not the central topic. Instead, we spent long nights discussing our families, our ambitions, our uncertainties.

I was absolutely amazed by our similarities. For the first time in literally years, I felt understood. I felt like someone had taken the time to understand me as a person instead of always trying to fix my problem first. To these three girls, I wasn't an anorexic needing treatment. I was just the fourth girl.

As my sense of belonging grew, I began to watch them. They were happy, attractive, smart and occasionally they ate cake mixture right out of the bowl. If I had so much in common with them, why couldn't I eat three meals a day too?

Pam, Julie and Liz never told me how to heal myself. They showed me every day, and they really worked to understand me before trying to cure me. By the end of my first term at university, they were setting a place for me at dinner. And I felt welcome.

Think of the influence these three girls had on the fourth girl because they tried to understand her instead of judging her. Isn't it interesting that once she felt understood and not judged, she immediately dropped her defences and was open to their influence? Contrast that with what might have happened had her flatmates turned preachy on her.

Have you ever heard the saying 'People don't care how much you know until they know how much you care'? How true it is. Think about a situation when someone didn't take the time to understand or listen to you. Were you open to what they had to say?

While playing football I developed some severe arm pain in my bicep for a time. It was a complex condition and I had tried a number of different techniques to fix it – ice, heat, massage, lifting weights and anti-inflammatory pills – but nothing worked. So

I went to see one of our more seasoned trainers for help. Before I had described my condition, however, he said to me, 'I've seen this thing before. This is what you need to do'. I tried to explain more, but he was already convinced he knew the problem. I felt like saying, 'What a minute. Hear me out, Doc. I don't think you understand'.

As you might have guessed, his techniques actually made my arm hurt worse. He never listened, and I never felt understood. I lost confidence in his advice and avoided him at all costs whenever I had an injury. I had no faith in his prescriptions, because he never diagnosed. I didn't care how much he knew, because he hadn't shown me that he cared.

You can show you care by simply taking time to listen without judging and without giving advice. This short poem captures how badly people just want to be listened to:

PLEASE LISTEN

When I ask you to listen to me
and you start giving me advice,
you have not done what I asked.
When I ask you to listen to me
and you begin to tell me why
I shouldn't feel that way,
you are trampling on my feelings.
When I ask you to listen to me
and you feel you have to do something
to solve my problem,
you have failed me,
strange as that may seem.
Listen! All I ask is that you listen.
Don't talk or do – just hear me.

FIVE POOR LISTENING STYLES

To understand someone you must listen to them. Surprise! The problem is that most of us don't know *how* to listen.

Imagine this. You're trying to decide what modules to take next year. You open up your schedule and look at what's available.

'Hmmm . . . Let me see . . . *Creative writing. Modern poetry. English*

literature. Listening. Wait a minute. Listening? A class on listening? Is this a joke?'

This would be quite a surprise, wouldn't it? But it really shouldn't be, because listening is one of the four primary forms of communication, along with reading, writing and speaking. And if you think about it, since birth you've been taking classes on how to read, write and speak better, but when have you ever taken a class on how to listen better?

When people talk we seldom listen because we're usually too busy preparing a response, judging or filtering their words through our own paradigms. It's so typical of us to use one of these five poor listening styles:

Five Poor Listening Styles

- Spacing out
- Pretend listening
- Selective listening
- Word listening
- Self-centred listening

EARTH TO BOB... ARE YOU LISTENING?

SPACING OUT

Spacing out is when someone is talking to us but we ignore them because our mind is wandering off in another galaxy. They may have something very important to say, but we're caught up in our own thoughts. We all space out from time to time, but do it too much and you'll get a reputation for being 'out of it'.

Pretend listening is more common. We still aren't paying much attention to the other person, but at least we pretend we are by making insightful comments at key junctures, such as 'yeah', 'uh-huh', 'cool', 'sounds great'. The speaker will usually get the hint and will feel that he or she is not important enough to be heard.

SO MY GIRLFRIEND DUMPED ME...

SOUNDS COOL.

PRETEND LISTENING

Selective listening is where we pay attention only to the part of the conversation that interests us. For example, your friend may be trying to tell you how it feels to be in the shadow of his talented brother in the army. All you hear is the word 'army' and say, 'Oh yeah, the army! I've been thinking a lot about it lately'. Since you'll always talk about what you want to talk about, instead of what the other person wants to talk about, chances are you'll never develop lasting friendships.

Word listening occurs when we actually pay attention to what someone is saying, but we listen only to the words, not to the body language, the feelings, or the true meaning behind the words. As a result, we miss out on what's really being said. Your friend Kim might say to you, 'What do you think of Richard?' You might reply, 'I think he's pretty cool'. But if you had been more sensitive, and listened to her body language and tone of voice, you would have heard that she was really saying, 'Do you think Richard likes me?' If you focus on words only, you'll seldom be in touch with the deeper emotions of people's hearts.

Self-centred listening happens when we see everything from our own point of view. Instead of standing in another's shoes, we want them to stand in ours. This is where sentences like 'Oh, I know exactly how you feel' come from. We don't know exactly how they feel, we know exactly how we feel, and we assume they feel the same way we do, like the shoe salesman who thinks that you should like the shoes because he likes them. Self-centred listening is often a game of one-upmanship, where we try to one-up each other, as if conversations were a competition. 'You think _your_ day was bad? That's nothin'. You should hear what happened to _me_.'

When we listen from our point of view, we usually reply in one of three ways, all of which make the other person immediately close up. We _judge_, we _advise_, and we _probe_. Let's take a look at each.

Judging. Sometimes, as we listen to others, we make judgements (in the back of our minds) about them and what they're saying. If you're busy judging, you're not really listening, are you? People don't want to be judged, they want to be heard. In the conversation below, notice how little listening and how much judging is going on in the mind of the listener. (The listener's judgements are enclosed in parentheses.)

   Peter: *I had a great time with Katherine last night.*
    Karl: *Oh, that's nice. (Katherine? Why would you want to go out with Katherine?)*
   Peter: *I had no idea how great she is.*
    Karl: *Oh, yeah? (Here you go again. You think every girl is great.)*
   Peter: *Yeah. I'm thinking about asking her to the dance!*
    Karl: *I thought you were going to ask Jessica. (Are you crazy? Jessica is much better looking than Katherine.)*
   Peter: *I was. But I think I'll ask Katherine now.*

Karl: *Well, ask her out then. (I'm sure you'll change your mind tomorrow.)*

Karl was so busy judging that he didn't hear a word Peter was saying and missed out on an opportunity to make a deposit into Peter's RBA.

Advising. This is when we give advice drawn from our own experience. This is the when-I-was-your-age speech you often get from your elders.

An emotional sister who needs a listening ear says to her brother:

'I don't like our new school at all. Ever since we moved I've felt like the biggest outcast. I wish I could find some new friends.'

Instead of listening to understand, the brother reflects upon his own life and says:

'You need to start meeting new people and get involved in sports and clubs like I did.'

Little sister didn't want any advice from a well-intentioned brother, no matter how good it was. She just wanted to be listened to, for heaven's sake. Once she felt understood, only then would she be open to his advice. Big brother blew a big chance for a big deposit.

Probing. Probing occurs when you try to dig up emotions before people are ready to share them. Have you ever been probed? Parents do it to teenagers all the time. Your mum, with every good intention, tries to find out what's going on in your life. But since you're not ready to talk, her attempts feel intrusive, and so you shut her out.

'Hi, honey. How was school today?'
'Fine.'
'How did you do on your test?'
'OK.'
'How are your friends?'
'Good.'
'Do you have any plans tonight?'
'Not really.'
'Have you been seeing any pretty girls lately?'
'No, Mum. Just leave me alone.'

No one likes to be interrogated. If you're asking a lot of questions and not getting very far, you're probably probing. Sometimes people just aren't prepared to open up and don't feel like talking. Learn to be a great listener and offer an open ear when the time is right.

GENUINE LISTENING

Luckily, you and I never exhibit any of these five poor listening styles. Right? Well, maybe just occasionally. There is a higher form of listening, fortunately, which leads to real communication. We call it 'genuine listening.' And it's the kind of practice we want to put to use. But to do genuine listening, you need to do three things differently.

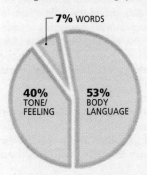

7% WORDS

40% TONE/ FEELING

53% BODY LANGUAGE

First, listen with your eyes, heart, and ears. Listening with just your ears isn't good enough, because only 7 per cent of communication is contained in the words we use. The rest comes from body language (53 per cent) and how we say words, or the tone and feeling reflected in our voice (40 per cent). For example, notice how you can change the meaning of a sentence just by emphasizing a different word.

_I_ didn't say you had an attitude problem.
I didn't say _you_ had an attitude problem.
I didn't say you had an _attitude_ problem.

To hear what other people are really saying, you need to listen to what they are _not_ saying. No matter how hard people may appear on the surface, most everyone is tender inside and has a desperate need to be understood. The following poem (one of my all-time favourites) captures this need.

PLEASE . . . HEAR WHAT I'M NOT SAYING

Don't be fooled by me. Don't be fooled by the mask I wear. For I wear a mask, I wear a thousand masks, masks that I'm afraid to take off, and none of them is me. Pretending is an art that is second nature with me, but don't be fooled.

. . . I give the impression that I'm secure, that all is sunny and unruffled with me, within as well as without; that confidence is my name and coolness is my game; that the waters are calm and that I'm in command and I need no one. But don't believe it; please don't.

I idly chatter with you in the suave tones of surface talk. I tell you everything that's really nothing, nothing of what's crying within me. So when I'm going through my routine, don't be fooled by what I'm saying. Please listen carefully and try to hear what I'm not saying; what I'd like to be able to say; what, for survival, I need to say but I can't say. I dislike the hiding. Honestly I do. I dislike the superficial phony games I'm playing.

I'd really like to be genuine, spontaneous and me; but you have to help me. You have to help me by holding out your hand, even when that's the last thing I seem to want or need. Each time you are kind and gentle and encouraging, each time you try to understand because you really care, my heart begins to grow wings. Very small wings. Very feeble wings. But wings. With your sensitivity and sympathy and your power of understanding, I can make it. You can breathe life into me. It will not be easy for you. A long conviction of worthlessness builds strong walls. But love is stronger than strong walls, and therein lies my hope. Please try to beat down those walls with firm hands, but with gentle hands, for a child is very sensitive, and I am a child.

Who am I, you may wonder. For I am every man, every woman, every child . . . every human you meet.

<u>Second, stand in their shoes.</u> To become a genuine listener, you need to take off your shoes and stand in another's. In the words of Robert Byrne, 'Until you walk a mile in another man's moccasins you can't imagine the smell'. You must try to see the world as they see it and try to feel as they feel.

Let's pretend for a moment that everyone in the world wears tinted glasses and that no two shades are exactly alike. You and I are standing on the banks of a river. I am wearing green lenses and you are wearing red. 'Wow, look how green the water is,' I say.

'Green? Are you crazy, the water is red,' you reply.

'Hello. Are you colourblind? That's as green as green gets.'

'It's red, you idiot!'

'Green!'

'Red!'

Many people look at conversations as a competition. It's my point of view versus yours; we can't both be right. In reality, since we're both coming from a different point of view, we both can be. Furthermore, it's silly to try to *win* conversations. That usually ends up in Win-Lose or Lose-Lose and is a withdrawal from the RBA.

My little sister was once told this story by a friend of hers named Toby. Notice what a difference standing in another's shoes made:

The worst part about going to school was having to ride the bus. I mean most of my friends had a car to drive (even if it was a wreck) but we couldn't afford a car for my own personal use, so I had to either take the bus or get a lift. Sometimes I would call my mum after school to come and pick me up, but she would take so long it drove me crazy. I remember many times screaming at my mum, 'What took you forever? Don't you even care that I've been waiting for hours?!' I never noticed

*how she felt or what she'd been doing. I
only thought about myself.*

*One day I overheard my mum talking
to my dad about it. She was crying and said
how much she wished they could afford a car
for me and how hard she had been working
to try to earn the extra money.*

*Suddenly my whole perspective changed. I
saw my mum as a real person with feelings –
fear, hopes, doubts and a great amount of love
for me. I vowed never to treat her badly again. I
even started talking more to her, and together we
figured out a way I could get a part-time job and
earn my way to a car. She even volunteered to drive me
to work and back. I wish I had listened to her earlier.*

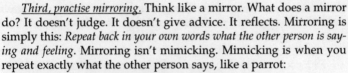

WHOA, I THINK
I UNDERSTAND
NOW...

<u>Third, practise mirroring.</u> Think like a mirror. What does a mirror
do? It doesn't judge. It doesn't give advice. It reflects. Mirroring is
simply this: *Repeat back in your own words what the other person is saying and feeling.* Mirroring isn't mimicking. Mimicking is when you
repeat exactly what the other person says, like a parrot:

'Tom. I'm having the worst time in school right now.'
'You're having the worst time in school right now.'
'I'm practically failing all of my subjects.'
'You're practically failing all of your subjects.'
'Man, stop saying everything I'm saying. What is it with you?'
Mirroring is different from mimicking in the following ways:

HELLO!
HELLO...

HELLO!

MIMICKING IS:	MIRRORING IS:
Repeating words	Repeating meaning
Using the same words	Using your own words
Cold and indifferent	Warm and caring

Let's take a look at an everyday conversation to see how mirroring works.

Your dad might say to you: 'No! You can't take the car tonight,
Son. And that's final.'

A typical seek-first-to-talk response might be: 'You never let me
take the car. I always have to get a lift. And I'm sick of it.'

This kind of response usually ends up in a big yelling match where neither side feels very good afterward.

Instead, try mirroring. *Repeat back in your own words what the other person is saying and feeling.* Let's try it again.

'No! You can't take the car tonight, Son. And that's final.'

'I can see that you're upset about this, Dad.'

'You bet I'm upset. The way your marks have been dropping lately, you don't deserve the car.'

'You're worried about my marks.'

'I am. You know how badly I want you to get into university.'

'University is really important to you, isn't it?'

'I never had the chance to go to university. And I've never been able to make much because of it. I know money's not everything, but it sure would help right now. I just want a better life for you.'

'I see.'

'You are so capable that it just drives me crazy when you don't take school seriously. I guess you can take the car if you promise me you'll do your homework later tonight. That's all I'm asking. Promise?'

Did you notice what happened? By practising the skill of mirroring, the boy was able to uncover the real issue. Dad didn't care so much about him taking the car; he was more worried about his future and his casualness toward school. Once he felt that his son understood how important results and university were to him, he dropped his defences.

I can't guarantee that mirroring will always lead to such perfect outcomes. It's usually, but not always, more complicated than this. Dad might have replied, 'I'm glad you understand where I'm coming from, Son. Now go do your homework.' But I can guarantee that mirroring will be a deposit into another's RBA and that you'll get further than you'd get using the 'fight or flight' approach. If you're still a sceptic, I challenge you to give it a try. I think you'll be pleasantly surprised.

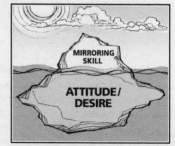

<u>Disclaimer.</u> If you practise mirroring but don't really desire to understand others, they will see through it and feel manipulated. Mirroring is a skill, the tip of the iceberg. Your attitude or desire to really understand another is the lurking mass of ice underneath the surface.

If your attitude is right but you don't have the skill, you'll be okay. But it doesn't work the other way around. If you have both the attitude and the skill, you'll become a powerful communicator!

Here are a few mirroring phrases you can use when trying to practise genuine listening. Remember, your goal is to *repeat back in your own words what another person is saying and feeling.*

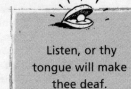

Listen, or thy tongue will make thee deaf.

NATIVE AMERICAN PROVERB

<u>Mirroring Phrases</u>
- 'As I get it, you felt that . . .'
- 'So, as I see it . . .'
- 'I can see that you're feeling . . .'
- 'You feel that . . .'
- 'So, what you're saying is . . .'

Important note: There is a time and a place for genuine listening. You'll want to do it when you're talking about an important or sensitive issue, like if a friend really needs help or if you're having a communication problem with a loved one. These conversations take time and you can't rush them. However, you don't need to do it during casual conversations or everyday small talk:

'Where's the bathroom? I've got go really badly.'

'So what you're saying is you're worried you won't find a bathroom in time.'

Genuine Listening in Action

Let's take another look at the sister who needs a listening ear from her big brother to illustrate how different genuine listening is.

Sister says, 'I don't like our new school at all. Ever since we moved I've felt like the biggest outcast. I wish I could find some new friends.'

The brother could use any one of the following responses:

'Pass the crisps?' (Spacing out)

'Sounds great.' (Pretend listening)

'Speaking of friends, my friend Bart . . .' (Selective listening)

'What you need to do is start meeting new people.' (Advising)

'You're not trying hard enough.' (Judging)

'Are you having trouble with your marks?' (Probing)

But if big brother is smart, he'll try mirroring:

'You feel that school's kind of tough right now.' (Mirroring)

'It's the worst. I mean I don't have any friends. And that Tabatha Jones has been so rude to me. Oh, I just don't know what to do.'

'You feel confused.' (Mirroring)

'Sure do. I've always been popular and then suddenly no one

knows my name. I've been trying to get to know people, but it doesn't seem to be working.'

'I can see you're frustrated.' (Mirroring)

'Yeah. I probably sound like I'm psycho or something. Anyway, thanks for listening.'

'No problem.'

'What do you think I should do?'

By listening, big brother made a huge deposit into his sister's RBA. In addition, little sister is now open to his advice. The time is now right for him to seek to be understood, to share his point of view.

A guy named Andy shared this:

I was going through communication problems with my girlfriend whom I cared very much about. We had been going out for a year and we had begun to fight and argue a lot, and I was really scared to maybe lose her. When I learned about seeking first to understand and then to be understood, and how to apply the relationship bank account to relationships, I took it very personal. I realized that I always had been trying to interpret what she was saying, but never really listened with an open mind. It saved our relationship and we are still together two years later. Our relationship is much more mature than most couples because we both believe in Habit 5. We use it for big decisions as well as little ones like going out to dinner. Every time I am together with her, I honestly keep saying to myself, 'Now shut up and try to understand her.'

• COMMUNICATING WITH PARENTS

Communication is hard enough by itself, but throw Mum or Dad into the mix and then you've got a tiger by the tail. I got along pretty

well with my parents as a teenager, but there were periods when I was convinced they had aliens living inside their bodies. I felt they didn't understand me or respect me as an individual, but just lumped me in with the rest of the kids. But no matter how distant your parents may seem at times, life will go so much better if you can communicate.

If you want to improve your relationship with Mum or Dad (and shock them in the process), try listening to them, just like you would a friend. Now, it may seem kind of weird to treat your parents as if they were normal people, but it's worth trying. We're always saying to our parents, 'You don't understand me. No one understands me.' But have you ever stopped to consider that perhaps you don't understand them?

You see, they have pressures too. While you're worrying about your friends and your upcoming history exam, they're worrying about their bosses and how they're going to pay for the family holiday. Like you, they have days when they get offended at work and go in the toilet to cry. They have days when they don't know how they're going to pay the bills. Your mum may seldom get a chance to go out on her own, let her hair down and enjoy herself. Your dad may get laughed at by the neighbours because of the car he drives. They may have unfulfilled dreams they've had to sacrifice so that you can reach yours. Hey, parents are people too. They laugh, they cry, they get their feelings hurt and they don't always have their act together, just like me and you.

If you take the time to understand and listen to your parents, two incredible things will happen. First, you'll gain a greater respect for them. When I turned nineteen, I remember reading one of my dad's books for the very first time. He was a successful author and everyone had always told me how great his books were, but I had never taken the time to even look at one until then. 'Wow,' I thought after finishing that first book, 'my dad is smart.' And for all those years I was convinced I was smarter.

Second, if you take time to understand and listen to your parents, you'll get your way much more often. This isn't a manipulative trick, it's a principle. If they feel that you understand them, they'll be much more willing to listen to you, they'll be more flexible and they'll trust you more. One mother once told me, 'If my teenage daughters simply took time to understand my hectic world and did little things around the house to help me, why I would give them so many privileges they wouldn't know what to do with them.'

So how can you better understand your parents? Start by asking them some questions. When is the last time you asked your mum or dad, 'How was your day today?' or 'Tell me what you like and don't like about your job' or 'Is there anything I could do to help around the house?'

You can also begin to make small deposits into their RBA. To do that, ask yourself, 'What do my parents consider a deposit?' Jump into their shoes and think about it from their point of view, not yours. A deposit to them might mean doing the dishes or hoovering without being asked, or keeping a commitment to be home on time, or, if you're living away from home, calling them every weekend.

Then Seek to Be Understood

I saw the results of a survey in which people were asked what their greatests fears were. 'Death' came out as number two. You'll never guess what the number-one fear was. It was 'speaking in public'. People would rather die than speak in public. Isn't that interesting?

It takes boldness to speak up in public, that's for sure. But it also takes boldness to speak up in general. The second half of Habit 5, Then Seek to Be Understood, is as important as the first half but requires something different of us. Seeking first to understand requires consideration, but seeking to be understood requires courage.

Practising only the first half of Habit 5, Seek First to Understand, is weak. It's Lose-Win. It's the doormat syndrome. Yet it's an easy trap to fall into, especially with parents. 'I'm not going to tell Mum how I feel. She won't listen and she'd never understand.' So we harbour these feelings inside while our parents carry on never knowing how we truly feel. But this isn't healthy. Remember, unexpressed feelings never die. They are buried alive and come forth later in uglier ways. You've got to share your feelings or they'll eat your heart out.

Besides, if you have taken the time to listen, your chances of being listened to are very good. In the following story, notice how Kelly practised both halves of the habit:

I was sick and missed a day of school. My parents were concerned that I wasn't getting enough sleep and that I was staying out too late. Instead of coming up with a bunch of excuses, I tried to understand their reasoning. And I agreed with them. But I also explained to them that I am trying to have a fun last year of school, and this includes spending time with my friends. My parents were willing to look at the situation from my point of view, and we reached a compromise. I was to stay in one of the days that weekend and rest. I don't think my parents would have been as lenient if I hadn't tried to understand them first.

Giving feedback is an important part of seeking to be understood. If done in the right way it can be a deposit in the RBA. If someone's zip is open, for instance, give feedback. They'll be very grateful, believe me. If you have a close friend who has bad breath (to the point of developing a reputation for it), don't you think he or she would appreciate some honest feedback, delivered tenderly? Have you ever returned home from a date only to discover that you had a big piece of meat between your teeth the whole evening? With terror you immediately recall every smile you made that night. Don't you wish your date had told you?

If your RBA with someone is high, you can give feedback openly without hesitation. My younger brother Joshua, in his last year at school, shared this:

> *One nice thing about having older brothers or sisters is the feedback they give you.*
>
> *When I come home from a school basketball or football game, Mum and Dad will meet me at the door and go over the game. Mum will rave about the talent that I have, and Dad will say it was my leadership skills that directed the team to victory.*
>
> *When my sister Jenny comes in the kitchen to join us, I'll ask her how I did. She'll tell me how ordinary I played, and I'd better get my act together if I want to keep my position, and she hopes I'll play better the next game and not embarrass her.*

Since Jenny and Josh are very close, they can share feedback candidly. Keep these two points in mind as you give feedback.

First, ask yourself the question 'Will this feedback really help this person or am I doing it just to suit myself and fix them?' If your motive for the feedback isn't with their best interest at heart, then it's probably not the time or place to do it.

Second, send 'I' messages instead of 'you' messages. In other words, give feedback in the first person. Say, '*I'm* concerned that you have a temper problem' or '*I* feel that you've been acting selfish lately'. 'You' messages are more threatening because they sound as if you're labelling. '*You* are so self-centred.' '*You* have a terrible temper.'

Well, that should pretty much wrap it up. I don't have a lot more to say about this habit, except to end with the thought that we began with: You have two ears and one mouth – use them accordingly.

COMING ATTRACTIONS

Next up, find out how 1 plus 1 can sometimes equal 3.
I'll see you there!

1 See how long you can keep eye contact with someone while they are talking to you.

2 Go to the high street, find a bench, and watch people communicate with each other. Observe what their body language is saying.

3 In your interactions today, try mirroring one person and mimicking another, just for fun. Compare the results.

4 Ask yourself, 'Which of the five poor listening styles do I have the biggest problem with – Spacing Out, Pretend Listening, Selective Listening, Word Listening or Self-Centred Listening (judging, advising, probing)?' Now, try to go one day without doing it.

The poor listening style I struggle with most: _____

5 Sometime this week, ask your mum or dad, 'How's it going?' Open up your heart and practise genuine listening. You'll be surprised by what you learn.

6 If you're a talker, take a break and spend your day listening. Only talk when you have to.

7 The next time you find yourself wanting to bury your feelings deep inside you, don't do it. Instead, express them in a responsible way.

8 Think of a situation where your constructive feedback would really help another person. Share it with them when the time is right.

Person who could benefit from my feedback: _____

HABIT 6

Synergize

1+1= 3

The
'High' Way

Alone we can do so little; together we can do so much.
HELEN KELLER

Have you ever seen a flock of geese heading south for the winter flying along in a **V** formation? Scientists have learned some amazing things about why they fly that way:

- By flying in formation, the whole flock can fly 71 per cent farther than if each bird flew alone. When a goose flaps its wings, it creates an updraught for the goose that follows.

- As the lead goose gets tired, he will rotate to the back of the **V** and allow another goose to take the lead position.

- The geese in the back honk to encourage those in the front.

- Whenever a goose falls out of formation, it immediately feels the resistance of trying to fly alone and quickly gets back into formation.

- Finally, when one of the geese gets sick or is wounded and falls out of formation, two geese will follow it down to help and protect it. They will stay with the injured goose until it is better or dies and then will join a new formation or create their own to catch up with the group.

Smart birds, those geese! By sharing in each other's draught, taking turns in the lead position, honking encouragement to each other, staying in formation and watching out for the wounded, they accomplish so much more than if each bird flew solo. It makes me wonder if they took a class in Habit 6, Synergize. Hmmm . . .

What does 'synergize' mean? In a nutshell, *synergy is achieved when two or more people work together to create a better solution than either could alone. It's not your way or my way but a better way, a higher way.*

Synergy is the reward, the delicious fruit you'll taste as you get better at living the other habits, especially at thinking Win-Win and seeking first to understand. Learning to synergize is like learning to form **V** formations with others instead of trying to fly through life solo. You'll be amazed at how much faster and farther you'll go!

To better understand what synergy is, let's see what synergy is not.

SYNERGY IS:	SYNERGY IS NOT:
Celebrating differences	Tolerating differences
Teamwork	Working independently
Open-mindedness	Thinking you're always right
Finding new and better ways	Compromise

SYNERGY IS EVERYWHERE

Synergy is everywhere in nature. The great sequoia trees (which grow to heights of 300 feet or more) grow in clumps and share a vast array of intermingled roots. Without each other, they would blow over in a storm.

Many plants and animals live together in symbiotic relationships. If you have ever seen a picture of a small bird feeding off the back of a rhinoceros, you've seen synergy. Each benefits: The bird gets fed and the rhino gets cleaned.

Synergy isn't anything new. If you've ever been on a team of any kind, you've felt it. If you've ever worked on a group project that really came together you've felt it.

A good band is a great example of synergy. It's not just the drums, or the guitar, or the sax, or the vocalist, it's all of them together that make up the 'sound'. Each band member brings his or her strengths to the table to create something better than each could alone. No instrument is more important than another, just different.

CELEBRATING DIFFERENCES

Synergy doesn't just happen. It's a process. You have to get there. And the foundation of getting there is this: Learn to celebrate differences.

I'll never forget encountering in school a Tongan named Fine (pronounced Fee-Nee) Unga. At first, I was scared to death of him. I mean the guy was built like a tank, was mean looking and was known as a street fighter. We looked, dressed, talked, thought and ate differently (you should have seen this guy eat). The only thing we had in common was football. So how in the world did we become best friends? Maybe it was because we were so different. I never quite knew what Fine was thinking or what he would do next, and that was terribly refreshing. I especially enjoyed being his friend when a fight broke out. He had strengths I didn't have and I had strengths he didn't have, so together we made a great team.

Boy, am I glad that the world isn't full of a bunch of clones who act and think exactly like me. Thank goodness for diversity.

When we hear the word *diversity*, we typically think of racial and gender differences. But there is so much more to it, including differences in physical features, dress, language, wealth, family, religious beliefs, lifestyle, education, interests, skills, age, style and on and on. As Dr Seuss said in *One Fish, Two Fish, Red Fish, Blue Fish:*

We see them come.
We see them go.
Some are fast.
And some are slow.
Some are high.
And some are low.
Not one of them
is like another.
Don't ask us why.
Go ask your mother.

The world is fast becoming a great melting pot of cultures, races, religions, and ideas. Since this diversity around you is ever increasing, you've got an important decision to make regarding how you're going to handle it. There are three possible approaches you can take:

Level 1: Shun diversity
Level 2: Tolerate diversity
Level 3: Celebrate diversity

Shunner's Profile

Shunners are afraid (sometimes even scared to death) of differences. It disturbs them that someone may have a different skin colour, worship a different God or wear a different brand of jeans than they do, because they're convinced their way of life is the 'best', 'right' or 'only' way. They enjoy ridiculing those who are different, all the while believing that they are saving the world from some terrible pestilence. They won't hesitate to get physical about it if they have to and will often join gangs, cliques or anti-groups because there's strength in numbers.

Tolerator's Profile
Tolerators believe that everyone has the right to be different. They don't shun diversity but don't embrace it either. Their motto is: 'You keep to yourself and I'll keep to myself. You do your thing and let me do mine. You don't bother me and I won't bother you.'

Although they come close, they never *get to synergy* because they see differences as hurdles, not as potential strengths to build upon. They don't know what they're missing.

Celebrator's Profile
Celebrators value differences. They see them as an advantage, not a weakness. They've learned that two people who think differently can achieve more than two people who think alike. They realize that celebrating differences doesn't mean that you necessarily agree with those differences, such as being Labour or Conservative, only that you value them. In their eyes, Diversity = Creative Sparks = Opportunity.

So where do you fall on the spectrum? Take a hard look. If someone's clothes don't match yours, do you value their unique clothing styles or do you think they're 'out of touch'?

Think about a group that has contrary religious beliefs to yours. Do you respect their beliefs or do you write them off as a bunch of weirdos?

If someone lives on a different side of town than you, do you feel they could teach you a thing or two or do you label them because of where they live?

The truth is, celebrating diversity is a struggle for most of us, depending on the issue. For example, you may appreciate racial and cultural diversity and in the same breath look down on someone because of the clothes they wear.

● WE ARE ALL A MINORITY OF ONE

It's much easier to appreciate differences when we realize that in one way or another, we are all a minority of one. And we should remember that diversity isn't just an external thing, it's also internal. In the book *All I Really Need to Know I Learned in Kindergarten*, Robert Fulghum says, 'We are as different from one another on the inside of our heads as we appear to be different from one another on the outside of our heads.' How do we differ on the inside? Well . . .

We learn differently. As you've probably noticed, your friend's or sister's brain doesn't work the same way yours does. Dr Thomas Armstrong has identified seven kinds of smarts and says that kids may learn best through their most dominant intelligence:

- *LINGUISTIC:* learn through reading, writing, telling stories
- *LOGICAL-MATHEMATICAL:* learn through logic, patterns, categories, relationships
- *BODILY-KINESTHETIC:* learn through bodily sensations, touching
- *SPATIAL:* learn through images and pictures
- *MUSICAL:* learn through sound and rhythm
- *INTERPERSONAL:* learn through interaction and communication with others
- *INTRAPERSONAL:* learn through their own feelings

One type isn't better than another, only different. You may be logical-mathematical dominant and your sister may be interpersonal dominant. Depending on your approach to diversity, you might say she's weird because she's so talkative, *or* you could take advantage of those differences and get her to help you in your speech class.

We see differently. Everyone sees the world differently and has a different paradigm about themselves, others and life in general. To understand what I mean, let's try an experiment. Look at the picture below for a few seconds. Now look at the picture on the bottom of

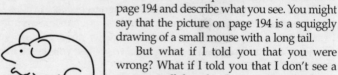

page 194 and describe what you see. You might say that the picture on page 194 is a squiggly drawing of a small mouse with a long tail.

But what if I told you that you were wrong? What if I told you that I don't see a mouse at all, but that I see a squiggly drawing of a man with glasses? Would you value my opinion or would you think I'm an idiot because I don't see the way you do?

To understand my point of view, turn to page 200 and study the picture on the bottom of that page for a moment. Then look at page 194 again. Now can you see what I see?

It goes to show that all the events of your past have formed a lens, or paradigm, through which you see the world. And since no one's past is exactly like anyone else's, no two people see alike. Some see mice and some see men, and both are right.

Once you catch on that everyone views the world differently, and that everyone can be right, it will increase your understanding and respect for differing viewpoints. (You might want to try this same experiment with a friend.)

We have different styles, traits and characteristics. The following exercise is not meant to be an in-depth diagnosis but a fun look at some of your general characteristics and personality traits. This exercise was developed by the Legislator's School in North Carolina, USA, and was adapted from _It's All in Your Mind_ by Kathleen Butler.

Read across each row and place a 4 in the blank that best describes you. Now place a 3 in the blank for the second word that best describes you. Do the same for the final words using a 2 and a 1. Do this for each row.

EXAMPLE:

| Imaginative | 2 | Investigative | 4 | Realistic | 1 | Analytical | 3 |

COLUMN 1		COLUMN 2		COLUMN 3		COLUMN 4	
Imaginative		Investigative		Realistic		Analytical	
Adaptable		Inquisitive		Organized		Critical	
Relating		Creating		Getting to Point		Debating	
Personal		Adventurous		Practical		Academic	
Flexible		Inventive		Precise		Systematic	
Sharing		Independent		Orderly		Sensible	
Cooperative		Competitive		Perfectionistic		Logical	
Sensitive		Risk-Taking		Hard-Working		Intellectual	
People-Person		Problem Solver		Planner		Reader	
Associate		Originate		Memorize		Think Through	
Spontaneous		Changer		Wants Direction		Judger	
Communicating		Discovering		Cautious		Reasoning	
Caring		Challenging		Practising		Examining	
Feeling		Experimenting		Doing		Thinking	

Now add up your totals (don't include the example, of course) for each column and place the total in the blanks below.

COLUMN 1 **Grapes**   COLUMN 2 **Oranges**   COLUMN 3 **Bananas**   COLUMN 4 **Melons**

If your highest score was in column 1, consider yourself a grape.
If your highest score was in column 2, consider yourself an orange.
If your highest score was in column 3, consider yourself a banana.
If your highest score was in column 4, consider yourself a melon.
Now find your fruit below and review what this may mean to you.

GRAPES

Natural abilities include:

- Being reflective
- Being sensitive
- Being flexible
- Being creative
- Preference for working in groups

Grapes may have trouble:

- Giving exact answers
- Focussing on one thing at a time
- Organizing

Grapes learn best when they:

- Can work and share with others
- Balance work with play
- Can communicate
- Are noncompetitive

To expand their style, Grapes need to:

- Pay more attention to details
- Not rush into things
- Be less emotional when making some decisions

ORANGES

Natural abilities include:

- Experimenting
- Being independent
- Being curious
- Creating different approaches
- Creating change

Oranges may have trouble:

- Meeting time limits
- Following a lecture
- Having few options or choices

Oranges learn best when they:

- Can use trial and error
- Produce real products
- Can compete
- Are self-directed

To expand their style, Oranges need to:

- Delegate responsibility
- Be more accepting of others' ideas
- Learn to prioritize

BANANAS

Natural abilities include:	***Bananas may have trouble:***

Natural abilities include:
- Planning
- Fact-finding
- Organizing
- Following directions

Bananas may have trouble:
- Understanding feelings
- Dealing with opposition
- Answering 'what if' questions

Bananas learn best when they:
- Have an orderly environment
- Have specific outcomes
- Can trust others to do their part
- Have predictable situations

To expand their style, Bananas need to:
- Express their own feelings more
- Get explanations of others' views
- Be less rigid

MELONS

Natural abilities include:
- Debating points of view
- Finding solutions
- Analyzing ideas
- Determining value or importance

Melons may have trouble:
- Working in groups
- Being criticized
- Convincing others diplomatically

Melons learn best when they:
- Have access to resources
- Can work independently
- Are respected for intellectual ability
- Follow traditional methods

To expand their style, Melons need to:
- Accept imperfection
- Consider all alternatives
- Consider others' feelings

● CELEBRATE YOUR OWN DIVERSITY

Our tendency is to ask, *Which fruit is best?* The answer is, *That's a stupid question.*

I have three brothers. Although we have much in common, like nose size and parents, we are very different. When I was younger, I was always trying to prove to myself that my talents were better than theirs: 'Sure, you may be more outgoing than me. But who cares? I'm better at school than you and that's more important.' I've since seen the stupidity of that kind of thinking and am learning to appreciate the fact that they have their strengths and I have mine. No one's better or worse, only different.

That's why you shouldn't feel so bad if a member of the opposite sex (whom you are just dying to go out with) doesn't go for you. You may be the must luscious and mouth-watering grape around, but he or she may be looking for a banana. And no matter how much you want a change of fruit, you're a grape and they want a banana. (But don't worry. A grape seeker is bound to drop by.)

Instead of trying to blend in and be like everyone else, be proud of and celebrate your unique differences and qualities. A fruit salad is delicious precisely because each fruit maintains its own flavour.

● ROADBLOCKS TO CELEBRATING DIFFERENCES

Although there are many, three of the largest roadblocks to synergy are ignorance, cliques and prejudice.

Ignorance. Ignorance means you're clueless. You don't know what other people believe, how they feel, or what they've been through. Ignorance often abounds when it comes to understanding people with disabilities, as Carrie Helms explained in an article she wrote:

My name is Carrie. I'm 5ft1in with blonde hair and hazel eyes. Big deal, right? What if I told you I was deaf?

In a perfect world, it wouldn't, shouldn't matter. We don't live in a perfect world, though, and it does matter. The moment someone knows I'm deaf, their whole attitude changes. Suddenly they look at me differently. You'd be surprised how people act.

The most common question I get is, 'How did you become deaf?' When I tell them, their reaction is as common as the question itself: 'Oh, I'm so sorry. That's so sad.' Whenever that happens I simply look them in the eye and I calmly inform them, 'No, really, it's not sad at all. Don't apologize.' No matter how good the intentions are, pity always makes my stomach churn.

Not all attitudes put me on the defensive. Some are just plain funny. I was signing with my friends and some bloke I didn't know came up to me and started talking.

'What's it like being deaf?'

'I don't know. What's it like being hearing? I mean, it isn't like anything. It just is.'

You see, the thing is this: if you meet someone who is deaf, don't write them off as disabled or disadvantaged. Instead take the time to get to know them and find out what being deaf is all about. By doing this, you open yourself to understanding not only others, but, more importantly, yourself.

<u>Cliques.</u> There's nothing wrong with wanting to be with those you're comfortable with; it becomes a problem only when your group of friends becomes so exclusive that they begin to reject everyone who isn't just like them. It's kind of hard to value differences in a close-knit clique. Those on the outside feel like second-class citizens, and those on the inside often suffer from superiority complexes. But breaking into a clique isn't hard. All you have to do is lose your identity, be assimilated, and become part of the Borg collective.

<u>Prejudice.</u> Have you ever felt stereotyped, labelled, or pre-judged by someone because your skin's the wrong colour, your accent's too heavy or you live on the wrong side of the tracks? Haven't we all, and isn't it a sick feeling?

Although we are all created equally, unfortunately, we are not all treated equally. It's a sad fact that minorities of all types often have additional hurdles to leap in life because of prejudices held by so many. Racism is one of the world's oldest problems. This is Natasha's experience:

Racism can make succeeding tougher. When you're a black student in the top 10 per cent of your class, a straight A student, some people have a tendency to feel threatened. I just wish that people would realize that everyone, no matter where they're from or what colour they are, deserves the same opportunities. As far as my friends and I are concerned, prejudice will always be a battle.

We aren't born with prejudices. They're learned. Kids, for instance, are colour blind. But as they mature they begin to pick up on the prejudices of others and form walls, as is explained in Rodgers and Hammerstein's lyrics to a song from the musical *South Pacific*:

> *You've got to be taught to be afraid*
> *Of people whose eyes are oddly made,*
> *And people whose skin is a diff'rent shade,*
> *You've got to be carefully taught.*
>
> *You've got to be taught before it's too late,*
> *Before you are six or seven or eight,*
> *To hate all the people your relatives hate,*
> *You've got to be carefully taught!*

The following poem by an unknown source tells the sad tale of what happens when people pre-judge one another.

THE COLD WITHIN

> *Six humans trapped by happenstance, in bleak and bitter cold,*
> *Each one possessed a stick of wood, or so the story's told.*
>
> *Their dying fire in need of logs, the first man held his back,*
> *For of the faces 'round the fire, he noticed one was black.*
>
> *The next man looking 'cross the way saw one not of his church,*
> *And couldn't bring himself to give the fire his stick of birch.*
>
> *The third one sat in tattered clothes, he gave his coat a hitch,*
> *Why should his log be put to use to warm the idle rich?*
>
> *The rich man just sat back and thought of the wealth he had in store,*
> *And how to keep what he had earned from the lazy, shiftless poor.*
>
> *The black man's face bespoke revenge as the fire passed from sight,*
> *For all he saw in his stick of wood was a chance to spite the white.*
>
> *The last man of this forlorn group did naught except for gain,*
> *Giving only to those who gave was how he played the game.*
>
> *Their logs held tight in death's still hand was proof of human sin,*
> *They didn't die from the cold without – they died from the cold within.*

● STICKING UP FOR DIVERSITY

Fortunately, the world is full of people who are warm within and who value diversity. The following story by Bill Sanders is a wonderful example of sticking up for diversity and showing courage:

A couple of years ago, I witnessed courage that ran chills up and down my spine.

At a school assembly, I had spoken about picking on people and how each of us has the ability to stand up for people instead of putting them down. Afterwards, we had a time when anyone could come up and have their say. Pupils could say thank you to someone who had helped them, and some people came up and did just that. A girl thanked some friends who had helped her through family troubles. A boy spoke of some people who had supported him during an emotionally difficult time.

Then a girl stood up. She stepped over to the microphone, pointed to the Lower Sixth and challenged her whole school. 'Let's stop picking on that boy. Sure, he's different from us, but we are in this thing together. On the inside he's no different from us and needs our acceptance, love, compassion and approval. He needs a friend. Why do we continually brutalize him and put him down? I'm challenging this entire school to lighten up on him and give him a chance!'

All the time she shared, I had my back to the section where that boy sat, and I had no idea who he was. But obviously the school knew. I felt almost afraid to look at his section, thinking the boy must be red in the face, wanting to crawl under his seat and hide from the world. But as I glanced back, I saw a boy smiling from ear to ear. His whole body bounced up and down, and he raised one fist in the air. His body language said, 'Thank you, thank you. Keep telling them. You saved my life today!'

> Differences create the challenges in life that open the door to discovery.
>
> American Sign Language symbol for
> **'WE ARE DIVERSE'**

Finding the 'High' Way Once you've bought into the idea that differences are a strength and not a weakness, and once you're committed to at least trying to celebrate differences, you're ready to find the High Way. The Buddhist definition of the Middle Way does not mean compromise; it means higher, like the apex of a triangle.

Synergy is more than just compromise or cooperation. Compromise is $1 + 1 = 1\frac{1}{2}$. Cooperation is $1 + 1 = 2$. Synergy is $1 + 1 = 3$ or more. It's creative cooperation, with an emphasis on the word *creative*. The whole is greater than the sum of the parts.

Builders know all about it. If one 2″ x 4″ beam can support 275 kilos, then two 2" x 4"s should be able to support 550 kilos. Right? Actually, two 2" x 4"s can support 830 kilos. If you nail them together, two 2" x 4"s can now support 2,200 kilos. And three 2' x 4's nailed together can support 3,855 kilos. Musicians know how it works too. They know that when a C and G note are perfectly in tune, it produces a third note, or an E.

Finding the High Way always produces more, as Elaine discovered:

In my physics lab the teacher was demonstrating the principle of momentum and our homework was to construct a catapult, like in medieval times. We called it a pumpkin launcher.

There were three of us in our group, two boys and me. We are all quite different, so we came up with a lot of different ideas.

One of us wanted to use bungee cords to make the launcher flip. Someone else wanted to use tension and ropes. We tried each without much success and then we figured out a way to use both of them together. It gave a lot more spring than either would have alone. It was cool because it doubled the length of our shot.

Synergy occurred as the founders of the United States of America were forming their government structure. William Paterson proposed the New Jersey Plan, which said that states should get equal representation in government regardless of population size. This plan favoured the smaller states. James Madison had a different idea, known as the Virginia Plan, which argued that states with greater populations should have greater representation. This plan favoured the larger states.

After several weeks of debate, they reached a decision that all parties felt good about. They agreed to have two branches of Congress. In one branch, the Senate, each state would get two representatives, regardless of population size. In the other branch, the House of Representatives, each state would get representatives based on population.

Although it is called the Great Compromise, this famous decision could really be called the Great Synergy, because it has proved to be better than either of the original proposals.

● **GETTING TO SYNERGY**

Whether you're arguing with your parents over dating and curfew guidelines or planning a school activity with your peers, or simply not seeing eye to eye, there is a way to *get to synergy*. Here's a simple five-step process to help you get there.

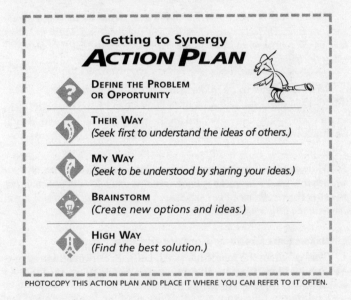

Getting to Synergy
ACTION PLAN

DEFINE THE PROBLEM OR OPPORTUNITY

THEIR WAY
(Seek first to understand the ideas of others.)

MY WAY
(Seek to be understood by sharing your ideas.)

BRAINSTORM
(Create new options and ideas.)

HIGH WAY
(Find the best solution.)

PHOTOCOPY THIS ACTION PLAN AND PLACE IT WHERE YOU CAN REFER TO IT OFTEN.

Let's give the action plan a try on a problem to see how it works.

The Holiday

Dad: *I don't care how you feel. You're going on this holiday whether you like it or not. We've had this planned for months, and it's important that we spend some time together as a family.*

You: *But I don't want to go. I want to be with my friends. I'll miss out on everything.*

Mum: *I don't want you staying here by yourself. I'd worry the whole time and it would ruin my holiday. We want you with us.*

DEFINE THE PROBLEM OR OPPORTUNITY

In this case, we have a problem. It's this:

My parents want me to holiday with the family, but I would rather stay home and go out with my friends.

THEIR WAY *(Seek first to understand the ideas of others.)*

Try using the listening skills you learned in Habit 5 so that you can really understand your mum and dad. Remember, if you want to have power and influence with your parents, they need to feel understood.

By listening, you learn the following:

This holiday is very important to my dad. He wants to have a family bonding time. He feels it won't be the same without me. Mum feels that they would worry so much about me being home alone that they wouldn't enjoy the holiday.

MY WAY *(Seek to be understood by sharing your ideas.)*

Now practise the second half of Habit 5 and have the courage to share your feelings. If you've taken the time to listen to them, they'll be much more likely to listen to you. So you tell your parents how you feel.

Mum and Dad, I want to stay home and be with my friends. They are very important to me. We have a lot of things planned, and I don't want to miss out on any of the fun. Besides, I go crazy when I have to drive in a crowded car all day with my little brother and sister.

BRAINSTORM *(Create new options and ideas.)*

This is where the magic happens. Utilize your imagination and create new ideas together that you could never think of alone. As you brainstorm, keep these tips in mind:

- *GET CREATIVE:* Throw out your wildest ideas. Let it flow.
- *AVOID CRITICISM:* Nothing kills the flow of creativity like criticism.
- *PIGGYBACK:* Keep building upon the best ideas. One great idea leads to another, which leads to another.

Brainstorming produces the following ideas:

- *Dad said we could go to a holiday spot that I would enjoy more.*
- *I mentioned that I could stay with relatives close by.*
- *Mum suggested I could take a friend with me.*
- *Mum was willing to cut the holiday short so it would be easier for me.*

- *I suggested staying home for part of the holiday and joining them later.*
- *Dad was willing to let me stay home if I would paint the fence while they were gone.*

HIGH WAY *(Find the best solution.)*

After brainstorming for a while, the best idea will usually surface. Now it's just a matter of going with it.

We all agreed that I could stay home during the first half of the week and then travel with a friend to join the family for the second half. They even offered to pay for my friend and me if I would paint the fence. It's not hard work, so I will still have time to hang out with my friends. They're happy, and so am I.

If you will follow the basics of the above formula, you'll be amazed at what can happen. But it takes a lot of maturity to get to synergy. You have to be willing to listen to the other point of view. You then need to have the courage to express your point of view. Finally, you've got to let your creative juices flow. See how this seventeen-year-old girl got to synergy:

> HEY, WILBUR, THIS SYNERGY STUFF IS GREAT! YOU PUSH, AND I'LL FLY!

The end of year school disco was coming up and I wanted to wear a certain style dress that I had found in a fashion magazine. The only problem was that it was short on me because I am real tall. I knew my mother would flip.

We sat down that evening and discussed the disco and who was going to take me out. I showed her the dress in a magazine, and, as I had anticipated, she said, 'Absolutely not. It's way too short'. I let her voice her opinion about what she thought I ought to do and where I should shop.

I didn't like anything she had to say, but it was obvious that she felt very strong about it. Then we started brainstorming ideas of what I could do. And one of the ideas was to find a seamstress and see if she could sew something that would satisfy us both. I made a quick phone call to a friend, found a seamstress and soon we were drawing up our ideas and shopping for fabric and pattern. The outcome was beautiful, very per-

sonal and different from everyone else's dress. I didn't spend as much money as I normally would have, and my friends loved the outfit too.

Go for It

The Getting to Synergy Action Plan can be used in all kinds of situations:

- You've just been given a group project for biology with three people you don't even know.
- You and your boyfriend can't decide whose family you should spend Christmas with.
- You want to go to university, but your parents aren't willing to help you pay for it.
- As a prefect, you and your team are in charge of planning the biggest dance of the year.
- You and your stepmother disagree on your curfew.
- You're always fighting with your brother about the computer.

The Getting to Synergy Action Plan is a guideline, nothing more. The steps don't always have to be in order, and you don't always have to do all of them. If your RBA is extremely high with

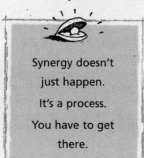

Synergy doesn't just happen. It's a process. You have to get there.

someone, you can virtually skip the first three steps and jump right into brainstorming. On the other hand, if your RBA is low, you may need to take more time listening. It may take several conversations to solve some problems, so be patient.

Despite herculean efforts on your part to find the High Way, sometimes the other party won't make any effort at all. You may just have to keep building the RBA in these situations.

How do you normally solve conflicts? Most of the time it's usually fight (with words or fists) or flight (you're silent or you take off). The Getting to Synergy Action plan offers an alternative.

Pretend you and your sister are in one continuous fight over who gets the car. Each of you feels you need it more than the other person, and it's created real bad feelings between you. Having recently learned about synergy, you decide to give the Getting to Synergy Action Plan a try.

DEFINE THE PROBLEM OR OPPORTUNITY

'Sis, I'm tired of fighting over the car all the time. Let's talk and see if we can come up with a Win-Win.'

'Oh, c'mon. Don't try that 7 Habits crap on me.'

'I mean it. I really want to work this out.'

'Fine. How do you suggest we do it? There's only one car and there's two of us.'

THEIR WAY *(Seek first to understand the ideas of others.)*

'Well, to start with, tell me why you need the car all the time.'

'You know why. I need a way to get home after practice.'

'Why can't you get a lift with your friends?'

'I can sometimes, but it always makes me feel embarrassed because I'm so far out of their way.'

'I see. Are there other reasons why you need the car?'

'Well, yeah. I sometimes like to stop by Jake's house on the way home.'

'That's important to you.'

'You bet.'

'So you don't like scrounging lifts home after practice and you want the freedom a car gives you to do things, such as seeing Jake. Does that pretty much sum it up?'

'Yeah.'

MY WAY *(Seek to be understood by sharing your ideas.)*

'Would you mind if I told you why I need the car?'

'I think I already know, but go ahead.'

'It's just work. I have to be to work by 6:00 every night and you usually don't get home until about 6:30. When I have Mum take me I'm always late and my boss has a fit.'

'Yeah, I know how it is with Mum.'

BRAINSTORM *(Create new options and ideas.)*

'Sis, how about if you were to get out of practice a little earlier? If you got home by quarter to six, then you could have the car first and then I'd take it to work.'

'I would if I could but I can't get out of practice early. What if you were to start work a little later?'

'Hey, now that I think about it, that might work. I'm sure my boss would let me start later if I ended later. Why don't we give it a try? You get the car till after practice and then I'll take it to work later.'

'But what if I want to see Jared?'

'If you want to see Jared, I'd just drop you off on my way to work and pick you up on the way home. Would that be all right?'

'Yeah, that'd be fine.'

HABIT 6

HIGH WAY *(Find the best solution.)*

'So, do we have a deal?'

'Deal.'

It's not always this easy. But, on the other hand, sometimes it is.

TEAMWORK AND SYNERGY

Great teams are usually made up of five or more different types of people, with each member playing a different but important role.

Plodders. Sure and steady, they stick to a job until it's done.

Followers. They are very supportive of leaders. If they hear a great idea, they can run with it.

Innovators. They are the creative, idea people. They offer the sparks.

Harmonizers. They provide unity and support and are great synergizers as they work with others and encourage cooperation.

Show-offs. Fun to work with, they can be tough at times. They often add the spice and momentum needed to bring the team overall success.

Great teamwork is like a great piece of music. All the voices and instruments may be singing and playing at once, but they aren't competing. Individually, the instruments and voices make different sounds, play different notes, pause at different times; yet they blend together to create a whole new sound. This is synergy.

The book you are holding is dripping with synergy. When I first decided to write it, I felt overwhelmed. So I started in the only way I knew how. I got help. I immediately asked a friend for assistance. I soon put together a bigger team. I identified a few schools and teachers from around the country who agreed to give feedback on drafts at different stages. I began interviewing teenagers one on one and in groups. I hired an artist. I put together contests asking for stories dealing with teenagers and the 7 Habits. By the end, there were well over 100 people involved in the creation of this book.

Slowly but surely it all came together. Each person brought his or her talents to the table and contributed in a different way. While I focussed on writing, others focussed on what they were good at. One was good at collecting stories. One could find great quotes. Another knew how to edit. Some were plodders, some innovators, some show-offs. It was teamwork and synergy to the max.

The wonderful by-product of teamwork and synergy is that it builds relationships. Basketball Olympian Deborah Miller Palmore said it well: 'Even when you've played the game of your life, it's the feeling of teamwork that you'll remember. You'll forget the plays, the shots and the scores, but you'll never forget your teammates.'

COMING ATTRACTIONS

If you keep reading, you'll discover the real reason why
Michelle Pfeiffer looks like a million pounds. Just a few more pages and
you're done!

BABY STEPS

1. When you meet a classmate or neighbour with a disability or impairment, don't feel sorry for them or avoid them because you don't know what to say. Instead, go out of your way to get acquainted.

2. The next time you are having a disagreement with a parent, try out the Getting to Synergy Action Plan. 1. Define the problem. 2. Listen to them. 3. Share your views. 4. Brainstorm. 5. Find the best solution.

3. Share a personal problem with an adult you trust. See if the exchanging of viewpoints leads to new insights and ideas about your problem.

4. This week, look around and notice how much synergy is going on all around you, such as two hands working together, teamwork, symbiotic relationships in nature and creative problem solving.

5. Think about someone who irritates you. What is different about them?

What can you learn from them?_____

_____

6. Brainstorm with your friends and come up with something fun, new and different to do this weekend, instead of doing the same old thing again and again.

7. Rate your openness to diversity in each of the following categories. Are you a shunner, tolerator, or celebrator?

	SHUNNER	TOLERATOR	CELEBRATOR
Race			
Gender			
Religion			
Age			
Dress			

PART IV

Renewal

Habit 7 – Sharpen the Saw
It's 'Me Time'

Keep Hope Alive!
Kid, You'll Move Mountains

HABIT 7

Sharpen the Saw

It's
'Me Time'

The time to repair the roof is when the sun is shining.

US PRESIDENT JOHN F. KENNEDY

Do you ever feel imbalanced, stressed-out or empty inside? If so, you're going to love Habit 7, because it was specially designed to help you deal with these problems. Why do we call it 'Sharpen the Saw'? Well, imagine that you're going for a walk in the forest when you come upon a guy furiously sawing down a tree.

'What are you doing?' you ask.

'I'm sawing down a tree,' comes the curt reply.

'How long have you been at it?'

'Four hours so far, but I'm really making progress,' he says, sweat dripping from his chin.

'Your saw looks really dull,' you say. 'Why don't you take a break and sharpen it?'

'I can't, you idiot. I'm too busy sawing.'

We all know who the real idiot here is, now, don't we? If the guy were to take a fifteen-minute break to sharpen the saw, he'd probably finish three times faster.

Have you ever been too busy driving to take time to get petrol?

Have you ever been too busy living to take time to renew yourself?

Habit 7 is all about keeping your personal self sharp so that you can better deal with life. It means regularly renewing and strengthening the four key dimensions of your life – your body, your brain, your heart and your soul.

BODY — **The Physical Dimension**
Exercise, eat healthy, sleep well, relax.

BRAIN — **The Mental Dimension**
Read, educate, write, learn new skills.

HEART — **The Emotional Dimension**
Build relationships (RBA, PBA), give service, laugh.

SOUL — **The Spiritual Dimension**
Meditate, keep a diary, pray, take in quality media.

● **BALANCE IS BETTER**

The ancient Greeks' famous saying 'Nothing overmuch' reminds us of the importance of balance and of keeping in touch with all four dimensions of life. Some people spend countless hours building the perfect body but neglect their minds. Others have minds that can bench-press 400 pounds but let their bodies waste away or forget about having a social life. To perform at your peak, you need to strive for balance in all four areas.

Why is balance so important? It's because how you do in one dimension of life will affect the other three. Think about it. If one of your car's tyres is out of balance, all four tyres will wear unevenly, not just the one. It's hard to be friendly (heart) when you're exhausted (body). It also works the other way. When you're feeling motivated and in tune with yourself (soul), it's easier to focus on your studies (mind) and to be more friendly (heart).

During my school years, I remember studying many of the great artists, authors and musicians, like Mozart, van Gogh, Beethoven and Hemingway. So many of them seemed to be emotionally messed up. Why? Your guess is as good as mine, but I think it was because they were out of balance. It seems they focussed so hard on just one thing, like their music or art, that they neglected the other dimensions of life and lost their bearings. As the saying goes, *Balance and moderation in all things.*

● **TAKE TIME FOR A TIME-OUT**

Just like a car, you too need regular services and oil changes. You need time out to rejuvenate the best thing you've got going for yourself – you! You need time to relax and unstring your bow, time to treat yourself to a little tender loving care. This is what sharpening the saw is all about.

Over the next several pages, we'll take a look at each dimension, the body, mind, heart and soul, and talk about specific ways to get that saw of yours razor sharp. So read on!

Caring for Your Body

I hated school. I felt awkward. I was unsure about who I was and how I fit in. And my body started undergoing all sorts of weird changes. I remember my first day in P.E. I had bought my first jockstrap ever, but I had no idea how to put it on. And all of us boys were so embarrassed at seeing each other naked for the first time that we just stood around in the showers and giggled.

During your teenage years, your voice will change, your hormones will run rampant and curves and muscles will begin springing up all over. Welcome to your new body!

Actually, this ever-changing body of yours is really quite a marvellous machine. You can handle it with care or you can abuse it. You can control it or let it control you. In short, your body is a tool, and if you take good care of it, it will serve you well.

Here is a list of ten ways teenagers can keep their physical selves sharp:

1. Eat good food
2. Relax in the bathtub
3. Bike
4. Lift weights
5. Get enough sleep
6. Practise yoga
7. Play sports
8. Take walks
9. Stretch out
10. Do an aerobics workout

The four key ingredients to a healthy body are good sleeping habits, physical relaxation, good nutrition and proper exercise. I'll focus here on nutrition and exercise.

You Are What You Eat

There's much truth to the expression 'You are what you eat'. I'm not an expert in nutrition, but I have found two rules of thumb to keep in mind.

First rule of thumb: Listen to your body. Pay careful attention to how different foods make you feel and from that develop your *own* handful of do's and don'ts. Everyone responds differently to food. For example, whenever I eat a big meal right before bed I feel horrible in the morning. And whenever I eat *too many* french fries, nachos or pizza I get a 'grease rush'. (Have you ever had one of those?) These are my *don'ts*. On the other hand, I've learned that eating lots of fruits and vegetables and drinking tons of water makes me feel sharp. These are my *do's*.

Second rule of thumb: Be moderate and avoid extremes. For many of us (me included), it's easier to be extreme than to be moderate, and so we find ourselves jumping back and forth between eating a rabbit-food and a junk-food diet. But extreme eating habits can be unhealthy. A little junk food on occasion isn't going to hurt you. (I mean, what would life be like without an occasional hamburger?) Just don't make it your everyday fare.

The USDA food pyramid is a balanced and moderate approach to nutrition that I highly recommend. It encourages eating more whole grains, fruits, vegetables and low-fat dairy products and eating less fast food, junk food and snacks, which are often loaded with fat, sugar, salt and other junk.

Remember, food affects mood. So eat with care.

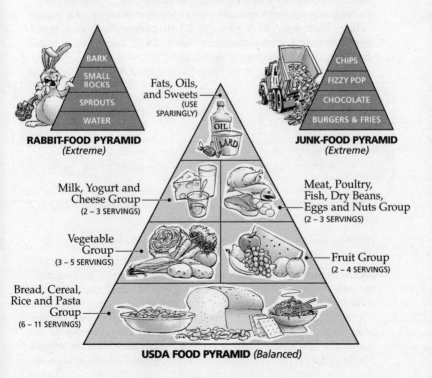

RABBIT-FOOD PYRAMID
(Extreme)

BARK
SMALL ROCKS
SPROUTS
WATER

JUNK-FOOD PYRAMID
(Extreme)

CHIPS
FIZZY POP
CHOCOLATE
BURGERS & FRIES

Fats, Oils, and Sweets
(USE SPARINGLY)

Milk, Yogurt and Cheese Group
(2 – 3 SERVINGS)

Meat, Poultry, Fish, Dry Beans, Eggs and Nuts Group
(2 – 3 SERVINGS)

Vegetable Group
(3 – 5 SERVINGS)

Fruit Group
(2 – 4 SERVINGS)

Bread, Cereal, Rice and Pasta Group
(6 – 11 SERVINGS)

USDA FOOD PYRAMID *(Balanced)*

● USE IT OR LOSE IT

One of my favourite movies is *Forrest Gump*. It's the story of a naive young man from Alabama with a good heart who keeps stumbling into success in spite of himself. At one point in the movie, Forrest is frustrated and confused about his life. So what does he do? He starts to run, and keeps on running. After running back and forth from one coast to the other two and a half times, Forrest feels better and is finally able to sort his life out.

We all feel depressed, confused or apathetic at times. And it's at times like these when perhaps the best thing we can do for ourselves is to do what Forrest did: exercise ourselves better. Besides being good for your heart and lungs, exercise has an amazing way of giving you a shot of energy, melting stress away, and clearing your mind.

There is no single best way to exercise. Many teenagers like to play competitive sports. Others prefer running, walking, biking, roller blading, dancing, stretching, aerobics or lifting weights. Still others just like to get outside and move around. For best results, you should exercise for twenty to thirty minutes a session at least three times a week.

Don't let 'pain' be the first thing that comes into your mind when you hear the word 'exercise'. Instead find something you enjoy doing, so that it's easy to maintain.

GARFIELD © 1982 Paws, Inc. Reprinted with permission of UNIVERSAL PRESS SYNDICATE. All rights reserved.

● IT'S ALL ABOUT HOW YOU FEEL, NOT HOW YOU LOOK

But be careful. In your quest for a better physique, make sure you don't get too obsessed with your appearance. As you've probably noticed, our society is hung up on 'looks'. To prove my point just walk into any newsagent and glance at the perfect people who adorn the covers of nearly every magazine. It kind of makes you feel self-conscious about all your physical imperfections, doesn't it?

As a young boy, I was very self-conscious about my fat cheeks. My dad told me that when I was born my cheeks were so fat the doctors didn't know which end to spank. I clearly remember a neighbourhood girl making fun of my cheeks one time. My brother David heroically tried to defend me by saying they were made out of muscle. It backfired and 'Muscle Cheeks' became my least favourite nickname of all.

When I was fourteen, my dad sent me on a long survival trek (a nice way of saying we hiked forever and starved) to try to toughen me up. The unexpected by-product was that I lost my cheeks. But as my teenage years unfolded, I became self-conscious about many other things, such as not having a perfect smile like some of my friends did or those spots that kept resurfacing like a bad habit that won't go away.

Before you start comparing yourself to the babes and hunks on the covers of *Cosmopolitan* and *Men's Health* and begin hating everything about your body and looks, please remember that there are thousands of healthy and happy teenagers who don't have high cheekbones, rock-hard abs or toned thighs. There are many successful singers, talk show hosts, dancers, athletes, actors and actresses who have all kinds of physical imperfections. You don't have to pop steroids or get your chest enlarged to be happy. If you don't have the 'look' or body type our society has stamped 'ideal', so what? What's popular today will probably change tomorrow anyhow.

The important thing is feeling good physically – and not so much your appearance. Talk show host Oprah Winfrey said it best: 'You have to change your perception. It's not about weight – it's caring for yourself on a daily basis.'

Real Life or Art?

Besides, if you didn't already know it, what you see on the covers of magazines isn't real. They're 'images'. Many years ago, actress and beauty queen Michelle Pfeiffer was featured on the front of *Esquire* magazine with the caption, 'What Michelle Pfeiffer needs . . . is absolutely nothing'.

She actually needed more help than meets the eye, as author Allen Litchfield revealed in *Sharing the Light in the Wilderness*:

But another magazine, Harper's, *offered proof in its edition the following month that even the 'beautiful people' need a little help.* Harper's *had obtained the photo retouchers' bill for Pfeiffer's picture on the* Esquire *cover. The retouchers charged $1,525 to render the following services: 'Clean up the complexion, soften smile line, trim chin, soften line under earlobe, add hair, add forehead to create better line and soften neck muscles.' The editor of* Harper's *printed the story because we are, he said, 'constantly faced with perfection in magazines; this is to remind*

the reader . . . there's a difference between real life and art.'

This is why you shouldn't be comparing your school photo or passport picture with the magazine cover faces. The photographer who is shooting your picture is getting paid the minimum wage, is bored, is in a hurry and may even hate you. Little wonder your picture comes out looking awful.

Remember, our fetish with chiselled bodies hasn't always been the trend. Wouldn't it be nice to have lived in eighteenth-century Europe, when being overweight was the 'in' thing, or during the Dark Ages, when everyone wore baggy robes and no one really knew what your body looked like? Boy, those were the days!

Of course, we should work hard to look our best and be presentable, but if we aren't careful, becoming obsessed with 'looks' can lead us to severe eating disorders such as compulsive eating, bulimia or anorexia or to addictions to performance-enhancing drugs such as steroids. Treating your body like a prisoner of war in order to be accepted by someone else is never worth it.

If you're struggling with an eating disorder, don't feel alone. It's a very common problem among teenagers. Admit you have a problem and get help. (At the back of the book I have listed some organizations that can help.)

I CAN QUIT WHENEVER I WANT

Just as there are ways to care for your body, there are also ways to destroy it. And using addictive substances such as alcohol, drugs and tobacco is a great way to do it. Alcohol, for example, is often associated with the three leading causes of death among teenagers: car accidents, suicide and homicide. And then there's smoking, which has been proven to cloud your eyes, cause your skin to prematurely age, yellow your teeth, cause bad breath, triple your cavities, cause receding gums, discolour the skin on your fingertips, create tiredness and cause cancer. (It's a wonder anyone dares smoke.) Moreover, it isn't popular. I once saw an anti-smoking advert that drove this point home:

Okay, there's (insert name of person you want to get with here) standing alone. The perfect opportunity. You check your clothes, your hair, light a cigarette, check your hair again and slowly walk towards them. You smile as they begin to speak, 'Could you do me a favour?' You lean a little closer, hanging on their words, 'Could you go smoke somewhere else?'

Smoking isn't as attractive as you think. In a study, 8 out of 10 guys and 7 out of 10 girls said they wouldn't date someone who smokes. So if you smoke, you better get used to kissing that cigarette.

Just remember, tobacco companies spend £500,000 every hour of every day promoting and advertising cigarettes. They want your money. A pack of cigarettes a day adds up to £1,800 a year. Just think about how many CDs you could buy for £1,800. Don't let them sucker you!

Now, of course, no one plans on getting addicted. It all starts so innocently. Yet too often playing with 'gateway drugs' like alcohol and tobacco leads to marijuana and then on to other deadly drugs like cocaine, LSD, PCP, opiates and heroin. Many begin drinking, smoking or doing drugs in an attempt to display their *freedom*, only to find that they eventually develop an addiction that *destroys* their freedom. Believe me, there are better ways to assert your individuality.

Perhaps the worst thing about picking up an addiction is this: You're no longer in control – your addiction is. When it says *jump*, you *jump*. You react. Say good-bye to the whole idea of being proactive. I always feel sorry for people at work who have to go outside to smoke because it's not allowed in the building. It's sad to see them standing outside in the heat of summer or the freeze of winter, puffing away, unable to control their urge.

We always think that addiction is something that happens to someone else and that we could quit anytime. Right? In reality, it's hard. As an example, only 25 per cent of teen tobacco users who try to quit are successful. I like what Mark Twain said about how easy it was for him to quit smoking: 'I've done it a hundred times.'

Here's a story of the struggle one teenage guy went through to overcome his drug addiction:

The first time I used any kind of drug or alcohol was when I was fourteen. I didn't even know what drugs were. I really didn't care. Everyone just told me how bad they were. My friend said, 'Here, take this. It's pretty cool'. So I took it. When I started, I wanted to be cool. After that, it wasn't peer pressure anymore. It was just me.

I started doing drugs and drinking more and more and my schoolwork started slipping. My relationships started to decrease. I was losing touch with my family, and I hated that. My attitude toward things turned around, you know – just a lot of negativity. I also started to see my girlfriend less.

Right after I started drinking and doing drugs, I noticed some physical problems, too. I felt real tired all the time. I also lost a lot of weight, about thirty pounds in two months.

The other thing was that I would go home and run out of toothpaste or something like that, and I'd cry. I was overreacting big time. My temper was really short.

About a month after my seventeenth birthday, I got caught with drugs in school. They suspended me for a week, and I knew that was the time I needed to get myself back together. So I tried to stop, but I couldn't. It's like when you smoke cigarettes. You can put one down and say you're going to quit, you're going to quit, but it is real hard to stop.

So I stopped hanging around my old friends and started going to Alcoholics Anonymous (AA) meetings and I got a sponsor. AA is a lifelong thing. You take one drink and it messes up everything you had built up to that point. A lot of my friends who came to AA have relapsed. But my sponsor really helped me out. Without this programme, I know I wouldn't have stopped.

Since I've been in this programme, it's been the greatest life. I don't drink. I don't do drugs. My schoolwork is going back up. My family is closer than ever now. Before, I worked at almost every fast-food place there is in town because I'd quit within two weeks at each one. Now, I've had just one job for about two months. I came back to school and I started to care. I was nice to people even when they weren't nice to me. I've totally changed my life around. I'm starting to think about university and doing all these things I would never think of before. It's real confusing to me why anyone would spend their school years drinking. It's a scary life.

● **THE REFUSAL SKILL™**

Staying away from drugs of all kinds is a lot easier said than done. Here are *The Refusal Skill™** steps that you might want to consider the next time you feel pressured to drink, smoke or do drugs, and don't really want to.

1. *Ask questions.* Ask tough questions that really make you think about what you're doing.

'Why would I want to smoke?'

'What will happen to me if I get stoned tonight?'

2. _Name the trouble._ Try to put a face on what you're doing.
'Smoking cannabis is illegal.'
'Smoking will ruin my breath.'

3. _State the consequences._ Think through the consequences of your actions.
'I could get arrested if I'm caught with drugs.'
'If I get wasted tonight, someone might take advantage of me.'

4. _Suggest an alternative._ Have your own list of fun alternatives ready to go whenever you're being lured in.
'Hey, why don't we go see a movie?'
'I'd rather play football.'

5. _Take off._ If you get caught in a situation that just doesn't look good, don't worry about what everyone might think of you, just get away . . . fast.
'Sorry, everyone. But I'm out of here.'

If you're creative enough, you'll be able to develop your own approach to avoiding the entire scene, as Jim did:

My friends and I just didn't want all that trouble that came from drinking and doing drugs, so we formed a group. We were about ten people who were committed to helping our friends stay out of trouble. We hung out a lot together, and weekly would go out for dinner and plan how we could support each other. The support mostly came in the form of talking to others when we saw them being tempted or floundering, and assuring them that they really didn't need to do those things to be cool, and then inviting them to come join us in our fun instead. It worked and really was very powerful.

SO HOW'S THE CARROT, DUDE?

WHOOA... WHAT A RUSH!

Believe me, you're not missing out on anything if you stay away from this stuff. 'Life itself,' said TV chef Julia Child, 'is the proper binge.' You don't need to even experiment. The short-term bang is never worth the long-term devastation that often follows. If you don't smoke, drink or do drugs, why even start? If you do, why not get help and quit? There are much better and more natural ways to get high. Why not give them a try? (See Info Central in the back of the book for more information.)

Caring for Your Brain

 I once heard a folklore story about a young man who came to Socrates, the great wise man, and said, 'I want to know everything you know.'

'If this is your desire,' said Socrates, 'then follow me to the river.' Full of curiosity, the young man followed Socrates to the nearby river. As they sat on the bank, Socrates said, 'Take a close look at the river and tell me what you see.'

'I don't see anything,' said the man.

'Look closer,' replied Socrates.

As the man peered over the bank and leaned closer to the water, Socrates grabbed the man's head and shoved it under the water. The man's arms flailed wildly as he attempted to escape, but Socrates' strong grip kept him submerged. About the time the man was about to drown, Socrates pulled him from the river and laid him on the bank.

Coughing, the man gasped, 'Are you crazy, old man? What are you trying to do, kill me?'

'When I was holding you under the river, what did you want more than anything else?' asked Socrates.

'I wanted to breathe. I wanted air!' he replied.

'Don't ever make the mistake of thinking wisdom comes so easily, my young friend,' said Socrates. 'When you want to learn as badly as you wanted air just now, then come to me again.'

The point here is clear. Nothing in life comes easy. You have to pay the price! Everyone has to pay the price. Write that down. Memorize it. Underline it. I don't care what people say, there are no free lunches! What a naive young man to think that he could gain a lifetime of learning without paying the price. But are we any less naive when we think that we can secure a good job and a promising future if we haven't paid the price to develop a strong mind?

In fact, getting a good education may just be the most important price you can pay – because, perhaps more than anything else, what you do with that mass of grey material between your ears will determine your future. In fact, unless you want to be flipping burgers and living with your parents when you're thirty years old, you'd better start paying the price now.

The mental dimension of Habit 7, Sharpen the Saw, means developing brain power through your schooling, extracurricular activities, hobbies, jobs, and other mind-enlarging experiences.

The Key to Unlocking Your Future

I once asked a group of teenagers in a survey 'What are your fears?' I was surprised by how many spoke about the stress of doing well in school, going to university, and getting a good job in the future. Said one, 'What can we do to be certain that we can get a job and support ourselves?' The answer is really rather simple. You could try to win the lottery. Your chances of doing that are about 1 in 1,000,000. Or you could develop an educated mind. By far, this offers your best chance of securing a good job and making a life for yourself.

What's an educated mind? It's much more than a certificate on a wall, even though that's an important part of it. A better definition is: An educated mind is like a well-conditioned ballerina. A ballerina has perfect control over her muscles. Her body will bend, twist, jump and turn perfectly, according to her command. Similarly, an educated mind can focus, synthesize, write, speak, create, analyze, explore, imagine and so much more. To do that, however, it must be trained. It won't just happen.

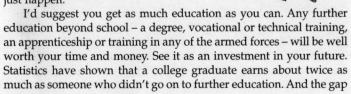

I'd suggest you get as much education as you can. Any further education beyond school – a degree, vocational or technical training, an apprenticeship or training in any of the armed forces – will be well worth your time and money. See it as an investment in your future. Statistics have shown that a college graduate earns about twice as much as someone who didn't go on to further education. And the gap seems to be widening. Don't let a lack of money be the reason you don't get more education. 'If you think education is expensive, try ignorance,' said Derek Bok, a former president of Harvard University, USA. Even if you have to sacrifice and work your tail off to pay for your education, it's well worth it. You'd also be amazed at the number of scholarships, grants and loans that are available if you search them out. In fact, millions of dollars of grant and scholarship money goes unclaimed each year because no one bothered to apply for it.

SHARPEN YOUR MIND

There are numerous ways to expand your mind. However, the best approach may simply be to read. As the saying goes, reading is to the mind what exercise is to the body. Reading is foundational to everything else and doesn't cost that much, unlike other methods, such as travelling. The following are twenty possible ways to sharpen your mind. I'm sure you can come up with another fifty if you try.

- Read a newspaper every day
- Subscribe to *National Geographic*
- Travel
- Plant a garden
- Observe wildlife
- Attend a lecture on an interesting topic
- Watch the Discovery Channel
- Visit a library
- Listen to the news
- Research your ancestors
- Write a story, poem or song
- Play challenging board games
- Debate
- Play a game of chess
- Visit a museum
- Comment in class
- Attend a ballet, opera or play
- Learn to play a musical instrument
- Have stimulating conversations with friends
- Solve crossword puzzles

FIND YOUR NICHE

While you may need to endure some subjects you don't enjoy at school, find the subjects you do enjoy and build upon them. Borrow books from the library, watch documentaries and do research on the internet on the topic. Don't let school be your only form of education. Let the world be your campus.

You should expect to have some trouble in some classes. Unless you're an Einstein, every subject won't be easy for you. Actually, I take back what I just said. The famous Albert Einstein actually failed math and was thought a fool for years.

If you ever get discouraged by school, please don't drop out. (You'll live to regret it.) Just keep plugging away. You're bound to eventually find something you enjoy about it or something you can excel at.

I once interviewed a heavily right-brained kid named Chris who shared how long it took him to fit in at school and find his niche:

Up until I went to school I was a happy child. Then kids found out that learning was difficult for me and they would point and call me names. I was slow at maths, English and grammar. I remember sitting in class one day, divided up into groups, when a girl in my group stood up and said, 'I'm not going to work with that retard', pointing to me. It made me feel terrible.

Through primary school, I could hardly read. A professional came to our home one day and after putting me through a number of tests told my mother that I would never be able to read. My mother was so angry that she told him to leave the house.

Years later, midway through secondary school, I picked up a science fiction book one day, and to my surprise it was suddenly easy to read. The stories in the book stimulated my imagination and then the words weren't words anymore but became pictures in my head. I read all the subsequent volumes and then I started to read other books and really got excited about reading and learning. I gained a big vocabulary. I started speaking better and using larger words.

It was about at this time that I began to excel at the arts. I learned that I have an incredible eye for shapes and colour. I've become gifted with watercolour, oil, painting, drawing and design. I can also write well. I write about my experiences. I write poetry. Toward the end of school, I won a lot of art gallery shows and gained a lot of confidence.

DON'T LET SCHOOL GET IN THE WAY OF YOUR EDUCATION

Grades are important, especially because they lead to future job and education options. But there is so much more to an education than grades.

My family is composed of a bunch of technical incompetents. I blame the bad gene on my dad. Several times I've seen him in 'technically challenging' situations, like when he lifts up the bonnet of the car (as if he could actually fix something) or when he attempts to change a light bulb. I've watched how, in these tough situations, his brain literally shuts down and ceases to function. It's a phenomenon! Being the proactive person that I am, I decided I wanted to overcome my inherited weakness and so I signed up for a car mechanics class during my last year of school. I was going to learn how to do an oil change if it killed me.

ER... **YOU** GOT AN **'A'** IN AUTO SHOP, DIDN'T YOU, SON?

Believe it or not, I got an A in that class. But I'm ashamed to admit that I hardly learned a thing. You see, instead of really paying the price to learn, I did a lot of watching and not a lot of doing. I never did my projects. And I crammed for all the tests, only to forget what I had learned two hours after taking them. I got the grade, but I failed to get an education.

Although qualifications are important, becoming truly educated is more important, so make sure you don't forget why you're going to school.

Over the years, I've seen so many people sacrifice their educations for so many stupid reasons, like thinking they don't need an education, or becoming obsessed with a part-time job, a girlfriend, a car or a rock group.

I've also seen many athletes sacrifice their education on the altar of sports. I've often been tempted to write letters to young athletes who become so sports-centred that they completely trash school. In fact, I actually wrote one, to an imaginary athlete. Though written to an athlete, it could apply to anyone who couldn't care less about developing their mind.

A LETTER TO AN

UNKNOWN
ATHLETE

Dear _____:

I'm a big believer in the benefits of sport. However, after meeting you, I am shocked to learn about your attitude toward school.

You say you're banking on a professional career and don't feel the need for an education. I say your chances of making it are about as good as my dad's chances of growing his hair back. 'A youngster gambling his future on a professional contract is like a worker buying a single Irish Sweepstakes ticket and then quitting his job in anticipation of his winnings.' Senator Bill Bradley, a former American basketball star, said that. Studies have shown that the chances of a school player making it professional are one in ten thousand.

Of the hundreds of university athletes I played with in university who hoped to make it, I can think of only a handful who made it. On the other hand, I can think of many who wasted their minds in the name of sports, and who were then thrown into the workforce without a chance or a clue.

I'll never forget the time one of my teammates delivered a psyche-up speech to our team the night before we played a rival university. Having neglected his education and having never learned to express himself, all he could do was uncork a barrage of vulgarities that could have cut down a forest. In a matter of three minutes it seemed he managed to use the f-word as a noun, a verb, an adjective, a pronoun, a conjunction and a dangling participle. I left that meeting thinking, 'Man, get a brain!'

Open your eyes! Your education is the key to unlocking your future.

You say you don't like school. I say, What does that have to do with it? Does anything good in life come easy? Do you like working out every day? Does a medical student enjoy studying for five years? Since when does liking something determine whether or not you should do it? Sometimes you just have to discipline yourself to do things you don't feel like doing because of what you hope to gain from it.

You say that you try to sit down and study but can't because your mind begins to wander. I say that unless you learn to control your mind you won't amount to anything. The discipline of the mind is a much higher form of discipline than that of the body. It is one thing to train your body to perform at peak levels; it is quite another to control your thoughts, to concentrate for sustained periods, to synthesize and to think creatively and analytically.

At times saying 'I try' is a lame excuse. Imagine how absurd it would sound if I asked you, 'Are you going to eat today or are you going to try to eat?' Just discipline yourself to do the thing.

You say you can get by without studying, that by cramming and finding ways to beat the system you can pull out pass marks. I say you reap what you sow. Can the farmer cram? Can he forget to plant his crops in the spring, loaf all summer long and then work real hard in the autumn to bring in the harvest? Can you improve your bench press by lifting weights once in a while? Your brain is no different than your bicep. To improve the strength, speed and endurance of your mind, you must work it out. There are no shortcuts. Don't expect to show up one day in the Land of Oz and have the Wizard hand you a brain.

Imagine five sets of hands. One set belongs to a concert pianist who can enthrall audiences with beautiful renditions of the classics. Another to an eye surgeon who can restore lost vision through microscopic surgery. Another to a professional golfer who consistently makes the clutch shot under pressure. Another to a blind man who can read tiny raised markings on a page at incredible speeds. Another to an artist who can carve beautiful sculptures that inspire the soul. On the surface, the hands may all look the same, but behind each set are years and years of sacrifice, discipline and perseverance. These people paid a price! Do you think they crammed? Did they beat the system?

One of my biggest regrets in life is that instead of reading 100 novels during high school, I read a bunch of Cliff Notes summaries. In contrast, I have a friend who during his teen years must have read hundreds of books. His brain can bench-press over four hundred pounds. Why, I would cut off one . . . no, two toes for such a brain.

If you don't pay the price you will earn a degree but fail to get an education. And there is a big difference between the two. Some of our best thinkers were degreeless, self-educated men and women. How did they do it? They read. It's only the single greatest habit you could ever develop. Yet few do it regularly. And many stop reading and learning when they finish school. That spells brain atrophy. Education must be a lifelong pursuit. The person who doesn't read is no better off than the person who can't.

You say you live for today and don't think about the future. I say the major difference between you and your dog is that you can think about tomorrow and he can't. Don't make long-term career decisions based on short-term emotions, like the student who chooses his or her university courses based on the shortest registration line. Develop a future orientation; make decisions with the end in mind. To have a good job tomorrow, you must do your homework tonight.

The Proverb sums up the whole matter: 'Take fast hold of instruction; let her not go: keep her; for she is thy life.'

You seem to be saying you don't need a brain. I say, get one!

I hope I haven't offended you. I mean well. It's just that ten years from now, I don't want you to find yourself singing, as did our friend the Scarecrow:

> I would not be just a nothin',
> My head all full of stuffin',
> . . . If I only had a brain.

Think about it,

SEAN

• POST–SCHOOL EDUCATIONAL OPTIONS

Don't get too worried about your degree or area of focus in school. If you can simply learn to think well, you will have plenty of career and education options to choose from. Admissions offices and companies that are hiring don't care so much about what you subjects you took. They want to see evidence that you have a sound mind. They will be looking at several different areas:

1. _Desire_ – How badly do you want to get into this particular university or programme? How much do you want this job?

2. _Standardized test scores_ – How well did you do in your SATs, GCSEs, AS and A-levels, etc.?

3. _Extracurricular_ – What other activities (sports, outside work, clubs, student government, church, community, etc.) were you involved in?

4. _Letters of recommendation_ – What do other people think of you?

6. _Communication skills_ – How well can you communicate in writing (based on your application essays) and verbally (based on an interview)?

If you can simply learn to think well, you will have plenty of career and education options to choose from.

Most important, they just want to see evidence that you will succeed at the next level. If your qualifications scores are lower than you would like, don't feel like you have to settle for second best. You can still get admitted to great universitys or get an A1 job if you're strong in other areas.

Also, don't be scared off by rumours about how hard it is to get into university. It's usually not as hard as you might think if you're willing to put some effort into your application. However, it will be harder than the following entrance exam would lead you to believe. (Hey, since I was a football player, I have the right to poke fun at myself.)

COLLEGE ENTRANCE EXAM
(Adapted for Football Players)

TIME LIMIT: 3 WEEKS

1. What language is spoken in France?

2. Would you ask William Shakespeare to
   ☐ build a bridge
   ☐ sail the ocean
   ☐ lead an army
   ☐ WRITE A PLAY

3. What religion is the pope?
   ☐ Jewish
   ☐ Catholic
   ☐ Hindu
   ☐ Polish
   ☐ Agnostic

4. What are the people in America's far north called?
   ☐ Westerners
   ☐ Southerners
   ☐ Northerners

5. Six kings of England have been called George, the last one being George the Sixth. Name the previous five.

6. How many commandments was Moses given (approximately)?

7. Can you explain Einstein's Theory of Relativity?
   ☐ yes
   ☐ no

8. What are coat hangers used for?

9. Explain Le Chatelier's Principle of Dynamic Equilibrium *or* spell your name in CAPITAL LETTERS.

10. Advanced maths: If you have three apples, how many apples do you have?

You must correctly answer three or more questions to qualify.

HABIT 7

● MENTAL BARRIERS

As you attempt to build a brain, you will need to overcome a few barriers. Here are three to consider:

Screentime. Screentime is any time spent in front of a screen, like a TV, computer, video game or cinema screen. *Some* time can be healthy, but *too much* time chatting on the internet, playing video games or watching TV can numb your mind. Did you know that the average teenager watches over twenty hours of TV a week? That equates to forty-three days each year and a total of eight years over a lifetime. Good thing you're not average! Just think what you could do with those forty-three days annually if you were to spend them doing something productive like studying French, ballroom dancing or computer programming.

Set guidelines for yourself regarding screentime, and don't let it get out of hand. Or try losing your remote control. That works too.

The Nerd Syndrome. Interestingly, some teenagers don't want to do too well in school because others might think they're too studious (nerds), and studious isn't cool. I've also heard girls tell me that they don't want to come across as 'brains' because it intimidates guys. What will we think of next, for crying out loud?! If having a mind intimidates someone, that probably tells you something about their own lack of neurons. Take pride in your mental abilities and the fact that you value education. I, for one, know a lot of wealthy and successful people who were once considered nerds.

Pressure. Sometimes we're scared of doing well in school because of the high expectations it creates. If we bring home a good school report and get praised for it, we've suddenly established the expectation that we'll do it again and again. And the pressure builds. If we do poorly, there's no expectation and no pressure.

Just remember this: The stress that results from success is much more tolerable than the regret that results from not trying your best. Don't sweat the pressure. You can deal with it.

● YOU GOTTA WANNA

In the end, the key to honing your mind will be your desire to learn. You've gotta really want it. You've gotta get turned on by learning. You've gotta pay the price. The following story is an example of someone who had an irresistible drive for learning and who paid a huge price for the simple joy of reading. Reading to this person was 'air'.

The kitchen door opened – and I was caught, cold. It was too late to hide the evidence; the proof was in the open, plain as could be, right there in my lap. My father, drunk, his face flushed, reeled before me, glowering, menacing. My legs started to tremble. I was nine years old. I knew I would be beaten. There could be no escape; my father had found me reading . . .

An alcoholic like his parents before him, my father had hit me before, many times and harder, and in the years that followed he would hit me again, many times and harder, until finally I quit school at sixteen and left home. His persistent rage about my reading when I was a boy, though, frustrated me more than all other abuse; it made me feel squeezed in the jaws of a terrible vice, because I would not, I could not, stop reading. I was drawn to books by curiosity and driven by need – an irresistible need to pretend I was elsewhere . . . Thus I defied my father – and, as I've recalled here, sometimes I paid a price for that defiance. It was worth it.

This account was written by Walter Anderson in his book *Read with Me*. Walter is now a successful editor, serves on the boards of many literacy organizations, and is the author of four books. Walter goes on to write:

When I was a child, I lived in a violent household, in a violent neighbourhood. But there was a place that I could go – a library – and all the librarians did was encourage me to read. I could open a book, and I could be anywhere. I could do anything. I could imagine myself out of a slum. I read myself out of poverty long before I worked myself out of poverty.

In the back of the book, I have compiled a list of fifty great books for teenagers. Take a look.

If you haven't paid the price to educate yourself so far, it's never too late to start. If you can learn to think well, the future will be an open door of opportunity. It's all about brain waves. Get some.

EXERCISE YOUR MIND

Caring for Your Heart

Late one afternoon there came a knock at the door.
'Who could that be?'
I opened the door and there stood my nineteen-year-old younger sister, heaving and sobbing.

'What's wrong?' I asked, leading her in, although I knew exactly what was wrong. This was the third sob-episode that month.

'He is so rude,' she snivelled, wiping her red, swollen eyes. 'I can't believe he did that to me. It was so mean.'

'What did he do this time?' I asked. I had heard some pretty good ones and couldn't wait to hear if this one was any better.

'Well . . . you know, he asked me to come over to his house to study,' she whimpered. 'And while we were studying some other girls came to visit him. And he acted like he didn't even know me.'

Let no one ever come to you without leaving better and happier. Be the living expression of God's kindness: kindness in your face, kindness in your eyes, kindness in your smile.

MOTHER TERESA

'I wouldn't worry about it,' I said wisely. 'I used to do that kind of thing all the time.'

'But I've been dating him for two years,' she blubbered. 'And when they asked him who I was, he told them that I was his sister.'

Ouch!

She was devastated. But I knew that in just a matter of hours or days she'd be thinking he was the greatest thing since sliced bread. Sure enough, a few days later she was crazy about him all over again.

Do you ever feel that, like my sister, you're riding an emotional roller coaster, up one day and down the next? Do you ever feel that you're the moodiest person in the world and that you can't control your emotions? If you do, then welcome to the club, because those feelings are pretty normal for teenagers. You see, your heart is a very temperamental thing. And it needs constant nourishment and care, just like your body.

The best way to sharpen the saw and nourish your heart is to focus on building relationships, or in other words, to make regular deposits into your relationship bank accounts and into your own personal bank account. Let's review what those deposits are.

<u>RBA (Relationship Bank Account) Deposits</u>

- Keep promises
- Do small acts of kindness
- Be loyal
- Listen
- Say you're sorry
- Set clear expectations

<u>PBA (Personal Bank Account) Deposits</u>

- Keep promises to yourself
- Do small acts of kindness
- Be gentle with yourself
- Be honest
- Renew yourself
- Tap into your talents

As you might have noticed, PBA and RBA deposits are very similar. That's because deposits you make into other people's accounts usually end up in your own as well.

As you set out each day, look for opportunities to make deposits and build lasting friendships. Listen deeply to a friend, parent, brother or sister without expecting anything in return. Give out ten compliments today. Stick up for someone. Come home when you told your parents you'd be home.

I like how Mother Teresa put it: 'Let no one ever come to you without leaving better and happier. Be the living expression of God's kindness: kindness in your face, kindness in your eyes, kindness in your smile.' If you approach life this way, always looking for ways to build instead of tear down, you'll be amazed at how much happiness you can give to others and find for yourself.

As you think about caring for your heart, here are a few other points to consider.

SEX AND RELATIONSHIPS

Said one young girl, 'I don't care what kind of relationship you are in or how devout you are . . . sex is always in the air. No matter if you are sitting in the car alone with that person or at home watching TV – the question hangs in the air.'

Sex is about a whole lot more than your body. It's also about your heart. In fact, what you do about sex may affect your self-image and your relationships with others more than any other decision you make. Before you decide to have sex or to continue having it, search your heart and think about it . . . carefully. The following excerpt from a pamphlet, published by Journeyworks Publishing, should help.

Think you're ready to go all the way? Are you sure? Sexually transmitted infections, unplanned pregnancy and emotional doubts are all good reasons to wait! Before you go too far, take a look at this list. Or make up your own ways to finish the sentence:

You're not ready to have sex if . . .

1. You think sex equals love.
2. You feel pressured.
3. You're afraid to say no.
4. It's just easier to give in.
5. You think everyone else is doing it. (They're not!)
6. Your instincts tell you not to.
7. You don't know the facts about pregnancy.
8. You don't understand how birth control works.
9. You don't think a woman can get pregnant the first time. (She can.)
10. It goes against your moral beliefs.
11. It goes against your religious beliefs.
12. You'll regret it in the morning.
13. You feel embarrassed or ashamed.
14. You're doing it to prove something.
15. You can't support a child.
16. You can't support yourself.
17. Your idea of commitment is a 3-day video rental.
18. You believe sex before marriage is wrong.
19. You don't know how to protect yourself from HIV – the virus that causes AIDS.
20. You don't know the signs and symptoms of sexually transmitted infections (STIs, also called STDs).
21. You think it will make your partner love you.
22. You think it will make you love your partner.
23. You think it will keep you together.
24. You hope it will change your life.
25. You don't want it to change your life.

26. You're not ready for the relationship to change.
27. You're drunk.
28. You wish you were drunk.
29. Your partner is drunk.
30. You expect it to be perfect.
31. You'll just die if it's not perfect.
32. You can't laugh together about awkward elbows and clumsy clothes.
33. You're not ready to take off your clothes.
34. You think HIV and AIDS only happen to other people.
35. You think you can tell who has HIV by looking at them.
36. You don't think teenagers get HIV. (They do.)
37. You don't know that abstinence is the only 100% protection against sexually transmitted infections and pregnancy.
38. You haven't talked about tomorrow.
39. You can't face the thought of tomorrow.
40. You'd be horrified if your parents found out.
41. You're doing it just so your parents will find out.
42. You're too scared to think clearly.
43. You think it will make you more popular.
44. You think you 'owe it' to your partner.
45. You think it's not OK to be a virgin.
46. You're only thinking about yourself.
47. You're not thinking about yourself.
48. You can't wait to tell everyone about it.
49. You hope no one will hear about it.
50. You really wish the whole thing had never come up.

It's OK to Wait.

HABIT 7

You're Gonna Make It It's totally normal to feel depressed at times. But there is a big difference between a case of the blues and sustained depression. If life has become a real pain for a long period of time and you can't seem to shake off that feeling of hopelessness, things are serious. Fortunately, depression is treatable. Don't hesitate to get help, either from medication or from talking with someone who is trained to deal with these issues.

If you are having thoughts of suicide, please listen closely to what I'm saying. Hold on for dear life. You're gonna make it. Life will get better . . . I promise. You are worth millions and you are needed. Bad times will pass . . . they always do. Someday you will look back on your situation and be glad you held on, as was the case with this young lady:

I am one of the many young people who comes from a wonderful home and really don't have any reason to have gotten into trouble. But I did. Friends became very important to me in school, and home life seemed very boring. I couldn't wait to get out of there every day just to be with my buddies and hang out. Within two years I probably tried every vice in the book, and it didn't make me feel any better. On the contrary.

I began having trouble even coming home. It was almost too painful to walk into that sunny, peaceful house with aromas of good cooking. They all seemed so good and perfect, and I felt like I couldn't fulfill their expectations. I somehow didn't fit in. I was not living a life they were proud of, and I would just make them unhappy. I began to wish I was dead. Then the thought led to actual suicide attempts.

I kept a diary and it really scares me today to see how close I came to ending it all. Today, just a few years later, I am in university getting top marks, I have a happy social life, I have a boyfriend who loves me very much, and I have a great relationship with my family. I have so many plans, so many things I am going to do. I love life, I have so much to live for, I cannot believe that I ever felt different, but I did. It took several serious wake-up calls to make me realize that I could be different. Thank heavens I'm still here.

Remember that the struggles you are now facing will eventually become a great source of strength for you. As the philosopher Kahlil Gibran wrote: 'That self-same well from which our laughter rises was often times filled with our tears. The deeper that sorrow carries into our being, the more joy it can contain.' (Please refer to the hotlines and websites in the back of this book if you need help.)

● LAUGH OR YOU'LL CRY

After all is said and done, there is one last key to keeping your heart healthy and strong. Just laugh. That's right . . . laugh. *Hakuna matata!* Don't worry, be happy! Sometimes life just stinks and there's not much you can do to change it, so you might as well laugh.

It's too bad that as we age we tend to forget what made childhood so magical. One study showed that by the time you reach primary school, you laugh about 300 times a day. In contrast, the typical adult laughs a wimpy seventeen times a day. No wonder children are so much happier! Why are we so serious? Maybe it's because we've been taught that laughing too much is childish. To quote the great Jedi master, Yoda, 'You must unlearn what you have learned'. We must learn to laugh again.

I read the most fascinating article by Peter Doskoch about the power of humour in *Psychology Today*. These were some of his key findings:

Laughter:
- Loosens up the mental gears and helps us think more creatively
- Helps us cope with the difficulties of life
- Reduces stress levels
- Relaxes us as it lowers our heart rate and blood pressure
- Connects us with others and counteracts feelings of alienation, a major factor in depression and suicide
- Releases endorphins, the brain's natural painkillers

Laughter has also been shown to promote good health and speed healing. I've heard several accounts of people who healed themselves from serious sickness through heavy doses of laughing therapy. Laughter can also help heal injured relationships. As entertainer Victor Borge put it, 'Laughter is the shortest distance between two people'.

If you're not laughing much, what can you do to start again? I suggest developing your own 'humour collection', a collection of books, cartoons, videos, ideas – whatever is funny to you. Then, whenever you're feeling down, or taking yourself way too seriously, visit your collection. For example, I like stupid movies. There are a few actors who make me laugh just at the thought of them. I have bought many of their low-budget movies and watch them whenever I need to 'lighten up'. Similarly, my brother Stephen has one of the largest collections of *The Far Side* cartoons ever known to man. He claims that these cartoons have kept him from going insane during high-stress periods.

Learn to laugh at yourself when strange or stupid things happen to you, because they will. As someone once said, 'One of the best things people can have up their sleeve is a good funny bone'.

Caring for Your Soul

What is it that moves your soul? A great movie? A good book? Have you ever seen a movie that made you cry? What was it that got to you?

What deeply inspires you? Does music? Art? Being in nature?

By soul, I mean that inner self that lurks far below the surface of your everyday self. Your soul is your centre, wherein lie your deepest convictions and values. It is the source for purpose, meaning, and inner peace. Sharpening the saw in the spiritual area of life means taking time to renew and awaken that inner self. As the famous author Pearl S. Buck wrote, 'Inside myself is a place where I live all alone and that's where you renew your springs that never dry up'.

How to Feed Your Soul

As a teenager, I got strength from writing in my diary, listening to good music and spending time alone in the mountains. This was my way of renewing my soul, although I didn't think of it that way at the time. I also got strength from inspiring quotes, such as this one by past US Secretary of Agriculture Ezra Taft Benson:

'Men and women who turn their lives over to God will find out that He can make a lot more out of their lives than they can. He will deepen their joys, expand their vision, quicken their minds, strengthen their muscles, lift their spirits, multiply their blessings, increase their opportunities and pour out peace.'

Your soul is a very private area of your life. Naturally, there are many different ways to feed it. Here are a few ideas shared by teenagers:

- Meditating
- Serving others
- Writing in my diary
- Going for a walk
- Reading inspiring books
- Drawing
- Praying
- Writing poetry or music
- Thinking deeply

- Listening to uplifting music
- Playing a musical instrument
- Practising a religion
- Talking to friends I can be myself with
- Reflecting on my goals or mission statement

Here are a couple of soul-nourishing techniques to especially consider.

GETTING BACK TO NATURE

There is something magical about getting into nature that just can't be matched. Even if you live in an inner city area far removed from rivers, mountains or beaches, there will usually be a park nearby that you can visit. I once interviewed a young man named Ryan who learned about the healing powers of Mother Nature in the midst of a really messed up home life.

At one point during school, I went through a dark period where it seemed that everything just caved in. That's when I found the river hole. It was just a bank off in some trees in the back of an old farmer's place and didn't look like much. But it became my escape. There was no one around, you couldn't hear people. It was beautiful. Just swimming around made me feel at peace with nature. Anytime I was stressed out I'd go there. It was like my life could come back to normal.

Some people turn to organized religion for direction, but it's been hard for me to turn to religion. I do have a religion and I'm strong in it. But sometimes it's just hard for me to get up and go to church, because I go and everyone says, 'Oh, just be happy. It will all work out. Just have faith. Things will work out with your family.' I just think that's bull. C'mon. Families don't always work out. My family's all messed up.

But by going to the river, that place didn't judge me. That place didn't tell me what to do. It was just there. And by following its example, the peacefulness and the serenity that existed there, that's all I needed to calm things down. It made me feel like everything was going to work out.

A TEENAGER'S BEST FRIEND

Like getting into nature, keeping a diary can do wonders for your soul. It can become your solace, your best friend, the only place where you can fully express yourself no matter how angry, happy, scared, love crazed, insecure or confused you feel. You can pour your heart out in your diary and it will just sit there and listen. It won't talk back. And it won't talk behind your back. Writing down your unedited thoughts can clear your mind, boost your confidence and help you find yourself.

Keeping a diary will also strengthen your tool of self-awareness. It's fun and enlightening to read past entries and realize how much you've grown, how stupid and immature you once sounded, or how caught up you were with some boy or girl. One girl told me about how reading her old diary entries gave her the insight to keep from returning to her former abusive boyfriend.

BOY, WHAT A MORON I WAS BACK THEN!

There is no formal way to keep a diary. Feel free to paste in mementos, ticket stubs, love notes and anything else that will preserve a memory. My old diaries are full of poor art, bad poetry and strange smells.

A diary is just a formal name for putting your thoughts down on paper. There are other names and forms. Allison writes little notes to herself that she keeps in a special box she calls her sacred box. Katie renews herself by keeping a 'gratitude book':

I have a book that helps me to be more positive in life. I call it my gratitude book. In this book, I write down something I'm grateful for or something positive that happened to me during the day. This book has changed my life and totally put things into perspective, because I try to pick out all the good things that happen and not the bad. This is not like a diary where you write what happens, both good and bad. I still keep a diary, but this is different. I have a page of my favourite songs, favourite touches (brother's hug), favourite sounds (Mum's laugh), favourite feels (cool breeze) and so on. I also write down small things like, 'Brian offered to clear the table for me', or 'John went out of his way to say hello to me today'. These things make you feel good. I look back at this book and remember these good things and the bad things are forgotten, erased and gone. They can't affect me anymore.

I've given a book to others and they say it has really helped them. It's my way of saying, 'You're the only one who can make you happy – no one else can'.

YOUR SPIRITUAL DIET

I've often wondered what would happen to someone who drank and ate only soft drinks and chocolate for several years straight.

What would they look and feel like after a while? Probably like scum. But why do we think the result would be any different if we fed our souls rubbish for several years straight? You're not only what you eat, you're also what you listen to, read and see. More important than what goes into your body is what goes into your soul.

So what is your spiritual diet? Are you feeding your soul nutrients, or are you loading it with nuclear waste? What kind of media do you allow yourself to take in? Have you ever even thought about it?

You see, we swim in a world of media and don't even know it. Try going 'media-free' for just one day and you'll see what I mean – one day without listening to any music, watching any TV or videos, reading any books or magazines, surfing the internet, or look at an advert (that's media too). You'll find it's virtually impossible, and you may even develop severe withdrawal pains.

Take music, for example. Studies show that the average teen listens to four hours of music a day. That's a lot of tunes! When you wake up in the morning, what do you do? You turn on your radio or stereo. Then you jump into your car and what do you do? You get angry with your parents, run to your room, and what do you do? Can you imagine watching a commercial, TV programme, or movie that isn't accompanied by music?

Now, if you think the media doesn't affect you, just think about your favourite song and what it does to your emotions. Or think about the last time you saw half-naked members of the opposite sex wiggling all over the screen or pictured on the page. Or think back to the last bottle of shampoo you bought. Why did you buy it? Probably because of the influence of a thirty-second TV commercial or a one-page magazine ad. And if a one-page ad can sell a bottle of shampoo, don't you think a full-length movie, magazine or CD can sell a lifestyle?

Like most things, there is a light and a dark side to the media. And you need to choose what you're going to allow in. My only suggestion is to follow your conscience and to treat your soul with the same respect that an Olympic athlete would treat his or her body. For example, if the music you listen to or the movies you watch make you feel depressed, angry, dark, violent or like you're on heat, then guess what? That's probably a sign that they're trash, and you don't need trash. On the other hand, if they make you feel relaxed, happy, inspired, hopeful or peaceful, then keep taking them. You'll eventually become what you view, hear, and read, so continually ask yourself the question 'Do I want this to be part of me?'

HABIT 7

You're Disturbing My Sleep

I ran across a letter from the YO! (Youth Outlook) website written by a girl named Ladie Terry who was fed up with all the rubbish on music television. She addressed the letter to 'the sisters who like to grind their way across my TV screen'. By permission, I've included parts of it here.

I guess it's exciting being in a music video. But do you know how you are affecting the minds and lives of your sisters? Do you think about the younger sisters, who learn fast and emulate you? Have you noticed the 12- and 13-year-olds dolled up to look like 20-year-olds? Or are times so hard that you don't care who you hurt?

I used to argue with my ex-boyfriend about watching MTV, because the majority of the videos consisted of not-even-half-naked girls wiggling and jiggling like a bowl of Jell-O . . . it hurt me to see my ex-boyfriend in a daze with his eyes moving up and down . . .

THAT'S IT! WE'RE SWITCHING TO NICKELODEON.

My neighbour used to tell me when she would watch music videos with her boyfriend he would say to her, 'That's how your body should look.' Another friend, who is 16, says boys ask her, 'Why can't you dance like that?'

Why are you on TV in tight, short clothing, moving your bodies around like you are freaks? . . . You sisters are very, very beautiful. You don't have to undress for success, or to get some attention. You want brothers to respect you? Show them why they should through your elegant, conservative dress – then back up your reasoning with your words. The way you dress tells people what is on your mind . . . when you upgrade your appearance and your mind set, a lot of brothers will upgrade their treatment of you.

So stop competing to see who is freakier than the next, and get your mind out of the bedroom, because you are disturbing my sleep.

Fried Frogs

Addictions of all kinds – whether it's to drugs, gossiping, shopping, overeating or gambling – have common characteristics.

Addiction:
- Creates short-term pleasure
- Becomes the primary focus of your life
- Temporarily eliminates pain
- Gives an artificial sense of self-worth, power, control, security and intimacy
- Worsens the problems and feelings you are trying to escape from

One of the more subtle but dangerous addictions is pornography, and it's available everywhere. Now, you can argue all you want about what pornography is and isn't, but I think that deep in your heart you know. Pornography may taste sweet for the moment, but it will gradually dull your finer sensitivities, like that inner voice called your conscience, until it's smothered.

You may be thinking, 'Take it easy, Sean. A little skin isn't going to hurt me'. The problem is that pornography, like any other addiction, sneaks up on you. It reminds me of a story I once read about frogs. If you put a frog in boiling water, it will immediately jump out. But if you put it in lukewarm water and then slowly turn up the heat, the frog will get cooked before it has the sense to jump out. It's the same with pornography. What you look at today may have shocked you a year ago. But because the heat was ever so slowly turned up, you didn't even notice that your conscience was being fried.

Have the courage to walk away, to turn it off, to throw it away. You are better than that. A boy shared this:

During the summer between my last two years of school, I worked for a construction company. One day the boss asked me to check on something with the building supervisor who had his office on the job site in a work trailer.

When I walked into the trailer there were pornographic pictures posted on all the walls. For a minute, I forgot what I had gone in there to ask the guys, because my attention was drawn to the pictures. It struck an interest in me. When I left the trailer I started thinking, where can I buy this stuff so I can see more of it? I soon found a place that sold them.

At first, when I looked at them, I felt very nervous and uneasy inside, like what I was doing was wrong, but it didn't take me long to get addicted to it. It began to consume me to the point where I was not thinking of anything else – my family, or work or sleep. I started to think and feel lower of myself.

During breaks at work, we would go to someone's vehicle, and someone would pull out a magazine, and we would laugh about it and carry on. The guys that were deeply involved in it were not satisfied with just looking. They would talk about all the girls they had slept with and they didn't seem to care about anything else in life. That was all their conversations were about, the magazines, films and sex.

Late one afternoon, as I was working, I heard some of my co-workers start whistling and calling out rude sexual remarks. I looked up to see what the commotion was, and there was my younger sister just getting out from her Volkswagen Beetle, looking for me. I overheard someone say, 'I'd like to get a piece of that!' I turned angrily and said, 'Shut up! That's my little sister!'

I was so disgusted. I left the job, just before quitting time, and drove around for a while by myself. I just kept thinking about how hurt my sister looked, to be treated so horridly when her intentions had been so innocent.

The next day, when I went back to the job, and the guys passed around the magazines, I got up and moved. At first it took a lot of strength, but as I did it more and more, it became easier. When conversations started that were crude and distasteful, I would walk away and go someplace else. I didn't think it was amusing anymore. I realized they were talking about somebody's sister.

● GET REAL

As we close this chapter, let me just share a couple of final thoughts. I once was talking to a girl named Clarissa about sharpening the saw, and she gave me an earful. 'Get real, Sean. Who has time? I'm at school all day, I have activities after school, and I study all night. I need to get good marks to get into university. What am I supposed to do, go to bed early and then fail my maths test tomorrow?'

Let me just say this. There is a time for everything. A time to be balanced and a time to be imbalanced. There are times when you'll need to go without much sleep and push your body to its limit, for a day, a week or a season. And there will be times when eating junk food out of the vending machine is your only alternative to starving. This is real life. But there are also times for renewal.

If you go too hard for too long, you won't think as clearly, you'll get cranky, and you'll begin to lose perspective. You may think you don't have time to exercise, build friendships or get inspired. In reality, you don't have time not to. The time you spend sharpening your saw will pay you back immediately, 'cause when you resume your normal routine, you'll cut that much faster.

You Can Do It (Y)ou're probably already doing a lot of saw sharpening without even knowing it. If you're working hard at school, you're sharpening your mind. If you're into sport or fitness, you're caring for your body. If you're working to develop friendships, you're nourishing your heart. Often you can sharpen the saw in more than one area at once. Melanie once told me how, for her, horseback riding did this. The physical nature of riding exercised her body. Thinking deeply while riding exercised her mind. And being in nature nurtured her soul. I then asked her, 'What about relationships? How does riding develop your heart?' She said, 'I get closer to my horse'. Well, I guess horses can be people too.

Sharpening the saw won't just happen to you. Since it's a Quadrant 2 activity (important but not urgent), you have to be proactive and happen to it. The best thing to do is to take out time each day to sharpen the saw, even if it's only for fifteen or thirty minutes. Some teenagers set apart a specific time each day – early in the morning, after school or late at night – to be alone, to think or to exercise. Others like to do it on the weekends. There's no one right way – so find what works for you.

Abraham Lincoln was once asked, 'What would you do if you had eight hours to cut down a tree?' He replied, 'I'd spend the first four hours sharpening my saw'.

COMING ATTRACTIONS

You'll like the next chapter because it's real short. You might as well just finish the book right now!

Body

1. Eat breakfast.

2. Start an exercise programme today and do it faithfully for 30 days. Walk, run, swim, bike, rollerblade, lift weights, etc. Choose something you really enjoy.

3. Give up a bad habit for a week. Go without alcohol, fizzy drinks, fried foods, sweets, chocolate or whatever else may be hurting your body. A week later, see how you feel.

Mind

4. Subscribe to a magazine that has some educational value, such as *Popular Mechanics* or *National Geographic*.

5. Read a newspaper every day. Pay special attention to the headline stories and the opinions page.

6. The next time you go on a date, visit a museum or eat at an ethnic restaurant you've never been to before. Expand your horizons.

Heart

7. Go on a one-on-one outing with a family member like your mum or your brother. Catch a football game, see a film, go shopping or get an ice cream.

8. Begin today to build your humour collection. Cut out your favourite cartoons, buy hilarious movies or start your own collection of great jokes. In no time, you'll have something to go to when you're feeling stressed.

Soul

9. Watch the sunset tonight or get up early to watch the sunrise.

10. If you haven't already done it, start keeping a diary today.

11. Take time each day to meditate, reflect upon your life or pray. Do what works for you.

Keep Hope Alive!

KID, YOU'LL MOVE MOUNTAINS

Several years ago the Reverend Jesse Jackson spoke at the US Democratic National Convention. He delivered a powerful message that set the convention on fire. He used only three words: 'Keep hope alive. Keep hope alive!

He kept saying these same words over and over and over for what seemed forever. The crowd swelled with applause. You could feel the sincerity in his voice. He inspired everyone. He created hope.

That's why I wrote this book . . . *to give you hope!* Hope that you can change, kick an addiction, improve an important relationship. Hope that you can find answers to your problems and reach your fullest potential. So what if your family life stinks, you're failing at school and the only good relationship you have is with your cat (and lately she's been letting you down). *Keep hope alive!*

If, after reading this book, you feel overwhelmed and don't have a clue where to start, I'd suggest doing this: Thumb through each chapter quickly for the key ideas, or ask yourself, 'Which habit am I having the most difficult time living?' Then choose just two or three things to

> So be sure when you step
> Step with care and great tact
> And remember that life's
> A Great Balancing Act.
>
> And will you succeed?
> Yes! You will, indeed!
> (98 and ¾ percent guaranteed)
> Kid, you'll move mountains.
>
> DR SEUSS
> FROM *OH, THE PLACES YOU'LL GO*

work on (don't get overzealous and choose twenty). Write them down and put them in a place where you can review them often. Then let them inspire you each day, not send you on a guilt trip.

You'll be amazed at the results a few small changes can bring. Gradually, you'll increase in confidence, you'll feel happier, you'll get high 'naturally', your goals will become realities, your relationships will improve and you'll feel at peace. It all begins with a single step.

If there was a habit or idea that really hit home, such as Be Proactive or the Relationship Bank Account, the best way to internalize it is to teach it to someone else while it's still fresh in your mind. Walk them through it using your own examples and words. Who knows, maybe you'll get them fired up and they'll want to work with you.

If you ever find yourself sliding or falling short, *don't get discouraged.* Remember the flight of an airplane. When an airplane takes off it has a flight plan. However, during the course of the flight, wind, rain, turbulence, air traffic, human error and other factors keep knocking the plane off course. In fact, a plane is off course about 90 per cent of the time. The key is that the pilots keep making small course corrections by reading their instruments and talking to the control tower. As a result, a plane reaches its destination.

If you keep getting knocked off your flight plan and feel as though you're off course 90 per cent of the time . . . so what? If you just keep coming back to your plan, keep making small adjustments, and keep hope alive, you'll eventually reach your destination.

Well, this is the end of the book. Thank you for journeying with me, and congratulations on finishing. I just want you to know that I truly believe in your future. You are destined for great things. Always remember, you were born with everything you need to succeed. You don't have to look anywhere else. The power and light is in you!

Before signing off, I'd like to leave you with a favourite quote of mine, by Bob Moawad, which sums it all up. I wish you all the best. Sayonara.

You can't make footprints in the sands of time by sitting on your butt. And who wants to leave buttprints in the sands of time?

ACKNOWLEDGMENTS

They say that writing a book is like eating an elephant. For some reason the two years I spent writing this book felt more like eating an entire herd of elephants. Luckily, I didn't have to eat them all by myself. There were many others who contributed in many ways to make this book possible. I would like to thank each of them:

Thank you, Annie Oswald, for being the ultimate project leader and for your tirelessness, leadership and initiative. Without a doubt, you were the key to making this book what it is.

Thank you, Trevor Walker, for your 'can-do' attitude and for helping me get this book off the ground in the beginning.

Thank you, Jeanette Sommer, for your unusual level of dedication to this project and for somehow always finding that impossible story.

Thank you, Pia Jensen, for contributing as a core team member for over two years and for your outstanding stories.

Thank you, Greg Link, for being a brilliant deal maker and a good friend, and for leading the PR and marketing efforts.

Thank you, Catherine Sagers, my sister, for your great work on the 'baby steps' and for contributing in many other ways. XOXO

Thank you, Cynthia Haller, my oldest sister and the 'mother hen', for your superb editorial assistance, stories and ideas. XOXO

Thank you, Mark Pett, for being the creative mind behind the majority of the illustrations in the book and for contributing several illustrations.

Thank you, Eric Olson (the book's primary illustrator) and Ray Kuik (the book's Art Director) of Raeber Graphics, Inc., for your creative genius and for fulfilling my vision of making this book a visual feast. All I can say about you guys is 'Wow!'

Thank you, Debra Lund, Janeen Bullock and team, for your proactive efforts in collecting all those lovely endorsements.

Thank you, Tony Contos and team at Joliet Township High School in Illinois, for serving as our primary test site. (Tony, your constant encouragement kept me afloat.) In particular, thanks to Sandy Contos, Flora Betts, Barbara Pasteris, Gloria Martinez, Linda Brisbin, Susan Graham, John Randich, Lynn Vaughn, Jennifer Adams, Marie Blunk, Cathe Ghilain, Marvin Reed, Bonnie Badurski, Judy Bruno, Richard Dobbs, Pat Sullivan, Shawna Kocielko, Reasie McCullough, Nichole Nelson, Michael Stubler, Nichol Douglas, Joseph Facchina, Kaatrina Voss, Joy Denewellis, Jordan McLaughlin, Allison Yanchick, Stephen Davis, Chris Adams, Neal Brockett and Marisha Pasteris.

Thank you, Rita Elliot and the other staff members and students of the North Carolina Legislator's School, for your insights and interviews. Specifically, thanks to Kia Hardy, Natarsha Sanders, Crystal Hall, Tarrick

Cox, Adam Sosne, Heather Sheehan, Tara McCormick and Terrence Dove.

Thank you, Kay Jensen and the Sanpete Child Abuse Prevention Team, for so courageously sharing your stories.

Thanks to the Heritage School administration, faculty, and students.

Thank you, Cindi Hanson and the Timpview High School Executive Tech class, for allowing me to teach you the 7 Habits. In particular, thanks to Kristi Borland, Spencer Clegg, Kelli Klein, Jennie Feitz, Brittney Howard, Tiffany Smith, Becky Tanner, Kaylyn Ellis, Rachel Litster, Melissa Gourley, T.J. Riskas, Willie Morrell, Brandon Kraus, Stephan Heilner, Monica Moore and Amanda Valgardson.

Thank you, students of Utah Valley High Schools, for your important participation in numerous focus groups. In particular, thanks to Ariel Amata, Brett Atkinson, Amy Baird, David Beck, Sandy Blumenstock, Megan Bury, Brittany Cameron, Laura Casper, Estee Christensen, Ryan Clark, Carla Domingues, Ryan Edwards, Jeff Gamette, Katie Hall, Liz Jacob, Jeff Jacobs, Jeremy Johnson, Joshua Kautz, Arian Lewis, Lee Lewis, Marco Lopez, Aaron Lund, Harlin Mitchell, Kristi Myrick, Chris Nibley, Whitney Noziska, Dianne Orcutt, Leisy Oswald, Laney Oswald, Jordan Peterson, Geoff Reynolds, Jasmine Schwerdt, Josie Smith, Heather Sommer, Jeremy Sommer, Steve Strong, Mark Sullivan, Larissa Taylor, Callie Trane, Kelli Maureen Wells, Kristi Woodworth and Lacey Yates.

Thanks to the many speakers, authors and youth leaders that assisted in one way or another, namely Brettne Shootman, Mona Gayle Timko, James E.H. Collins, Brenton G. Yorgason, James J. Lynch, Matt Clyde, Dan Johnson, Deborah Mangum, Pat O'Brien, Jason Dorsey, Matt Townsend, Vanessa Moore, Dr Cheryl Gholar and John Bytheway and Premier School Agenda and team.

A special thanks to all those who contributed interviews and stories, including Jackie Gago, Sara Duquette, Andy Fries, Arthur Williams, Christopher Williams, Tiffany Tuck, Dave Boyer, Julie Anderson, Liz Sharp, Renon Hulet, Dawn Meeves, Chris Lenderman, Jacob Sommer, Kara Sommer, Sarah Clements, Jeff Clements, Katie Sharp, Brian Ellis, Donald Childs, Heidi Childs, Patricia Myrick, Naurice Moffett, Sydney Hulse, Mari Nishibu, Andrew Wright, Jen Call, Lena Ringheim Jensen, Bryan Hinschberger, Spencer Brooks, Shannon Lynch, Allison Moses, Erin White, Bryce Thatcher, Dermell Reed, Elizabeth Jacob, Tawni Olson, Ryan Edwards, Ryan Casper, Hilda Lopez, Taron Milne, Scott Wilcox, Mark C. Mcpherson, Igor Skender, Heather Hoehne, Stacy Greer, Daniel Ross, Melissa Hannig, Colleen Petersen, Joe Jeagany, Tiffany Stoker Madsen, Lorilee Richardson, Stephanie Busbey, Robert Clack, Adkins Jones, Todd Lucas, Andrea McNear, Mary Beth Sylvester, Dr Cheryl Gholar and Vanessa Moore.

And finally, thank you to the hundreds of others who contributed in different ways.

Info Central

You or a friend or loved one may be in a situation and feel hopeless or confused about what to do. There are many people out there who want to help. You don't have to do it alone. Please call or visit the websites listed below. The numbers are free to call. If you don't get the kind of help you want or need with the first phone call or visit, please try again. Remember: Keep Hope Alive!

Substance Abuse

If you suspect that you may be drinking too much and you don't know what to do or you are worried about a family member or friend who drinks too much, call Alcoholics Anonymous or visit the website (*www.alcoholics-anonymous.org.uk*) **0845 769 7555**

If you or a friend are using illegal drugs or abusing any drug, visit the Narcotics Anonymous website for information and help *www.ukna.org*

You may also want to visit the following websites for information: Cocaine Anonymous *www.cauk.org.uk*
Drugscope *www.drugscope.org.uk*

Eating Disorders

If you suspect that one of your friends may have anorexia, bulimia or an overeating disorder and you want to get help, call the Eating Disorders Association Youthline (or visit their website at *www.edauk.com*) **0845 634 7650**

Physical and Mental Health

If you or a friend are considering suicide, PLEASE call the Samaritans (*www.samaritans.org.uk*). They are available 24 hours a day **08457 90 90 90**

ChildLine also operates a free, 24 hour helpline for children or young people. Counsellors are trained to help with bullying, child abuse, domestic violence, eating disorders, pregnancy, STDs and suicide **0800 1111**

If you or your friends are concerned about having a venereal disease or contracting AIDS, call the AIDS and Sexual Health Helpline (*www.aidshelpline.org.uk*) **0800 137 437**

The National Aids Trust can also provide information *www.nat.org.uk*

If you need to know where to go to get help on abortion, contraception, pregnancy or sexually transmitted diseases then contact the FPA (*www.fpa.org.uk*) **0845 310 1334**

Another website aimed at young people looking for information or advice on having sex is *www.ruthinking.co.uk*. They also operate a helpline **0800 282 930**

Abuse

If you or a friend (male or female) are a victim of rape, incest or any form of sexual abuse, either call ChildLine, listed above, or the NSPCC Child Protection Helpline (*www.nspcc.org.uk*) **0808 800 5000**

Education

If you are considering further education then visit the following website for information on higher education in the UK .... *www.hero.ac.uk*

50 GREAT BOOKS FOR TEENAGERS

Old Classics

Across Five Aprils
Irene Hunt

Little Women
Louisa May Alcott

The Wonderful Wizard of Oz
Frank Baum

The Adventures of Huckleberry Finn
Mark Twain

The Lord of the Rings trilogy
J. R. R. Tolkien

Anne of Green Gables
Lucy Maud Montgomery

The Foundling and Other Tales of Prydain
Lloyd Alexander

The Chronicles of Narnia
C. S. Lewis

Animal Farm
George Orwell

Anne Frank: The Diary of Young Girl
Anne Frank

To Kill a Mockingbird
Harper Lee

Cry, the Beloved Country
Alan Paton

The Yearling
Marjorie Kinnan Rawlings

The Farthest Shore
Ursula K. Le Guin

Of Mice and Men
John Steinbeck

The Red Badge of Courage
Stephen Crane

The Greatest Salesman in the World
Og Mandino

New Classics

Sounder
William H. Armstrong

Island of the Blue Dolphins
Scott O'Dell

Along the Tracks
Tamar Bergman

Night
Elie Wiesel

Red Scarf Girl: A Memoir of the Cultural Revolution
Ji-Li Jiang

Hiroshima
John Hersey

Bless Me, Ultima
Rudolfo Anaya

Anthony Burns: The Defeat and Triumph of a Fugitive Slave
Virginia Hamilton

Behind the Secret Window
Nellie S. Toll

Parrot in the Oven—Mi Vida
Victor Martinez

Walk Two Moons
Sharon Creech

I Heard the Owl Call My Name
Margaret Craven

The Color of Water: A Black Man's Tribute to His White Mother
James McBride

Point of Departure: 19 Stories of Youth and Discovery
Robert S. Gold

Rising Voices: Writings of Young Native Americans
Arlene B. Hirschfelder and Beverly R. Singer

The Watsons Go to Birmingham—1963
Christopher Paul Curtis

Self-Help

The Book of Virtues
William J. Bennett

Chicken Soup for the Teenage Soul
Jack Canfield, Mark Victor Hansen, and Kimberly Kirberger

Making College Count
Patrick S. O'Brien

The Measure of Our Success
Marian Wright Edelman

A Book of Your Own: Keeping a Diary or Journal
Carla Stevens

Death Is Hard to Live With
Janet Bode and Stan Mack

The Fiske Guide to Getting Into the Right College: The Complete Guide to Everything You Need to Know to Get Into and Pay for College
Edward B. Fiske and Bruce Hammond

Detour for Emmy
Marilyn Reynolds

There Are No Children Here
Alex Kotlowitz

How Could You Do That?
Dr Laura Schlessinger

Where Are My Birth Parents?
Karen Gravelle and Susan Fischer

Different Worlds: Interracial and Cross-Cultural Dating
Janet Bode and Iris Rosoff

Love and Sex in Plain Language: Responsible Sex and Common Sense
Eric W. Johnson

Kids in Jail
Paul Vasey

Are You Dying for a Drink?
Laurel Graeber

Real Gorgeous: The Truth About Body and Beauty
Kaz Cooke

Teen Power
Norm Hull, Mark Scharenbroich, Eric Chester, C. Kevin Wanzer, and Gary Zelesky

BIBLIOGRAPHY

PARADIGMS AND PRINCIPLES

Greyling, Dan P. 'The Way the Cookie Crumbles'. Reprinted with permission from the July 1980 *Reader's Digest*. Copyright © 1980 by The Reader's Digest Association, Inc.

MacPeek, Walter. *Resourceful Scouts in Action*. Nashville: Abingdon Press, 1969.

THE PERSONAL BANK ACCOUNT

Barton, Bruce. *The Man Nobody Knows*. New York: Collier Books, 1925.

MAN IN THE MIRROR. Words and Music by Glen Ballard and Siedah Garrett. © Copyright 1987 Music Corporation of America, Aerostation Corporation and Yellowbrick Road Music. All rights for Aerostation Corporation Controlled and Administered by MCA Music Publishing, A Division Of Universal Studios, Inc. International Copyright Secured All Rights Reserved

HABIT 1

Lemley, Brad. 'The Man Who Won't Be Defeated'. New York: *Parade*. Reprinted with permission from *Parade*. Copyright © 1989.

Nelson, Portia. 'Autobiography in Five Short Chapters'. From *There's a Hole in My Sidewalk*. Copyright © 1993 by Portia Nelson. Hillsboro, Oregon: Beyond Words Publishing, Inc., 1-800-284-9673.

HABIT 3

Nelson, Portia. *There's a Hole in My Sidewalk*. Copyright © 1993 by Portia Nelson. Hillsboro, Oregon: Beyond Words Publishing, Inc., 1-800-284-9673.

HABIT 4

Lusseyran, Jacques. *And There Was Light*. Edinburgh: Parabola Books, 1985. Reprinted with permission.

HABIT 6

Armstrong, Thomas. *7 Kinds of Smart*. New York: Plume, 1993.

Rodgers, Richard, and Oscar Hammerstein II. 'You've Got to Be Carefully Taught'. Copyright © 1949 by Richard Rodgers and Oscar Hammerstein II. Copyright Renewed. WILLIAMSON MUSIC owner of publication and allied rights throughout the world. International Copyright Secured. Reprinted by Permission. All Rights Reserved.

Sanders, Bill. *Goalposts: Devotions for Girls*. Grand Rapids, Mich.: Fleming Revel, a division of Baker Book House, 1995.

HABIT 7

Litchfield, Allen, contributor. From the Especially for Youth recording *Sharing the Light in the Wilderness*. Salt Lake City: Deseret Book, 1993.

Anderson, Walter. *Read with Me*. Boston: Houghton Mifflin Co., 1990.

INDEX

SEND IN YOUR STORY!

Stories are a powerful source of learning and hope. Stories can give you new ideas, suggest choices and options, and are just fun to read. Stories can also illustrate principles and habits that have applications in all our lives. Perhaps you have a story of using one or more of the 7 Habits and how you applied that to overcoming challenges in your own life, either at school or work or home. Or perhaps you've heard of one. If you would like to share your story and submit if for possible inclusion in a future book, please send it to:

FranklinCovey Co.
7 Habits for Teens
MS 0734
2200 West Parkway Boulevard
Salt Lake City, UT 84119-2331
USA
Fax: +1 801-817-8069
Attn: 7 Habits for Teens
E-mail: stories@7Habits.com
Web site: www.franklincovey.com

ABOUT FRANKLINCOVEY CO.

FranklinCovey provides many of the world's foremost private and public sector organizations with professional services, with one mission: to help improve the effectiveness of their people and their enterprise, significantly and measurably.

Consolidated in 1997 in a merger of the Franklin Institute and the Covey Leadership Centre, the company had its foundations in the works of Stephen R. Covey, author of global bestseller *The 7 Habits of Highly Effective People*, and Hyrum Smith, author of *The 10 Natural Laws of Successful Time and Life Management*.

FranklinCovey's approach goes to the heart of success both personal and business, and over the past 15 years the company has become a global leader in its field. In the USA alone, the client list includes 90 percent of the Fortune 100, more than 75 percent of the Fortune 500, and thousands of small and mid-sized businesses, as well as numerous government entities and educational institutions.

The company has grown worldwide rapidly through a network of direct offices and licensed partners (details overleaf). Now FranklinCovey is a firm with 39 offices covering 95 countries, and trains over 300,000 people around the world every year in effectiveness, leadership and productivity programmes.

Franklincovey Co. Global Offices

Country	Licensee	Tel/Fax	Email/Web

Southeast Asia / Pacific

Country	Licensee	Tel/Fax	Email/Web
India	FranklinCovey South Asia Leadership Knowledge Consulting Pte Ltd #955, Sector 17B Defence Colony Gurgaon (National Capital Region New Delhi) Haryana, India 122001	Tel No: +91 124 5013032 +91 981 1174447 +91 981 1174446 Mumbai: +91 982 0340000 Fax No: +91 124 5013032 +91 981 1789799	Email: lavleen@franklincoveyindia.com franklincoveyindia@hotmail.com Web: www.franklincoveysouthasia.com
Indonesia	Dunamis Organization Services Jl. Bendungan Jatiluhur No. 56 Bendungan Hilir Jakarta 10210 Indonesia	Tel No: +65 21 5720761 Fax No: +65 21 5720762	Email: info@dunamis.co.id Web: www.dunamis.co.id
Malaysia	Leadership Resources (Malaysia) Sdn. Bhd. Suite 5.02, Level 5, PJ Tower Amcorp Trade Center No. 18, Jalan Persiaran Barat 46050 Petaling Jaya Selangor Darul Ehsan Malaysia	Tel No: +603 7958 6418 +603 7955 1148 Fax No: +603 7955 2589	Email: info@franklincoveymalaysia.com Web: www.franklincoveymalaysia.com
Philippines	Center for Leadership and Change, Inc. G/F Hoffner Building Ateneo de Manila University Loyola Heights, Quezon City 1108 Philippines	Tel No: +632 426 6121 +632 924 4490 Fax No: +632 426 5935	
Singapore	Centre for Effective Leadership (Asia) Pte Ltd 19 Tanglin Road #05-18 Tanglin Shopping Centre Singapore 247909	Tel No: +65 6838 0777 Fax No: +65 6838 9211	Email: training@cel-asia.com Web: www.highlyeffectiveleaders.com
	Centre for Effective Leadership (HK) Ltd Room 1502, 15/F, Austin Tower 22 – 26A Austin Avenue, Tsimshatsui Kowloon, Hong Kong	Tel No: +852 2541 2218 +852 2802 2939 Fax No: +852 2544 4311 +852 3009 7585	Email: product@asiacel.com Web: www.highlyeffectiveleaders.com
	Strategic Paradigm Consulting Co., Ltd 7F-1, No. 183, Section 4 Chung Hsiao E. Rd. Taipei 106 Taiwan	Tel No: +886 2 2751 1333 Fax No: +886 2 2889 9390	Email: sns@tpts1.seed.net.tw Web: www.highlyeffectiveleaders.com
	Centre for Effective Leadership Asia Pte Ltd **Beijing office** Room 1201A, The Gateway No. 10 Yabao Road Chaoyang District Beijing 100020 P.R. of China	Tel No: +86 10 65951326 Fax No: +86 10 65925186	Email: fcclisa@public3.bta.net.cn Web: www.highlyeffectiveleaders.com
	Shanghai office Unit AH, 8F 25 Chong Qing Road (M) Shanghai 200020 P.R. of China	Tel No: +86 21 6387822 Fax No: +86 21 63870188	Email: fccliang@sh163.net Web: www.highlyeffectiveleaders.com

Country	Licensee	Tel/Fax	Email/Web
	Guangzhou office Room 1309, Peace World Plaza No. 362–366 Huanshi Road East Guangzhou 510060 P.R. of China	Tel No: +86 20 83878706 Fax No: +86 20 83752205	Email: wangyum@public.guangzhou.gd.cn Web: www.highlyeffectiveleaders.com
South Korea	Korea Leadership Center 2-3F Jeil Building 88–9 Nonhyun-Dong Kangnam-Ku Seoul, 135-010 Korea	Tel No: +82 2 2106 4100 Fax No: +82 2 2106 4001	Web: www.eklc.co.kr
Thailand	PacRim Leadership Center Co., Ltd 59/387–389 Moo 4 Ramkhamhaeng Road Sapansoong, Bangkok 10240 Thailand	Tel No: +66 2 728 1224 Fax No: +66 2 728 0211	Email: plc@pacrimgroup.com Web: www.pacrimgroup.com

Americas

Country	Licensee	Tel/Fax	Email/Web
Argentina	FranklinCovey Organizational Services LFCA S.A. Cerrito 774, Piso 11 C1010AAP, Buenos Aires Argentina	Tel No: +54 11 4372 5648 Fax No: +54 11 4383 0226	
Bermuda	Effective Leadership Bermuda 4 Dunscombe Road Warwick, WK08 Bermuda	Tel No: +1441 236 0383 Fax No: +1441 236 0192	Email: franklincovey.bda@cwbda.bm
Canada Quebec	Big Knowledge 360 St.-Jacques St. West, Suite 111 Montreal, Quebec H3C 1L5 Canada	Tel No: +1 514 844 2300 Fax No: +1 514 844 0706	Web: www.bigknowledge.com
Colombia	CLC Colombia, SA Calle 90 No. 11 A-34 Oficina 101 Santa Fe de Bogota Colombia	Tel No: +57 1 610 2736 Fax No: +57 1 610 2723	Email: franklincoveyco@fcla.com
Latin America	Advantage Management International, Inc. 3377 Forsyth Road Winter Park, FL 32792, USA	Tel No: +1 407 644 7117 Fax No: +1 407 644 5919	Email: franklincovey@fcla.com Web: www.fcla.com
Panama	Leadership Technologies, Inc. Bella Vista, Avenida Federico Boyd Edificio Alfaro – 1er Piso Panama, Republic de Panama	Tel No: +507 264 8899	Web: www.fcla.com
Puerto Rico	FranklinCovey Puerto Rico Suite 112 MSC 388 100 Gran Bulevar Paseos San Juan, Puerto Rico 00926-5955	Tel No: +1787 977 4065 +1787 977 4068 +1787 644 9094 Fax No: +1787 977 4067	Email: coveypr@coqui.net
	Guatemala office 5ª, Avenida 5-55 Zona 14 Edificio EuroPlaza Torre II, Oficina 404A Guatemala	Tel No: +502 385 3494 +502 385 3495,+502 385 3496, +502 385 3497 Fax No: +502 385 3407	Email: franklincoveygu@fcla.com ordenesgu@fcla.com fcguatemala@hotmail.com Web: www.fcla.com

Country	Licensee	Tel/Fax	Email/Web
Trinidad & Tobago	Leadership Consulting Group Limited #23 Westwood Street San Fernando Trinidad, West Indies	Tel No: +1868 652 6805 +1868 653 4313 Fax No: +1868 657 4432	Email: lcg@rave-tt.net
Uruguay	FranklinCovey Uruguay Torre Nauticas Torre 24 / Of. 1204 Calle Publica 1234 Montevideo, 11300 Uruguay	Tel No: +598 2 628 6139 Fax No: +598 2 628 6117	Email: franklincoveyur@fcla.com Web: www.fcla.com

Europe/ Middle East/ Africa

Country	Licensee	Tel/Fax	Email/Web
Benelux	FranklinCovey Benelux Ruimtesonde 3 3824 MZ Amersfoort The Netherlands	Tel No: +31 33 453 0627 Fax No: +31 33 456 76 36	Email: info@franklincovey.nl Web: www.franklincovey.nl
Egypt	Egyptian Leadership Training Center 122 Mohi El-Din Abou El-Ezz Str. Mohandessin Giza, Egypt	Tel No: +20 2 33 68 911 Fax No: +20 2 76 15 181	Email: fc_eltc@sofiocom.com.eg Web: customerservice@eltc.com.eg
Estonia	7H Eesti OU Kreutzwaldi 12 10124 Tallinn Estonia	Tel No: +372 6 830315 Fax No: +372 6 830314	Email: 7H@7harjumust.ee Web: www.7harjumust.ee
France	FranklinCovey France Cegos SA Unité FranklinCovey 11, rue René Jacques 92798 Issy-les-Moulineaux cedex 9 France	Tel No: +33 1 55 00 94 01 Fax No: +33 1 40 95 28 05	Email: info@franklincoveyfrance.com Web: www.franklincoveyfrance.com
Germany	FranklinCovey®GSA (Germany, Switzerland, Austria) Focus & Execution Ltd c/o FranklinCovey GSA Gustav-Stresemann-Ring 1 65189 Wiesbaden, Germany	Tel No: +49 611 9777 4215 Fax No: +49 611 9777 4111	Email: info@franklincovey.de Web: www.franklincovey.de
Greece	**Athens office** 26 Perikou Str. Paleo Psixiko 115 24 Athens Greece	Tel No: +30 210 69 85 946 Fax No: +30 210 69 85 947	Email: dms@sparknet.gr Web: www.franklincoveygreece.gr
	Thessaloniki office 19 Karolou Dil Str. 546 23, Thessaloniki Greece	Tel No: +3 231 0273 979 Fax No: +3 231 0271 945	
Israel	Momentum Training Ltd. Moshav Kfar Hess, 40692 Israel	Tel No: +972 9 7961055 Fax No: +972 9 7961055	Email: goz@momentumtraining.co.il

Country	Licensee	Tel/Fax	Email/Web
Italy	Cegos Italia S.p.A Piazza Velasca 5 20122 Milano Italy	Tel No: +39 2 80 67 21 Fax No: +39 2 72 00 16 47	Email: servizio.clienti@cegos.it Web: www.cegos.it
Lebanon	Starmanship & Associates Badaro Street Komeir Bldg(CNSS) P.O. Box 167089 Beirut, Lebanon	Tel No: +961 1 393 494 Fax No: +961 1 386 451	Email: starman@cyberia.net.lb
Nigeria	FranklinCovey Organisation Services, Nigeria ReStraL Limited 12th Floor, St. Nicholas house Catholic Mission Street Lagos, Nigeria	Tel No: + 234 1 2645885 +234 1 2632239 +234 1 2632850 +234 1 4705124 +234 1 2880883 Fax No: +234 1 2635090	Email: enquiries@restral.com Web: www.franklincoveynig.com www.restral.com
Nordic Region	FranklinCovey nordic approach k/s Tuborg Boulevard 12 DK-2900 Hellerup Denmark	Tel No: +45 7022 6612 Fax No: +45 7022 6712	Email: info@franklincovey.dk Web: www.franklincovey.dk
Poland	Polska – FranklinCovey Poland BIURO GŁÓWNE NA EUROPĘ CENTRALNĄ WSCHODNIĄ FC PL Sp. z o.o. 02-384 Warszawa ul. Włodarzewska 33	Tel No: +48 22 824 11 28 IFax No: +48 22 824 11 29	Email: biuro@franklincovey.pl Web: www.franklincovey.pl
	Ceská republika – FranklinCovey Czech Republic Výhradní zastoupení pro Ceskou a Slovenskou republiku FC CZECH, s.r.o. Ohradni 1424/2B, 140 00 Praha 4	Tel No: +420 2 61 099 341 +420 2 61 099 342 Fax No: +420 2 61 099 343	Email: info@franklincovey.cz Web: www.franklincovey.cz
	Węgry – FranklinCovey Hungary FC HU 1134 Budapest, Lehel utca 11 BankCenter	Tel No: +36 1 4121884 Fax No: +36 1 4748181	Email: office@franklincovey.hu Web: www.franklincovey.hu
Portugal	Cegoc – Tea, Lda Avenida António Augusto de Aguiar, Nº 21 – 2º 1050-012 Lisboa Portugal	Tel No: +351 21 319 19 60 Fax No: +351 21 319 19 61	Email: mfonseca@cegoc.pt mceitil@cegoc.pt amrocha@cegoc.pt Web: www.cegoc.pt
South Africa	FCSA Organisation Services (Pty) Ltd 45 De La Rey Road Rivonia, 2128, Johannesburg South Africa	Tel Nö: +27 11 807 2929 Fax No: +27 11 807 2871	Email: info@franklincovey.co.za Web: www.franklincovey.co.za
Spain	TEA-CEGOS, S.A. FranklinCovey Division Fray Bernardino de Sahagún, 24 28036 Madrid Spain	Tel No: +34 912 705 000 Fax No: +34 912 705 001	Email: ctyden@tea-cegos.es Email: franklincovey@tea-cegos.es Web: www.tea-cegos.es

Country	Licensee	Tel/Fax	Email/Web
Turkey	ProVista Mithatpasa Cad. No: 1190/2 35260 Guzelyali, Izmir Turkey	Tel No: +90 232 247 50 21 Fax No: +90 232 247 50 22	Email: provista@bilgilink.com Web: www.bilgilink.com/provista.html
UAE	FranklinCovey – Qiyada Consultants Kendah House, Suite 3102 Sheikh Zayed Road P.O. Box 53703 Dubai, UAE	Tel No: +971 4 332 2244 Fax No: +971 4 332 2282	Email: info@franklincoveyme.com

**SIMON &
SCHUSTER**

More **Stephen R. Covey** and **Simon & Schuster** titles are available
from your book shop or can be ordered direct from the publisher.

Books

0 684 85839 8	The 7 Habits of Highly Effective People	£10.99
0 684 85840 1	First Things First	£10.99
0 684 85841 X	Principle Centered Leadership	£10.99
0 684 86008 2	The 7 Habits of Highly Effective Families	£10.99
0 7432 0906 0	Living the 7 Habits	£10.99
0 684 85609 3	The 7 Habits of Highly Effective Teens	£9.99
0 684 87060 0	Daily Reflections for Highly Effective Teens	£6.99
0 671 88717 3	Daily Reflections for Highly Effective People	£4.99
0 684 84240 8	First Things First Everyday	£4.99
0 7432 3234 8	The 7 Habits Journal	£7.99

Audio cassettes

0 7435 0107 1	The 7 Habits of Highly Effective People	£9.99
0 671 85322 8	First Things First	£9.99
0 671 01113 8	Principle Centered Leadership	£8.99
0 671 03808 7	Living the 7 Habits	£9.99
0 671 01110 3	Daily Reflections for Highly Effective People	£8.99

Please send cheque or postal order for the value
of the book, **free postage and packing within
the UK**, to SIMON & SCHUSTER CASH SALES
PO Box 29, Douglas Isle of Man, IM99 1BQ
Tel: 01624 677237, Fax: 01624 670923
www.bookpost.co.uk

Please allow 14 days for delivery. Prices and availability
subject to change without notice